Mastering UltraEdit

Functions and Possibilities of the Most Flexible, Powerful, and Secure Text Editor

Devid Espenschied

Apress®

Mastering UltraEdit: Functions and Possibilities of the Most Flexible, Powerful, and Secure Text Editor

Devid Espenschied
Berlin, Berlin, Germany

ISBN-13 (pbk): 979-8-8688-1159-3   ISBN-13 (electronic): 979-8-8688-1160-9
https://doi.org/10.1007/979-8-8688-1160-9

Managing Director, Apress Media LLC: Welmoed Spahr
Acquisitions Editor: Ryan Byrnes
Desk Editor: Laura Berendson
Editorial Project Manager: Gryffin Winkler

Cover designed by eStudioCalamar

Cover Image by Pexels from Pixabay

Distributed to the book trade worldwide by Springer Science+Business Media New York, 1 New York Plaza, Suite 4600, New York, NY 10004-1562, USA. Phone 1-800-SPRINGER, fax (201) 348-4505, e-mail orders-ny@springer-sbm.com, or visit www.springeronline.com. Apress Media, LLC is a California LLC and the sole member (owner) is Springer Science + Business Media Finance Inc (SSBM Finance Inc). SSBM Finance Inc is a **Delaware** corporation.

For information on translations, please e-mail booktranslations@springernature.com; for reprint, paperback, or audio rights, please e-mail bookpermissions@springernature.com.

Apress titles may be purchased in bulk for academic, corporate, or promotional use. eBook versions and licenses are also available for most titles. For more information, reference our Print and eBook Bulk Sales web page at http://www.apress.com/bulk-sales.

Any source code or other supplementary material referenced by the author in this book is available to readers on GitHub. For more detailed information, please visit https://www.apress.com/gp/services/source-code.

If disposing of this product, please recycle the paper

I would like to dedicate this book to my long-term girlfriend Caroline, who has always stood by my side and thus contributed to the success of this book. We went through a difficult phase and that brought us closer together. Our daughter Catharina will always connect us and I am very grateful that we found each other – I love you with all my heart.

Table of Contents

About the Author

Devid Espenschied lives in Berlin, Germany, and has been working in software development for more than 30 years. As a freelance author and developer, he has written many articles for IT magazines and programmed his own system diagnostic tool. His previous books include the German-language book *System Programming with Delphi.*

About the Technical Reviewer

 **Ben Schwenk** is the Chief of Staff at Idera, Inc., where he plays a key role in driving business performance across product, sales, and marketing functions for UltraEdit and several other tech brands. With nearly 20 years of experience in the industry, Ben has a deep understanding of software tools especially in desktop software and web development. He is passionate about empowering developers by eliminating coding roadblocks and ultimately becoming more productive. Ben is also a regular speaker in various ministries at his church and in his community. He lives near Cincinnati, Ohio, with his wife and three sons.

Acknowledgments

First and foremost, I would like to thank the people at UltraEdit, who have been doing a great job for 30 years and hopefully for the next 30 years. In particular, I would like to mention Ben Schwenk, Jan Sloboda, and Troy Pennington, who have repeatedly offered me inputs and ideas as well as their support, without which the first book on UltraEdit in this form would not have been possible.

At the same time, I would like to thank Apress, who supported me in every way during the realization of this project. I would particularly like to mention Ryan Byrnes, Shobana Srinivasan, Gryffin Winkler, and Laura Berendson.

Introduction

UltraEdit is one of the most flexible, powerful, and secure text editors on the market and has been continuously developed for 30 years. Its success story and increasing popularity is reflected in the number of customers, which, at 4+ million users worldwide, is unique among text editors.

Despite this outstanding market success, not a single book about UltraEdit has been written in the last 30 years, and the idea of starting this book project arose in the course of the 30th anniversary. During the writing process, however, I had to realize that UltraEdit contains so many functions and features that one book was not enough for a detailed description. The idea of writing two books arose.

This first book contains the most important functions in ten chapters, which describe UltraEdit as a whole and already enable a smooth workflow. This includes the introduction, including the history and installation options, detailed descriptions of the user interface, program navigation, the very extensive and flexible customizations in the settings, the arrangement of windows, and the basics of file management. Furthermore, the core functions are described, including editing, inserting, column mode, viewing, formatting, and find/replace. The description of more advanced functions includes syntax highlighting, multi-caret editing, the Command palette, FTP integration, and editing extremely large files. In each section, the practical relevance is established, and the program functions are supplemented with useful notes and hints.

The second volume of this UltraEdit book will be written after the publication of the first book and will cover advanced topics such as macros, scripting, plug-ins, project management, using UEStudio for development, and data comparisons with UltraCompare.

Together, the two books form the ideal complement to each other and provide a fully comprehensive description of the functionality for which UltraEdit has become so popular and widely used.

I hope all readers enjoy reading this book and that you too can discover UltraEdit for yourself, as I did, and how it can demonstrably increase your daily work success.

Devid Espenschied, November 2024

CHAPTER 1

General Basics

UltraEdit was first released in 1994 and has become the most flexible, powerful, and secure text editor in its 30 years. The areas of application are almost endless and cover most of the required functions and user scenarios.

Although a great deal of knowledge about UltraEdit exists in digital form – sometimes as wiki, tutorials, power tips, and white papers – no printed book has been published to date. This circumstance was also the reason for writing this book in time for the 30th anniversary. I have tried to write a well-founded introduction and at the same time address as many user groups as possible.

The chapters therefore provide a structured guide to the program interface, navigation, file management and file editing, as well as the advanced functions. This includes syntax highlighting, multi-caret editing, the command palette, FTP integration, the Powershell terminal and the processing of very large files.

If you are missing a particular topic or if it is not included in the desired form, please do not hesitate to write to me so that i can take this into account in a potential next edition of this book – thank you.

History of UltraEdit

UltraEdit was originally developed and founded by Ian D. Mead. It was released in the spring of 1994, and at that time Microsoft Windows 3.11 was on the market – not yet as an operating system of its own, but as an operating system extension based on (MS)DOS.

© Devid Espenschied 2025
D. Espenschied, *Mastering UltraEdit*, https://doi.org/10.1007/979-8-8688-1160-9_1

When UltraEdit proved to be a commercial success, he officially founded the company as "IDM Computer Solutions, Inc." – which represented his initials. When he retired in 2021, the company was then reincorporated as "UltraEdit."

Historically, this was followed in 2004 by the IDM software UltraCompare, which enabled a powerful comparison of files and folders. We will discuss this application in more detail later.

This was followed in 2005 by UEStudio, which enabled team-capable possibilities including UltraEdit editing capability, integration of version control systems, project managers, and control of external development environments and compilers. This also addressed the target group of software developers, and we will discuss this powerful software in more detail later.

Licensing has also been expanded, although perpetual licensing has always been available. Subscription licensing was then added in 2015, which enabled the use of all applications with the "IDM All Access" subscription. This was followed shortly afterward by individual subscriptions for UltraEdit and UEStudio. Basically, subscriptions were a trend in which users do not have to invest higher acquisition costs and can use all applications, including support, for an annual rental fee.

A few months after the release of the "IDM All Access" subscription, the All Access Manager was released, with which all desktop and portable versions of the UltraEdit series could be installed within a single installer application. We will also discuss this powerful tool in more detail.

UltraEdit was then acquired by Idera Inc. in August 2021, whereby Idera is divided into three divisions: Data Tools, Developer Tools, and Test and Security Tools. UltraEdit was integrated into the Developer Tools division and is recommended, for example, as a parallel tool for software development using Embarcadero's RAD Studio. The latter consists of the C++ builder and Delphi.

Further milestones in the company's history were a Mac/Linux version of UltraEdit and UltraCompare in 2011 and 2012, as well as the additional applications UltraFinder (2012) and UltraFTP (2017).

Now in 2024, UltraEdit is celebrating its 30th birthday and is still as popular as it was in the beginning, and even more powerful than it was originally. The integration of the various tools allows for workflow optimization, and a variety of powerful features not found in competitors make UltraEdit a unique and powerful tool.

Licensing and Distribution

UltraEdit is available in two license models, referred to as subscription and perpetual license. The main difference is defined in the pricing structure and duration of use.

A one-off investment is required for the perpetual license, while subscription licenses incur lower costs at regular intervals.

In terms of the duration of use, the software may be used indefinitely with a perpetual license, but with the subscription license only for a defined period of time (usually one year).

Further license conditions are listed by the manufacturer, which concern updates and maintenance, flexibility, and costs over time.

With a subscription license, all updates are included for the duration of the subscription, and you also receive priority technical support on an ongoing basis.

For the respective flexibility, the subscription licenses offer more of it than perpetual licenses, because you can opt out or switch to another product or service at any time. With a perpetual license, you are tied to the product you have purchased and will no longer have access to new versions and updates when maintenance expires.

In the short term, subscription licenses may seem more expensive than perpetual licenses because you are paying for continued access to the products. However, over time, the total cost of ownership for a perpetual license is often higher due to maintenance and support costs.

The license matrix in Table 1-1 compares both license models with each other, and your own requirements ultimately decide which license model is more suitable.

Table 1-1. *License models compared in a matrix*

	Subscription	Perpetual
License duration and eligibility	Yearly	Permanent (with maintenance)
Technical support	Yes	Yes
Number of unique installs (*)	Up to five installs	Up to three installs
Multi-user licenses	Yes	Yes
Multi-year plans	Yes	No
Concurrent licensing (floating licenses)	Available via sales quote	Yes
Free UltraCompare (**)	Yes	Yes
Admin tools	Yes, for All Access	No
Available on Windows	Yes	Yes
Available on Mac	Yes	Yes
Available on Linux	Yes	Yes
Qualifies for auto-renewals	Yes	Yes

Please also note the additional notes on the number of unique installations and UltraCompare:

- * An instance of the application on each device is counted as a unique install. Applies to singular personal license plans only.

- ** Available for UltraEdit or UEStudio only.

Installation

In this chapter, we describe the installation under Microsoft Windows, which can be realized in two ways. One way is the single installation of the corresponding application (e.g., UltraEdit or UltraCompare), and the other way is the convenient use of the All Access Manager.

Single Installation

For a single installation, the corresponding application is first downloaded from the home page www.ultraedit.com by selecting the application in the Products category and pressing the download button. Depending on the application, downloads are available in different languages and for the Windows platform for 32 and 64 bits.

You can either download the corresponding executable file (exe extension) and start it manually or let the browser you are using take care of this task by pressing the download button.

When the installer is executed, the Windows User Account Control (UAC) opens and requests higher rights. This request must be confirmed with *Yes* in order to start the actual installer. The installer starts with a welcome page in Figure 1-1, in which the license agreement must be accepted and the advanced installation can also be selected. As soon as you click on the plus symbol in front of the advanced installation, additional fields are displayed:

- The installation folder can be customized.

- The installation can be carried out either for all users or only for the current user (if the latter is selected, the installation is not carried out in the general program directory, but in the profile directory of the current user and the subfolder for documents).

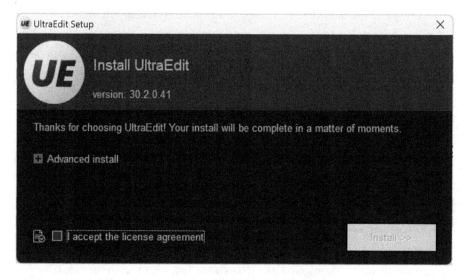

Figure 1-1. Welcome screen of the UltraEdit installer

After pressing the Install button, the installer starts the installation process and then offers the combined installation of UltraCompare Professional.

Both applications are supplied together, i.e., UltraCompare is supplied free of charge with UltraEdit, but can also be obtained as a stand-alone application. Figure 1-2 shows the selection of UltraEdit Professional directly after the UltraEdit installation.

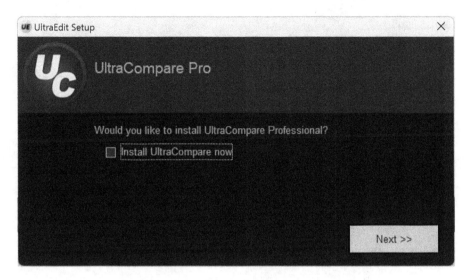

Figure 1-2. *Selection screen for the installation of UltraCompare Professional*

If you activate the *Install UltraCompare now* check box at this point, the installation program downloads the UltraCompare application directly after pressing the *Next* ➤ button and then installs it. Either with or without UltraCompare, the installer displays a result message at the end to indicate whether the installation was successful (see Figure 1-3).

Figure 1-3. *Result screen after the installation process*

This installation process is admittedly relatively simple and only contains the most necessary settings. The All Access Manager, which can be downloaded from the home page www.ultraedit.com/products/ue-all-access, offers even more installation options, if you have the All Access license instead of individual single licenses. This powerful tool is described in more detail in the next section.

Note   For the Windows platform, a separate MSI download is also offered, which is suitable for silent/scripted installations. The Windows Installer, which is delivered as the file *msiexec.exe* with Windows, can be used for this purpose, on the one hand with the regular command-line parameters and on the other hand with some additional user-defined parameters that have been added at the request of customers. This type of installation is generally used for mass deployment, for example, for many machines/users within a working group in a company.

Combined Installation with the All Access Manager

After downloading the executable program file and starting the program, the All Access Manager presents itself with a simple interface. In the upper area, you have the option of installing all applications using the *Install all* button, and the language of the installed applications can be selected directly below this button. This language setting should be made correctly before installation, as it cannot be changed afterward and requires a new uninstallation and subsequent reinstallation in a different language.

While the *Install all* button downloads and installs all Desktop apps in an automatic process, the All Access Manager downloads the respective installer for the Portable apps and starts it so that the user can specify the target directory.

Figure 1-4 shows the All Access Manager after starting the program.

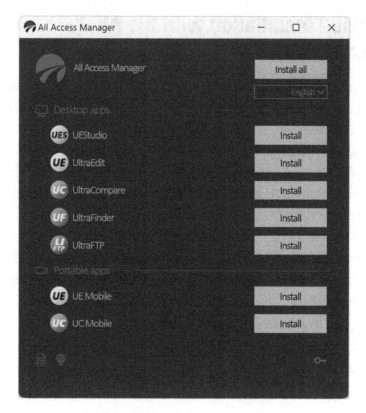

Figure 1-4. *All Access Manager*

The icons in the footer area have a special meaning. The list icon on the left opens a log window to the right of the All Access Manager, and clicking on this symbol again closes the log window. The network symbol next to it allows you to define a proxy server. This can either be done manually or the All Access Manager will attempt to automatically detect and use the proxy settings, if these are configured on the host system.

At the bottom right is the most important option that should be discussed before an installation – the key symbol and the associated license ID. If you don't enter a license ID and password here before installation, all applications will be installed as 30-day trial versions. Although you can activate the installed trial versions separately with the license ID, the All Access Manager offers the option of automatic activation for all installed applications. Pressing the key symbol opens a window (see Figure 1-5) in which the license ID and the corresponding password can be entered. If the data is correct, a blue check mark is displayed next to the key symbol. This means that the All Access Manager can install full versions of the applications.

Figure 1-5. *Entering the license ID and password (ideally before the installation process)*

Note   Clicking on the key symbol (when the blue check mark is displayed next to it) opens the license details including the license name, license ID, and the end date of the subscription.

Figure 1-6 shows what the result can look like with fully installed desktop apps, where the version number is displayed directly next to the program name after installation.

Figure 1-6. *All Access Manager with fully installed desktop apps*

The respective application is installed if the corresponding button contains the text *Uninstall*. In this case, the application can be started via the start menu or the desktop icon.

Uninstallation

The reverse way of an installation, the uninstallation, can be done either via the All Access Manager or via the Windows Settings and the installed apps.

Within the All Access Manager, simply select the relevant application and click the *Uninstall* button. In this case, the application is uninstalled completely automatically without any further asking.

Alternatively, you can uninstall via the usual Windows mechanisms, such as the Control Panel ➤ Programs and Features, or via the Windows Settings ➤ Apps ➤ Installed Apps. By using this way and the associated UltraEdit uninstaller, it allows two options before the uninstallation process (see Figure 1-7). On the one hand, an existing activated license can be deactivated, whereby the license is then reported back to the UltraEdit servers and could be used for another new installation. On the other hand, all program settings that were adjusted while working with UltraEdit can be removed. It is therefore recommended to activate both options in order to leave the system as clean as possible after uninstallation.

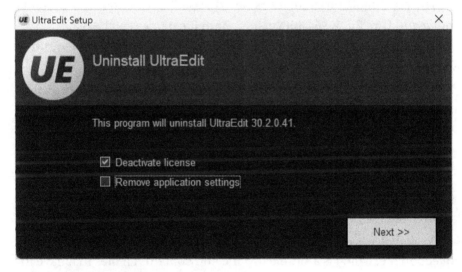

Figure 1-7. UltraEdit Uninstall page

Command-Line Parameters

UltraEdit can be invoked with various command-line parameters, which makes it even more flexible to use.

To do this, open the Windows command prompt and either change to the UltraEdit directory (e.g., *C:\Program Files\IDM Computer Solutions\ UltraEdit*) or restart Windows after the installation. The latter is mostly necessary due to the fact that the UltraEdit directory is appended to the PATH environment variable during installation in order to call UltraEdit from any directory. Unfortunately, this change of the environment variable is not automatically updated after installation. Therefore, you must either log out the logged-in Windows user and then log in again or alternatively restart Windows.

The executable program file is called *uedit32.exe* for the 32-bit version and *uedit64.exe* for the 64-bit version. Both file names can be used without an extension followed by a space and the possible command-line parameters.

Basically, UltraEdit supports files specified via the command line that are opened with UltraEdit. This can either be a single file or multiple files, each file separated by a space. If the file name is long and contains spaces, it must be enclosed in double quotation marks.

In addition, UltraEdit supports two methods for opening files via the command line. The first method is based on wildcards, which are also known from the normal command line. For example, the parameter "*.txt" opens all files with the txt extension. The second method is based on a collection file, which is a simple text file and contains all files that have to be opened in a list. In this case, each file to be opened must appear in a separate line within the collection file. With the command-line parameter "/f" followed by a space and the collection file name, UltraEdit then opens all files that can be accessed in the file.

Other practical command-line parameters exist and are summarized in Table 1-2.

Table 1-2. *Command-line parameters for the usage with UltraEdit*

Parameter	Description
/r	Opens the file read-only
/n	Suppresses the notification if a file has been deleted that is to be opened via the command line
/p	Opens the file, prints it on the default printer, and then closes UltraEdit
/m	Allows macros to be automatically invoked
/s	Allows scripts to be invoked
/foi	Is used to open a file in the original instance
/fni	Is used to open a file in a new instance
/i	Permits the INI file used for UltraEdit settings to be specified by the user
-s	Performs a Find in the specified file and this MUST be the last parameter on the command line

Summary

In this chapter, UltraEdit was introduced as a powerful and versatile editor, which is supplemented by other products from the manufacturer's portfolio.

We discuss the history, license, and distribution options, as well as installation and uninstallation. Convenient handling of these steps is possible and recommended via the All Access Manager.

This chapter concludes with the command-line parameters, which provide additional ways to open files flexibly.

In the next chapter, we will take a closer look at the user interface and its components because it represents the daily interface for working with UltraEdit.

CHAPTER 2

User Interface

In this chapter, we will take a closer look at the UltraEdit user interface and discuss which fundamental concepts have been implemented and which settings should be made once before starting work. We will also discuss the license activation, which is necessary when starting the program for the first time or after the 30-day free trial has expired in order to legitimize yourself with the software manufacturer.

License Activation

The license must be activated immediately after first starting the program, if a license for a full version has been purchased and the activation has not already been done via the All Access Manager. To do this, the Activate window opens (see Figure 2-1), in which the user can either enter the license key or activate a 30-day trial version.

© Devid Espenschied 2025
D. Espenschied, *Mastering UltraEdit*, https://doi.org/10.1007/979-8-8688-1160-9_2

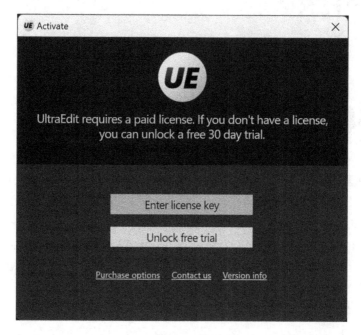

Figure 2-1. *License activation during the first program start*

Further links at the bottom area open web pages for the purchase options and contact possibilities. Version and copyright details are displayed via the third option *Version info.*

If the decision is made to enter the license key, the next window "License activation" appears, in which the license ID and the corresponding password can be entered. The license is then activated via the button *Activate,* and all program functions are available starting from this point. In the best case, the license activation has worked, and a short status window informs about the success.

Welcome Page

The Welcome page appears immediately after starting UltraEdit and can also be opened later at any time via *File* ➤ *Help* ➤ *Show welcome page*. If the menu mode is used instead of the ribbon mode, the Welcome page can be opened via the menu *Help* ➤ *Show welcome page*.

In this screen, the visual properties that represent the appearance of UltraEdit are defined. This is due to the fact that UltraEdit wants to appeal to as many user groups as possible with predefined templates. Some users like it lighter, others darker. One user likes a clean layout, the other a multi-window display. Some users prefer a classic menu; others are used to ribbons. This contrast existed already in Microsoft Office, which contained classic menu bars until version 2003 but then switched to a new interface with ribbons from version 2007. In order to stay up to date and use the latest version, everybody had to get used to ribbons. UltraEdit makes this way more flexible and allows both the one and the other visualization – this ultimately makes a real display flexibility for productivity.

Tip   Every user should take the time to configure this properly once, as it will have a noticeable impact on the subsequent experience and efficiency. If someone is used to working with menus, it makes no sense to adopt the default setting for ribbons.

The Welcome page is divided into four areas: *Theme, Layout, Ribbon or menu/toolbars*, and *other settings*, which we will discuss below.

Themes

First of all, it should be mentioned that a change to the display property is applied in real time so that the user can see the result immediately. This is advantageous for clicking through the display variants and comparing them.

Themes refer to the color properties of the UltraEdit interface, and as Figure 2-2 shows, there are five options: Studio Dark, One Dark, Monokai Pro, Charcoal, and Predawn.

Figure 2-2. *Theme selection from the Welcome page*

This selection is of course not complete, and a complete list can be found in *Layout* ➤ *Themes* or, if the menu display is active instead of the ribbons, in *View* ➤ *Themes* (see also Figure 2-3).

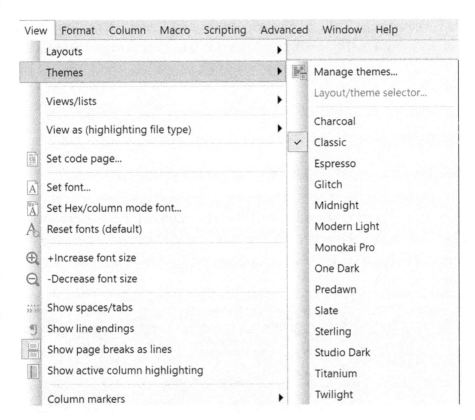

Figure 2-3. *Theme selection from the menu*

Note   Since only five dark themes can be selected via the Welcome page, but UltraEdit offers considerably more themes (especially lighter ones), it can be seen that the dark themes should be used according to the manufacturer's recommendation. Of course, this can be configured individually for each user.

We therefore use the classic theme in the following chapters, not only to save printer ink but also to adjust the contrast between the figures and the book background. Nevertheless, it should also be mentioned here that the Welcome page is always displayed in the dark theme – regardless of the theme setting. For this reason, the following screenshots in this chapter are still dark, and from the next chapter onward, they will be shown in a classic light color scheme.

Layouts

There are four predefined templates for the layout, and these define which frames and associated program functions are displayed and how these elements are arranged in the UltraEdit program interface. Basically, a layout includes ribbon commands, customized menus, toolbars, and dockable windows as well as customized templates for selected layouts (see Figure 2-4).

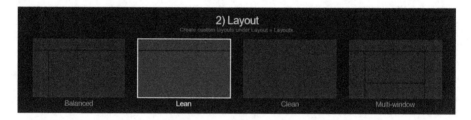

Figure 2-4. *Layout selection from the Welcome page*

In the Lean layout, a minimalist display is selected, with the ribbons or the menu with optional toolbars at the top and the input area below in the rest of the UltraEdit window. No dockable windows are used in the display. This theme is preselected as the default setting.

In the Balanced layout, in addition to the Lean layout, an area is displayed in the left pane that can be configured individually. In the default setting, a file explorer is displayed in this pane, which can be used to navigate through drives and folders in order to edit files and perform various actions. In the lower area, this function can be switched to a project view, open files, and a file list. We will discuss these functions in more detail later. The file explorer in particular is a useful extension, which means the user doesn't have to constantly switch to Windows Explorer or another file manager but can control everything from one interface.

In addition to the Balanced layout, the Multi-window layout displays an area in the right pane that can be configured individually. In the default setting, a function list is displayed in this pane, which provides quick access to certain UltraEdit functions. In the lower area of this right-hand pane, this function can be switched to an XML manager and a template list. We will also discuss these functions in more detail later. While the input area of UltraEdit is displayed in the middle area, an area below it contains an output window. This window is used to capture and display output from external user tools (configurable via *Tools ➤ Configuration*) and to display the output of the *Find in Files* function.

As the name suggests, the Clean layout defines a classic compact top area, which can consist of a menu bar or ribbons. The input area of UltraEdit then follows directly below. In comparison to the Lean layout, a potentially displayed toolbar is hidden so that only a narrow ribbon bar or the menu remains visible. This layout is suitable for displaying the largest possible input area and hiding all program functions in a compact ribbon or menu bar.

These layouts can be configured as required, and the associated Layout Manager can be opened from *Layout ➤ Layouts* (see Figure 2-5).

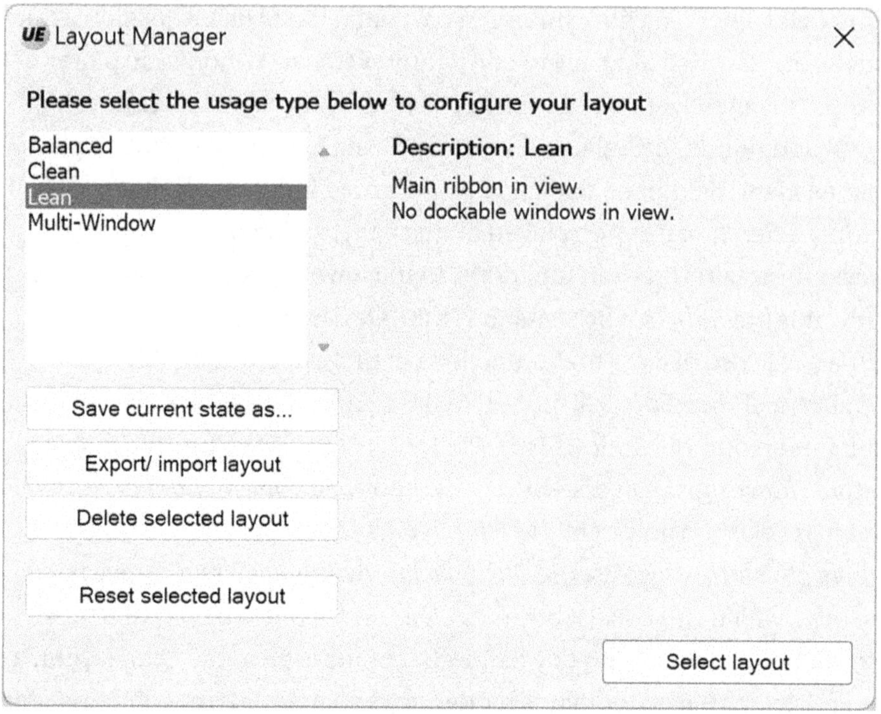

Figure 2-5. *Layout Manager for selecting, saving, importing/ exporting, and deleting layouts*

In this layout manager, the user can save the current status of the UltraEdit program interface as a customized layout with the corresponding description text – and delete existing or saved layouts. Any layout can also be imported and exported as well as activated using the *Select layout* button.

To restore the initial state, the *Reset selected layout* can be used, which not only resets the four predefined layouts but also deletes any additional layouts that have been created. This button is therefore useful if the predefined layouts were configured in such an unfortunate way that using a fresh starting point makes more sense.

Ribbon or Menu (Including Toolbars)

UltraEdit allows access to its program functions via ribbons, as known from Microsoft Office version 2007. Alternatively, menus can be used, either as menus in combination with toolbars or without toolbars (see Figure 2-6).

Figure 2-6. *Ribbon or menu/toolbars selection from the Welcome page*

This setting in particular has a significant impact on productivity, because users with a preference for ribbons work less productively with menus, and vice versa. It is therefore advisable to reflect on the user's previous personal use and test both ways with this option.

This setting can be changed later by right-clicking on a ribbon or the menu. If the ribbon view is activated (which is also the default setting), the option *Toolbar/menu mode* with its two sub-options, *Contemporary menus* and *Traditional menus*, appears in the context menu when clicking with the right mouse key on a ribbon. The difference between both menu types is that traditional menus are based on traditional menu structures that are common in other applications (and previous versions of UltraEdit/ UEStudio). The traditional menu structure is often familiar and contains the standard menu items *File, Edit, Search, Insert*, etc.

Contemporary menus in contrast are based on the ribbon structure. These menus follow the ribbon categories (like *File, Home, Edit, Format, View*, etc.), and in general, all functionality and commands follow the organization of the ribbon.

Note   The toolbars for toolbar/menu mode are the same with both menu types.

If the menu display is active (either Contemporary or Traditional menu), the *Ribbon mode* can be selected via the context menu with the right mouse button on the menu bar, as well as the other menu display that is not currently active.

Backup and Tab Settings

In the last lower section of the Welcome page, a few settings can be defined, which are divided into the groups *Backups* and *Tabs*. Figure 2-7 shows the exemplary arrangement of these options.

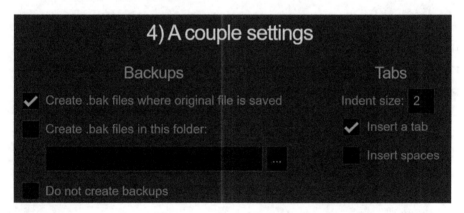

Figure 2-7. *Backup and Tab options selection from the Welcome page*

Backups are intended to prevent files or file areas from being lost or overwritten. UltraEdit therefore offers to create backup files with the extension .bak for each saved file (in the same directory). For the backup process, this means that the previous file is saved as a bak file (e.g., *Test.txt* to *Test.bak*) and the new file is given the current file name (in this example case, *Test.txt*). This means that two backup versions are automatically available.

The option *Create .bak files in this folder* can be used to customize the folder in which all backup files with the .bak extension are saved. This is advantageous if another backup software is used in which this folder can be added for a backup (e.g., with Microsoft Backup or Acronis True Image – to name just two solutions). Another key benefit is that it keeps .bak files from being created all over the file system, which might be especially important for something like Git repositories.

If no backups are required at all and the resulting risk possibilities are known, the option *Do not create backups* can be used.

Another setting affects the behavior of UltraEdit when the tabulator key (abbreviation: tab key) is pressed on the keyboard during file editing. The tab key is used in many ways, for example, in the command line, in graphical shells, dialogs, and generally in text editing. In this last category, the tab key is used to move the caret by a specified distance and to insert a tab stop.

The field *Indent size* defines the number of digits (default value 2) to which a caret jumps as soon as the tab key is pressed. The user can also specify whether a tab should be inserted up to the indent size when the tab key is pressed or whether the position up to the indent size should be filled with spaces.

Note   The tab setting only applies to text adjustments that are made after the tabulator settings have been changed. Previously existing files are not subsequently adjusted.

Edit Window

The middle and often largest area is the edit window, in which data from files is opened and displayed. The display can be a simple text display or a hexadecimal display (if hex mode is activated).

We will discuss this area in detail in the next chapter for the program navigation, including the associated keyboard shortcuts.

Status Bar

The status bar is displayed at the bottom of the UltraEdit window and is activated by default. Manual activation/deactivation can be done via the layout settings and the corresponding check box *Status bar*.

In terms of content, the status bar consists of various tabs that contain frequently used status values during text editing. Starting from the left, these are the following status tabs:

- Help prompts: Describes actions of menu items as the user uses the arrow keys to navigate through menus or hover the mouse pointer over menu items. This area similarly shows messages that describe the actions of toolbar buttons as the user hovers the mouse pointer over them or depresses them before releasing them.

- Macro recording: If macro recording is in progress, a red dot and the word "Macro" will be displayed in the rightmost portion of this field as well.

- Line/column number: The line number (if enabled) of the caret in the file and the column number are displayed together in a single panel. The active clipboard is shown in the Status Bar following the Line and Column indicator separated with a comma.

C0 indicates the standard Windows Clipboard is active, while C1-C9 indicates one of the user clipboards is active. If UltraEdit runs in hex mode, this displays the caret position in Hex and Decimal values.

- File format (line terminator): The File Format indicates if the file contains DOS, UNIX, or MAC (legacy) line terminators.

- Encoding type: The Encoding Type control allows users to change the encoding used to display the active file. This does not actually affect the underlying content of the file. No conversion is done. This merely changes the encoding used to display the file in the editor.

- Highlighting type: The Highlighting Type control allows users to specify what type of highlighting should be applied to the active file if this is not detected by the editor when the file is loaded. If the file extension of the active file matches one of those specified in the wordfile, this field will also indicate the syntax highlighting type (related to the active Language from the wordfile) currently being used.

Note   UltraEdit applies syntax highlighting from definitions and configurations, which are contained in so-called wordfiles. These wordfiles are loaded on startup, or when modified in an integrated editor dialog. UltraEdit provides approx. 30 predefined word files in the subdirectory "wordfiles", which have the extension .uew and are text files with a predefined syntax. This allows defined syntax areas to be highlighted in color.

- Date/time: This control contains the date and time the active file was last modified (prior to the current session). For new files, the date and time shown is the creation date and time. The date format is read from the system "short date" setting, which can be configured in the Regional Settings of the Windows Control Panel.

- File size: Contains the file size of the active file and is updated when UltraEdit writes any changes to the disk. If a selection is made in the file, this field will indicate the number of bytes/lines selected. For performance reasons, the number of lines selected is not displayed if the total file size exceeds 10 MB.

- Read only status: This field contains the state of the current file, and the values R/O for Read-Only and R/W for Writable are possible. The user can also click on this field to change the status – this is particularly useful if sensitive documents need to be protected. Switching from R/W to R/O will prevent editing in the editor until this setting is changed. This does not affect the underlying file attribute unless the option *Change file attribute when toggling read-only for active file* is selected in the program configuration under *File Handling* ➤ *Miscellaneous.*

- Insert/overstrike status: This control allows users to toggle between Insert and Overstrike mode, which affect all documents (not just the active document).

- Column mode status: This control allows users to toggle between column and normal editing modes, which affect all documents (not just the active document).

- CAP status indicator: The rightmost area of the status bar shows CAP if the Caps Lock key is turned on, and will be subdued if Caps Lock is turned off.

Summary

After the UltraEdit license has been activated, the program opens with the Welcome page, which should be configured once and properly. This includes definitions for color themes, the window layout, the ribbon or menu display (the latter as Contemporary or Traditional menus), as well as further options for the document backup and the handling of the tab key.

The middle frame represents the input area, which is used for the central handling of text editing.

At the bottom is a convenient status bar with various status tabs, which are helpful for editing and workflow.

All settings on the Welcome page can be adjusted later and invite the user to experiment until the most efficient customized program interface is defined.

In the next chapter, we will look at the program navigation and which functions are available for this. To do this, we will look at the left, middle, right, and bottom program areas and discuss the mechanisms behind them.

CHAPTER 3

Program Navigation

In this chapter, we will look at the program navigation, which, in addition to the central edit window, includes further areas to the left, right, and below the edit window and provides many additional navigation options for any type of text editing. The middle edit window is supplemented by numerous keyboard shortcuts, which can be used to access the most important program functions very quickly in order to increase efficiency. Extensive context menus are available for each program function, which we will discuss in detail.

Left Program Area

The left program area is called *File View* and can be displayed using the keyboard shortcut Ctrl+U. In principle, this is a child window that contains a tree-style display of the files in different panes. These panes can be used to switch between the modes for *File explorer*, *Project*, *Open files*, and *File lists*.

Individual panes can be shown or hidden via the layout settings, and there are three additional icons at the top right for displaying the panel:

- Window position: Allows the position to be defined, with the possible values *Floating*, *Docking*, *Auto hide*, and *Hide*. In addition, the option *Undockable* can be used to prevent the pane from being docked to other positions in UltraEdit.

- Auto hide: Hides the pane on the left side and only the pane names appear. The pane is made visible again by moving the mouse over the names.

- Close: Closes the entire pane.

File Explorer

The File Explorer can be used to navigate on all existing internal and connected external drives (e.g., on removable media). The drive list is displayed alphabetically for this purpose and normally contains two panes, which are split horizontally, with the upper pane showing the default file tree view and the lower pane showing the contents of the selected folder.

The header area of the File Explorer contains various buttons, which are shown in Figure 3-1. All displayed files can be filtered using a filter, and the default value *.* displays all files. Alternative values are known from the command line, such as *.txt or *.csv. If several file types are to be filtered here, they must be separated by a semicolon.

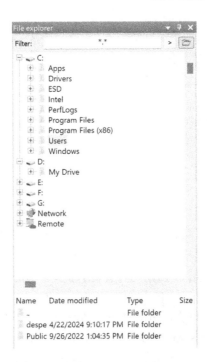

Figure 3-1. *File explorer with filter settings and pane split*

The button to the right of the filter field (right arrow) can be used to execute predefined filter groups, which are available as examples for C/C++ and assembler files. The menu item *Edit list* opens the *Extension Groups window*, in which further groups can be added manually. As can be seen in Figure 3-2, the subgroups are listed below a file group (in square brackets), which can then also be activated via submenus. The default list can be reset with the *Default extension list* button.

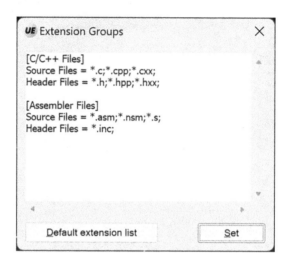

Figure 3-2. *Extension Groups with subcategories*

The button on the right with a folder icon in Figure 3-1 defines whether the File explorer pane is split horizontally, with the upper section showing the standard file tree view and the lower section showing the contents of the selected folder – this separation is displayed in Figure 3-1. If splitting is deactivated, there is only one File explorer pane, and this allows simultaneous navigation through directories and file lists.

For basic navigation in the panes, you should know that a double-click on a file in the lower pane will cause it to be opened for editing. Double-clicking on a folder will navigate into that folder. Double-clicking on the folder labeled "." at the top of the lower pane will navigate to the parent folder.

If a file is selected, right-clicking in the File Tree View presents a context menu, which is described in Table 3-1.

Table 3-1. *Context menu for a selected file in the File Tree View*

Context menu item	Description
System explorer menu	Presents applicable parts of the Windows Explorer context menu
Add file(s)/folder(s) to favorites	Adds all selected file(s) and folder(s) to either the favorite files or project
Rename file	Moves focus to active file name to allow renaming
New folder	Creates a new folder in the selected folder
New file	Creates a new file in the selected folder
Open file	Opens the active file in the edit window
Open with default	Opens the active file in the application registered with Windows for the file type
Properties	Displays the Windows properties dialog for active file
Delete file(s)	Deletes the selected file(s). This is a permanent system-level delete, and the files are not sent to the Recycle Bin
Make folder active file path	Switches to the selected file's parent folder in the Explorer pane
Insert into file	Opens a submenu where the user can choose to insert the selected file's full path, path only, or name only into the active file
Show hidden files/folders	Toggles the visibility of hidden files/folders

If a folder is selected, right-clicking in the File explorer presents an alternative context menu, which is described in Table 3-2.

Table 3-2. *Context menu for a selected folder in the File Tree View*

Context menu item	Description
System explorer menu	Presents applicable parts of the Windows Explorer context menu
Add file(s)/folder(s) to favorites	Adds all selected file(s) and folder(s) to either the favorite files or project
Refresh	Updates listing of all hard drives and removable media
Set directory as root	Sets the active directory as root on right click and selection
Find in files in this directory	Launches the *Find in Files* dialog with the directory set to selected directory
Replace in files in this directory	Launches the *Replace in Files* dialog with the directory set to selected directory
Open command prompt here	Opens the command prompt set to the path for the selected directory
Rename folder	Moves the focus to the active folder name to allow renaming
New folder	Creates a new folder in the selected folder
New file	Creates a new file in the selected folder
Open files	Opens the *Open Files* dialog where the user can sort a filtered list of files in the active folder or in all selected folders based on file name, file path, or modified date, and then open any number of files from the list by double-clicking or clicking the *Open* button
Properties	Displays the Windows properties dialog for the selected folder

(*continued*)

Table 3-2. (*continued*)

Context menu item	Description
Delete folder(s)	Deletes the selected folder(s). This is a permanent system-level delete, and the folders are not sent to the Recycle Bin
Make folder active file path	Sets the selected folder as active file path
Windows directory	Switches focus to the Windows directory
System directory	Switches focus to the System directory
My Documents	Switches focus to the My Documents directory for the current user
Insert into file	Opens a submenu where the user can choose to insert the selected folder's full path, path only (parent folder), or name only into the active file
Show hidden files/ folders	Toggles the visibility of hidden files/folders

Especially the option *Open Files* in the context menu for a selected folder opens the *Open Files* dialog, in which all files in this folder are listed with name, path, and modification date. Figure 3-3 shows that a Quick Search can be performed and the list can be copied to the clipboard. A double-click on a file or the button *Open* opens the file directly in UltraEdit.

UE Open Files			×
Quick files search:		Clipboard	Open

▾ Name	Path	Modified
changes_ues.txt	C:\Program Files\IDM Computer Solutions\UEStudio\changes_ues.txt	04/19/2024, 02:24 AM
dbghelp.dll	C:\Program Files\IDM Computer Solutions\UEStudio\dbghelp.dll	04/19/2024, 02:24 AM
icudt68.dll	C:\Program Files\IDM Computer Solutions\UEStudio\icudt68.dll	04/19/2024, 02:24 AM
icuin68.dll	C:\Program Files\IDM Computer Solutions\UEStudio\icuin68.dll	04/19/2024, 02:24 AM
icuuc68.dll	C:\Program Files\IDM Computer Solutions\UEStudio\icuuc68.dll	04/19/2024, 02:24 AM
idm_tidylib.dll	C:\Program Files\IDM Computer Solutions\UEStudio\idm_tidylib.dll	04/19/2024, 02:24 AM
idmcl.exe	C:\Program Files\IDM Computer Solutions\UEStudio\idmcl.exe	04/19/2024, 02:24 AM
IDMUpdate.exe	C:\Program Files\IDM Computer Solutions\UEStudio\IDMUpdate.exe	04/19/2024, 02:24 AM
KEYLIB32.dll	C:\Program Files\IDM Computer Solutions\UEStudio\KEYLIB32.dll	04/19/2024, 02:24 AM
lmeditor.exe	C:\Program Files\IDM Computer Solutions\UEStudio\lmeditor.exe	04/19/2024, 02:24 AM
lua5.1.dll	C:\Program Files\IDM Computer Solutions\UEStudio\lua5.1.dll	04/22/2024, 02:30 PM
mymake.exe	C:\Program Files\IDM Computer Solutions\UEStudio\mymake.exe	04/19/2024, 02:24 AM
PLUSNative.dll	C:\Program Files\IDM Computer Solutions\UEStudio\PLUSNative.dll	04/19/2024, 02:24 AM
ProtectionPlusDLL.dll	C:\Program Files\IDM Computer Solutions\UEStudio\ProtectionPlusDLL.dll	04/19/2024, 02:24 AM
taglist.uet	C:\Program Files\IDM Computer Solutions\UEStudio\taglist.uet	04/19/2024, 02:24 AM
UACHelper.exe	C:\Program Files\IDM Computer Solutions\UEStudio\UACHelper.exe	04/19/2024, 02:24 AM
UEDOS32.exe	C:\Program Files\IDM Computer Solutions\UEStudio\UEDOS32.exe	04/19/2024, 02:24 AM
UEFeaturesDLL.dll	C:\Program Files\IDM Computer Solutions\UEStudio\UEFeaturesDLL.dll	04/19/2024, 02:24 AM
uehh.exe	C:\Program Files\IDM Computer Solutions\UEStudio\uehh.exe	04/19/2024, 02:24 AM
uejs.dll	C:\Program Files\IDM Computer Solutions\UEStudio\uejs.dll	04/19/2024, 02:24 AM
ues64ctmn.dll	C:\Program Files\IDM Computer Solutions\UEStudio\ues64ctmn.dll	04/22/2024, 02:30 PM
uesctmn.dll	C:\Program Files\IDM Computer Solutions\UEStudio\uesctmn.dll	04/22/2024, 02:30 PM
uespawn.dat	C:\Program Files\IDM Computer Solutions\UEStudio\uespawn.dat	04/19/2024, 02:24 AM
uesres.dll	C:\Program Files\IDM Computer Solutions\UEStudio\uesres.dll	04/19/2024, 02:24 AM
UEStudio.chm	C:\Program Files\IDM Computer Solutions\UEStudio\UEStudio.chm	04/19/2024, 02:24 AM
uestudio.com	C:\Program Files\IDM Computer Solutions\UEStudio\uestudio.com	04/19/2024, 02:24 AM
UEStudio.exe	C:\Program Files\IDM Computer Solutions\UEStudio\UEStudio.exe	04/19/2024, 02:24 AM

Double-click on the file in list to open the file and keep this window open

Figure 3-3. *Open Files dialog with Quick files search and a list of all available files in the selected folder*

The File Explorer is particularly suitable if the user wants to navigate through files and folders and have everything combined within one interface instead of an external file manager (such as Windows Explorer or from third-party manufacturers). This concept also focuses on efficiency, as the user doesn't have to switch between two windows, but UltraEdit provides this functionality.

Project

The Project pane displays all files and directories of the activated project. The project concept has existed within UltraEdit for a long time, and in general, the user can assign various files and folders to a project and add groups to structure all data sets – as a result, this Project pane displays this structure for further text editing.

A project can therefore be understood as a kind of container and is saved in UltraEdit with the file extension .prj. Figure 3-4 shows the exemplary structure of the project pane.

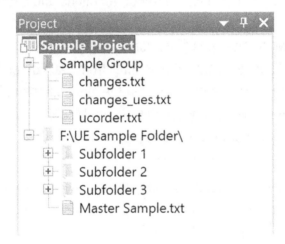

Figure 3-4. *Project pane with the project structure (files, folders, and groups)*

The advantage of this project concept is that the entire project structure is visible while working with UltraEdit and individual files can be opened in the middle edit window by double-clicking. This structure is particularly helpful for larger projects that span over several drives, folders, and files, because everything is clearly accessible from one single location.

In UltraEdit's initial state, no project is loaded. In this case, double-clicking the empty Project pane will open the dialog *Open project*.

To open an existing project, it must first be created once. This creation is done via *Project* ➤ *New project* (Ribbon mode), via *Project* ➤ *New project/workspace* (Traditional menu mode), or via *Project* ➤ *New project* (Contemporary menu mode). Both options open the *Specify Project File* dialog, in which firstly a project file name and its path need to be specified. UltraEdit automatically adds the extension .prj to the file name and later saves the project structure in this text file using a special syntax.

Note   Within this book, we will always separate the ribbon and menu mode for the discussed UltraEdit functions and describe both access paths. Since we learned in Chapter 2 that the menu mode exists with two menu types (Traditional and Contemporary), these two types will be listed explicitly if they differ from each other. If a certain UltraEdit function can be accessed via the identical menu item in both menu types, we simply call this "Menu Mode" – i.e., without the addition Traditional or Contemporary.

For all three ways – in ribbon and both menu modes – the *Project Settings* dialog opens, in which the project directory and elements can be added. This includes groups, folders, files, the currently active file, and all currently open files (see Figure 3-5).

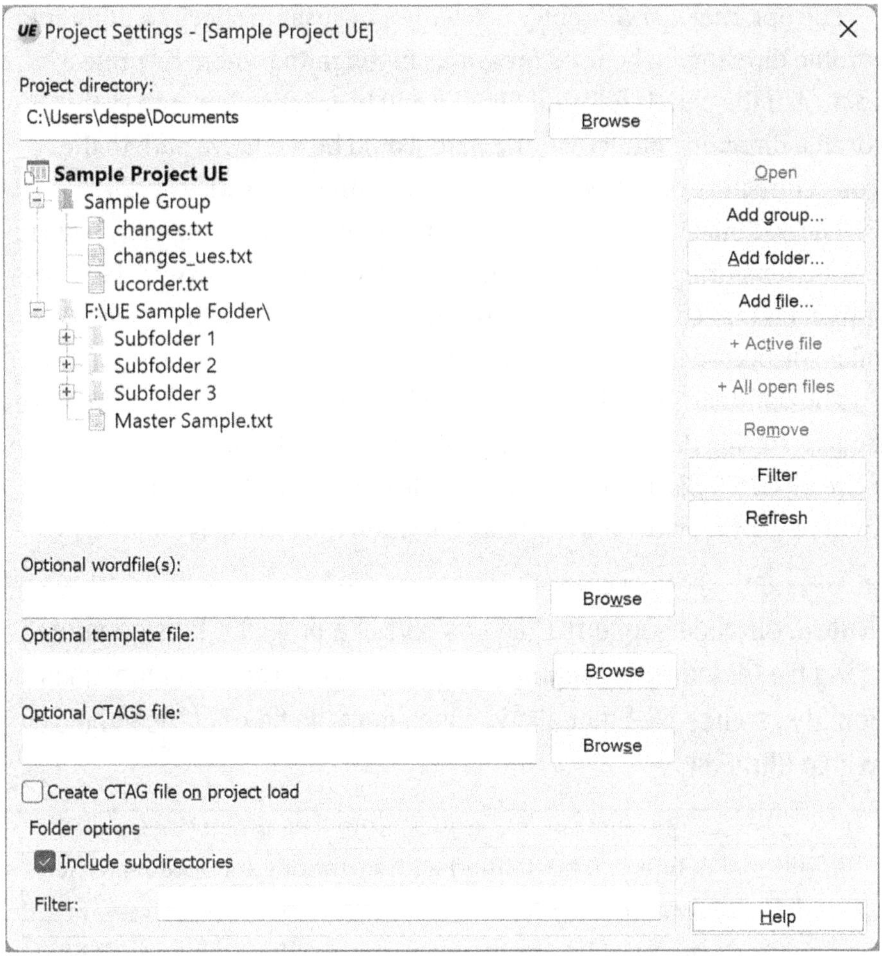

Figure 3-5. *Project Settings while creating a new UltraEdit project*

The buttons on the right allow the elements to be added, and at the same time individual elements can be moved using drag and drop (e.g., files into a group). There is a definable filter and a refresh function.

The optional *wordfile* entry box allows the user to specify a different wordfile directory to be used for syntax highlighting when the project is active. If the path is fully qualified, it will be an absolute path to the wordfile directory; otherwise, the path would be a relative path to the project directory or project file (based on settings above).

The optional template file entry box allows the user to specify a file to be used for storing templates to be used only with the active project. When a project is loaded with this option specified, an additional Project node will be displayed in the Template List.

The optional CTAGS file entry box allows the user to specify a file to be used for storing data for CTAGS functions. The option may also be selected to *Create CTAG file on project load*. If this item is checked, UltraEdit will automatically create the CTAGS tag file when the project is loaded.

Note   UltraEdit supports Ctags as part of a project. Ctags generates a tag file (or index) of programming language objects and functions found in source files that allows these items to be referenced quickly within UltraEdit.

Additional details can be defined with further folder options. When selected, the *Include subdirectories* causes UltraEdit to recursively include all subfolders when a folder is added to a project. If a filter is specified (e.g., *.txt), only files with matching extensions will be considered as part of the project. If a filter is specified for a folder in the file tree view, this filter will apply only to the selected folder and will override the filter defined for the project as a whole in the *Project Settings* dialog.

Finally, we will discuss the context menu that appears with the right mouse click. A distinction is made here as to whether the focus is in an empty area of the Project pane or whether a file or directory is selected. If a folder in an active project is connected to a remote server directory, there are additional options.

If the focus is in an empty area, right-clicking presents a context menu, which is described in Table 3-3.

Table 3-3. *Context menu for an empty area in the Project pane*

Context menu item	Description
Explore	Opens the Windows Explorer window to the active project directory
Refresh	Updates the project information (committing the changes) and refreshes the project list
Edit project file	Opens the active project file (INI based) in the editor
Add folder	Opens the *New folder* dialog for adding a folder from the file system to the project
Add group	Opens a dialog allowing the user to specify the name of a new virtual group folder for the project. Group folders are not real folders but act as virtual containers within the project
Add new file	Opens a dialog allowing the user to specify the name of a new file, which will be added to the project
Add active file	Adds the file currently opened in the edit window to the active project
Add all open files	Adds all currently opened files to the active project
Add files to project	Opens a file browser where the user can choose files to be added to the active project. If no group is selected in the *Project group* drop-down, the selected file(s) will be added to the root of the project

(continued)

Table 3-3. (*continued*)

Context menu item	Description
List files in project	Opens a dialog listing all files in the project, including files from all subfolders. The user can filter files by typing them in the field *Quick file search*. Multiple files may be selected via Ctrl or Shift + mouse click. The button *Open* opens all selected files
Settings	Opens the *Project Settings* dialog
Select active file	Defines the currently focused file as the active file

If a folder in the active project is linked to a remote server directory in the *New Folder* dialog and that folder is selected in the Project pane, the additional options shown in Table 3-4 will be available in the context menu.

Table 3-4. *Additional context menu options for a remote server directory in the Project pane*

Context menu item	Description
Download from server	Downloads all files in the remote path specified to the folder linked to in the active project. Any files with the same name are overwritten regardless of their timestamps
Download with Sync	Downloads only newer files from the server to the folder linked to in the active project
Upload to server	Uploads all files in the remote path specified to the folder linked to in the active project. Any files with the same name on the server are overwritten regardless of their timestamps
Upload with Sync	Uploads only newer files from the local folder to the linked server directory

If a file or folder is selected in the Project pane, the items shown in Table 3-5 are available in the context menu.

Table 3-5. *Context menu for a selected file or folder in the Project pane*

Context menu item	Description
Open/Filter	Opens the selected file in the active project. If a folder is selected, the option *Filter* allows a separate filter that is applied to all displayed sub-elements (e.g., *.txt)
Explore	Opens the Windows Explorer to the selected file/folder directory
Set open file at	Only appears for files and allows to place the caret at the position of the last editing position or the start or end of the file
FTP settings	Only appears for directories and allows a local directory to be linked to an FTP server directory. The dialog *FTP Folder Properties* appears for this purpose, in which an FTP account and remote path are specified
Include subfolders	Only appears for directories and includes/excludes all subfolders that exist below the currently focused folder
Filter 'dot' files/ directories	Filters files and folders that begin with a dot
Remove item(s) from project	Removes selected file(s) and/or folder(s) from the active project
Show (relative) file paths	Will show the relative file path if the path is resolvable to the project directory. If not, the fully qualified path is shown

(*continued*)

Table 3-5. (*continued*)

Context menu item	Description
Find in files in this directory	Only appears for directories and opens the dialog *Find and Replace* with the tab *Find in Files*. Here the user can search in files in this directory for search terms
Replace in files in this directory	Only appears for directories and opens the dialog *Find and Replace* with the tab *Replace in Files*. Here the user can search and replace in files in this directory

Note   It should be mentioned that these context menus are also used in UEStudio, but there are many additional entries in the file/folder context menu in particular. These primarily concern the handling of files/folders with version systems, which are frequently used for the program development in teams. One of the best-known systems is Git, and UEStudio offers several options for dealing with branches. This includes commits, adding files to a repository, viewing the log, comparing two file versions (local and from the repository), and removing files/folders from a repository. These terms are frequently used in program development, and we will discuss them in more detail in the later chapter on UEStudio.

Open Files

The Open files pane displays all currently open files. The user can select multiple items in this pane with Ctrl+Click or Shift+Click and then act upon these items via the context menu.

Figure 3-6 shows an example of this pane, which is of course heavily dependent on the files currently open and provides a good overview. This list offers a better navigation option, especially with many open files that can be accessed with their horizontal tabs, as the arrangement in this Open Files pane is vertical.

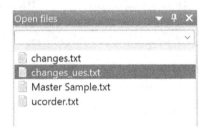

Figure 3-6. *Open files pane with currently opened files*

If a file is selected from the Open files pane, right-clicking opens a context menu, which is described in Table 3-6.

Table 3-6. *Context menu for a selected file in the Open files pane*

Context menu item	Description
Close file	Closes selected file(s)
Save file	Saves selected file(s)
Print file	Prints selected file(s)
Rename file	Renames the selected file
Add files to project	Adds the selected file to an existing UltraEdit project
Tile windows horizontally	Horizontally tiles all open files
Tile windows vertically	Vertically tiles all open files
Make folder active file path	Sets the active file path to the path of the currently selected file
Show names only	If selected, only file names (and not paths) are displayed
Sort by extension	Sorts listed files by extension

File Lists

The File lists pane displays the favorite files, recently opened files, and user-created file groups as collapsible file lists. Figure 3-7 shows an example of these file lists, which may look different depending on the scenario and requirements as well as previous UltraEdit use.

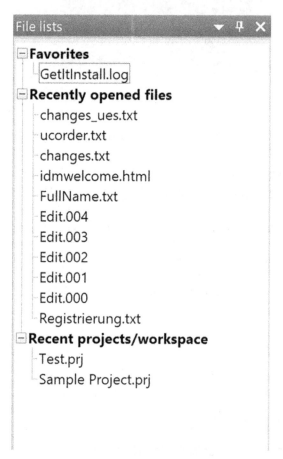

Figure 3-7. *File lists with Favorites, Recently opened files, and projects/workspaces*

The user can create new groups of files by right-clicking on the *Favorites* heading and selecting *Add group*. After a new group name is entered, it will be created as a subgroup of the *Favorites* group. Files can be added with drag and drop to the *Favorites* or other subgroups. Also, items within the list can be dragged to rearrange them as everyone needs it.

The items shown in Table 3-7 are available in the context menu.

Table 3-7. *Context menu in the File lists pane*

Context menu item	Description
Add group	If *Favorites* is selected, this will be enabled and allow you to create a new subgroup of the main *Favorites* group
Add top level group	Adds a top-level group to the File lists view that is on the same top level as other top-level groups (e.g., *Favorites*)
Add folder	Opens a folder browser where the user can select a folder to add to favorites (or subgroup)
Add file	Opens a file browser where the user can select one or more files to add to favorites (or subgroup)
Add active file	Adds active file to favorites (or subgroup)
Add all open files	Adds all open files to favorites (or subgroup)
Show names only	If checked, shows only the file names in the File lists pane and if unchecked, the full file/folder paths are shown
Rename file	Makes the selected file name editable for renaming
Remove selected items	Removes selected file(s)/folder(s) from favorites

Middle Program Area

The middle program area is referred to as the editor window and represents the visible section in which file content is displayed and edited.

The editing process includes, for example, writing new text or code, copying existing texts or sections, and removing texts. To do this, you navigate through the text or code flow, and the more you deal with it, the more efficient your own workflow will be.

Edit Window

Although UltraEdit can be handled entirely with the mouse and this is the most comfortable way for the majority of users, it is still an editor that expects characters entered with the keyboard for text editing. It therefore makes sense to make the most important program functions accessible via keyboard shortcuts so that the focus is not shifted away from the keyboard during text input and efficiency is increased at the same time.

Figure 3-8 shows an example of the edit window, which contains the open files arranged in horizontal tabs. For each file, the line numbering is located vertically on the left, and the column position scale is located horizontally at the top. The latter allows precise navigation through the individual characters of the file content.

Figure 3-8. *Edit window with line numbers, position scale, and document map*

The *changes.txt* and *changes_ues.txt* files opened in Figure 3-8 are located in the UltraEdit and UEStudio directories and contain a comprehensive list of version changes. This starts with UltraEdit from version 8.0 and with UEStudio from the first published version. Both files provide technical insights into how both applications have changed over the years, including which optimizations and new features have been integrated, as well as which bugs have been fixed.

The vertical area on the right is the document map, which is a compact and minimized display of the file content with the currently visible section of the edit window highlighted in gray. Convenient navigation is also possible here by holding down the mouse button and moving the focus marker down/up, thereby influencing the display of the visible edit window in real time. It is also possible to click directly on a specific position in the document map and the edit window automatically adjusts itself. Clicking the right mouse button opens a context menu with further options (see Table 3-8).

Table 3-8. *Context menu for the document map*

Context menu item	Description
Zoom in (show less)	Shows less of the file in the document map at once
Zoom out (show more)	Shows more of the file in the document map at once
Show – Active line	Toggles the visibility of the active line in the document map
Show – Bookmarks	Toggles the visibility of bookmarks in the document map when they exist in the active file
Show – Code folding	Toggles the visibility of folding nodes in the document map when they exist in the active file
Reposition caret on click	Sets the caret at the beginning of the line in the edit window when clicking in the document map
Close document map	Closes the document map. This can be reactivated via *View* ➤ *Document map* (Ribbon mode) or *View* ➤ *View/lists* ➤ *Document map* (Traditional menu mode) or *View* ➤ *Document map* (Contemporary menu mode)

The display of the edit window can be switched from normal ASCII mode to hex mode, which can be done using the key shortcut Ctrl+H and is discussed in more detail in later chapters. Hex mode is normally used for non-ASCII files or binary files, which generally contain nonprintable characters and do not represent text files.

The following tables therefore list the keyboard shortcuts while working in the edit window, which are divided into the categories *Document Navigation* (Table 3-9), *Select/Delete/Insert* (Table 3-10), *Hex Mode* (Table 3-11), *Bookmark* (Table 3-12), and menus. The latter category contains the menu items *File* (Table 3-13), *Edit* (Table 3-14), *Search*

(Table 3-15), *View* (Table 3-16), *Format* (Table 3-17), *Macro* (Table 3-18), *DOS* (Table 3-19), and *Help* (Table 3-20). Most of the menu functions will be discussed in more detail later in this book, so the keyboard shortcuts for the most efficient editor navigation will primarily be described here.

Table 3-9. *Document navigation shortcuts*

Keyboard shortcut	Description
Ctrl + Up	Scroll up one line keeping the caret in view
Ctrl + Down	Scroll down one line keeping the caret in view
F4	Toggle focus between the active file and the Tree View if shown
Alt + Right	Position the caret at the first non-space character of the next paragraph
Alt + Left	Position the caret at the first non-space character of the current paragraph (if positioned mid-paragraph) or previous paragraph
Alt + Page Up	Position the caret at the beginning of the first line of the display
Alt + Page Down	Position the caret at the beginning of the last line of the display
Alt + '-' (*NM)	Position the line with the caret at the top of the window
Alt + '+' (*NM)	Position the line with the caret at the bottom of the window
Alt + "*" (*NM)	Position the line with the caret at the center of the window
Ctrl + '1' (*NM)	Position the caret at the end of the previous word
Ctrl + '2' (*NM)	Position the caret at the end of the next word
Ctrl + F6	Make the next document window as active
Ctrl + Shift + F6	Make the previous document window as active

Note description for *NM: This will only work on the numeric keypad.

Table 3-10. *Select/Delete/Insert shortcuts*

Keyboard shortcut	Description
Ctrl + Shift + Left (or Right)	Select the word preceding (or following) the caret
Ctrl + Backspace	Delete the word preceding the caret
Ctrl + Delete	Delete the word following the caret
Ctrl + I	Insert a literal character at the caret position
INS	Toggle between Insert and Overstrike mode

Table 3-11. *Hex Mode shortcuts*

Keyboard shortcut	Description
Ctrl + H	Toggle Hex editing mode
Ctrl + D	Insert or delete characters in Hex editing mode

Table 3-12. *Bookmark shortcuts*

Keyboard shortcut	Description
Ctrl + F2	Toggle bookmark on and off
F2	Go to next bookmark

Table 3-13. *File menu shortcuts*

Keyboard shortcut	Description
Ctrl + N	Create a new document file
Ctrl + O	Open an existing document file
Ctrl + Q	Open an existing document without showing the *File Open* dialog
Ctrl + F4	Close an existing document file
Ctrl + S	Save the active document
F12	Save the active document as a new file
Ctrl + P	Print the active document

Table 3-14. *Edit menu shortcuts*

Keyboard shortcut	Description
Ctrl + X	Cut text from the document into the clipboard
Ctrl + C	Copy text from the document into the clipboard
Ctrl + V	Paste text from the clipboard into the active document
Ctrl + 0-9	Select active clipboard
Ctrl + A	Select all text in the active document
Ctrl + Z	Undo the last action if possible
Ctrl + Y	Reverse the last undo action if possible
Ctrl + J	Join several selected lines into one line
Ctrl + E	Delete line the caret is on
Ctrl + F11	Delete from the caret to start of line
Ctrl + F12	Delete from the caret to end of line
Ctrl + W	Toggle Word Wrap on/off
F7	Insert time/date at caret

Table 3-15. *Search menu shortcuts*

Keyboard shortcut	Description
Alt + F3 or Ctrl + F	Find a character string
Ctrl + F3	Repeat last find toward beginning of file
F3	Repeat last find toward end of file
Ctrl + B	Find matching brace (,[,{ or },],)
Ctrl + R	Find and replace a character string with another
Ctrl + G	Go to the specified line (or hex address)

Table 3-16. *View menu shortcuts*

Keyboard shortcut	Description
Ctrl + U	Toggle File Tree View
Ctrl + F8	Toggle Tag List

Table 3-17. *Format menu shortcuts*

Keyboard shortcut	Description
Ctrl + T	Reformat the current paragraph or selected text
Ctrl + F5	Convert selected text to lowercase
Alt + F5	Convert selected text to uppercase
F5	Capitalize the first character of each word in selected text
Shift + F5	Invert case of all characters in selected text
Ctrl + K	Invoke the spelling checker
Alt + C	Toggle column/block mode

Table 3-18. *Macro menu shortcuts*

Keyboard shortcut	Description
Ctrl + M	Replay a macro
Ctrl + L	Replay a macro the specified number of times

Table 3-19. *DOS menu shortcuts*

Keyboard shortcut	Description
F9	Run DOS Window command
Ctrl + F9	Repeat last DOS Window command
F10	Execute Windows Program

Table 3-20. *Help menu shortcuts*

Keyboard shortcut	Description
Shift + F1	Invoke the context-sensitive help

Right Program Area

If the *Multi-window* layout is selected, the right program area contains three tabs, which are called *Function List*, *XML manager*, and *Template List*.

Individual panes can be shown or hidden via the layout settings, and there are three additional icons at the top right for displaying the panel:

- Window position: Allows the position to be defined, with the possible values *Floating*, *Docking*, *Auto hide*, and *Hide*. In addition, the option *Undockable* can be used to prevent the pane from being docked to other positions in UltraEdit.

- Auto hide: Hides the pane on the right side and only the pane names appear. The pane is made visible again by moving the mouse over the names.

- Close: Closes the entire pane.

Function List

The Function List shows a list of functions from the active source file (or for all project files if enabled). This distinction can be toggled in the Layout settings. The results are displayed either in an alphabetical order or in an order they occur in the document.

Navigation within the Function List is intuitive:

- The user can double-click on an item and UltraEdit will jump to the occurrence of – and move focus to – that item in the file.

- If an item in the Function List is selected and the Enter key is pressed, UltraEdit will jump to the occurrence but keep focus in the Function List.

- If the keyboard shortcut Ctrl+Enter is pressed, UltraEdit will jump to the definition and move the focus to the item (this is the same effect as double-clicking).

The drop-down field at the top of the Function List allows the user to search for items in the Function List by typing any number of characters to match all or part of an item. All items matching the typed string are populated into the drop-down field, which can be opened by clicking the down-arrow button on the right. Opening and selecting any of the items in the drop-down list will jump to that particular item in the active file.

After typing a string in the drop-down's input, the user can press Enter to immediately jump to the first matched item in the Function List and active file. It is also possible to use the down arrow key to scroll down through other matches and jump to them as well.

While navigating through a file containing Function List items, UltraEdit will highlight the function in which the caret is positioned. This is done by locating the function occurring immediately before the current caret position. If the caret is outside of a function definition, the previous function will be highlighted, and if the Function List is configured to show functions for all project files, this behavior is disabled.

While the Function List is designed primarily to list function definitions, because of its generic design, it can actually be used to list any text string that matches a regular expression pattern. These regular expression patterns are defined as function strings in the wordfile that defines the active file's syntax highlighting. While it is possible to modify these by directly editing the wordfile, it is recommended to make modifications through the special configuration dialog called *Modify groups*.

Figure 3-9 shows an example of how the Function List can be structured using the UltraEdit Welcome page as an example. It should be mentioned that the Welcome page is technically positioned as an HTML-based file including various images, JavaScript string files, and Cascading Style Sheets (CSS) documents. These files are located in the UltraEdit subdirectory *\extras\welcome*.

Figure 3-9. *Function List with found functions and categories (e.g., External Links, Anchors, Images, Scripts, Stylesheets, and Named Functions)*

Right-clicking in the Function List presents a context menu, which is described in Table 3-21.

Table 3-21. *Context menu for the Function List*

Context menu item	Description
Sort list	Sorts all functions alphabetically. If unchecked, functions are sorted in the order they occur in the file
Automatically expand functions	If checked, all functions containing subgroups will automatically expand in the Function List when the user moves the caret onto or into them in the editor
Collapse all	Collapses all functions in the Function List to hide their subgroups
Expand all	Expands all functions in the Function List to show their subgroups
List for all project files	Lists all functions for all files in the active project. If unchecked, the functions listed are limited to the active file
Copy to clipboard	Copies the entire content of the Function List to the clipboard
Refresh function list	Refreshes the Function List (the same with F8)
Flat list	Toggles the display of functions between flat and hierarchical tree-style modes
Configuration	Opens the dialog *Modify groups* where the user can add, remove, and modify regular expressions used to match functions

XML Manager

The UltraEdit XML manager is a dockable window or right pane tab which provides a parsed, visual, tree-style representation of the active XML file with options for modifying the XML structure.

Navigation within the XML manager is straightforward:

- Double-clicking on an item will move the caret to the related XML element in the active file.

- Pressing Shift+double-click with the caret on a node will select the text corresponding with that node in the active file.

- Expanding a node in the XML manager will also cause the corresponding source code to be expanded in the editor if folded.

The button on the upper right corner with a folder icon will split the XML manager into two panes; the upper pane will display the active XML document tree, while the lower pane will display a table with an Attribute and Value column. When a node is selected in the top pane, it will be scanned for attributes, and any found attributes are listed in the lower pane along with their values.

If a node (means an element or attribute) is selected, after a momentary delay, the user can click a second time on it to make it editable. When editing an element in the XML manager, the Enter key saves the changes to the document tree and appropriately updates the open and close tag for the element in the active document.

The combobox at the top can be used to navigate quickly within the document tree of the active XML document. Typing an element or attribute name and then pressing Enter will jump to and select the first matching node.

It's also possible to drag and drop elements in the XML tree to reposition them in the active XML document. If the user uses drag and drop with nodes in the XML manager, the corresponding text in the active file will be moved accordingly.

Note   The XML manager will always highlight the current/active XML node under the caret in the main edit window.

Figure 3-10 shows an example of the XML manager using the UltraEdit Command Palette XML file. This file is called *commandpalette.xml*, located in the UltraEdit subdirectory *\extras\commandpalette*, and contains all the UltraEdit commands.

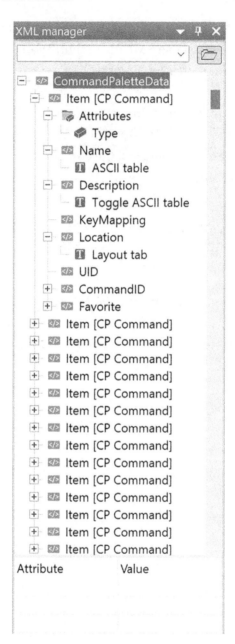

Figure 3-10. *XML manager with XML interpretation and structure of the current XML file*

Right-clicking in the XML manager presents a context menu, which is described in Table 3-22.

Table 3-22. *Context menu for the XML manager*

Context menu item	Description
Automatically expand nodes	Automatically expands all nodes in the XML manager for a fully visible list
Up	Moves the selected node up in the document tree
Down	Moves the selected node down in the document tree
Copy	Copies the selected node to the clipboard
Select	Selects the active node in the document tree
Copy XPath	Copies the selected node's XPath to the clipboard
Format file	Reformats the active XML document into a more human-readable structure by adding/removing line breaks and indentation where necessary
Parse file	Parses the active XML document and updates the XML document tree
Cut	Cuts the selected node to the clipboard
Replace with clipboard	Replaces the selected node with the contents of the clipboard
Paste before	Pastes the node in the clipboard before the active node
Paste after	Pastes the node in the clipboard after the active node
Duplicate	Duplicates the selected node below the active node in the document tree

Template List

The Template List is a dockable window or right pane tab that displays all templates that have been configured in the dialog *Modify templates*.

Navigation within the Template List and adding templates is very easy:

- Double-clicking a template in the Template List will insert it into the active file at the caret position.

- Templates can be inserted via *Edit ➤ Insert template* (Ribbon mode) or *Insert ➤ Template* (Traditional menu mode) or *Edit ➤ Insert template* (Contemporary menu mode)

- Coding templates can be integrated via *Coding ➤ Code template* (Ribbon mode) or *Advanced ➤ Display/ modify templates* (Traditional menu mode) or *Coding ➤ Code template* (Contemporary menu mode)

Templates are in general organized into four groups: *Global, Layout, Language,* and *Project*. All template groups are differently available:

- Global templates are always available.

- Layout templates are only available when the layout they're associated with is loaded.

- Language templates are associated with languages specified for syntax highlighting and are only available when editing files with extensions included in the language's wordfile.

- Project templates are only available when the project they're associated with is loaded.

Figure 3-11 shows an example of a template list that is generated when a C++ source code file was opened. The two templates in the *Global* and *Lean* areas were created manually, and the templates below the *C/C++* area were created by UltraEdit.

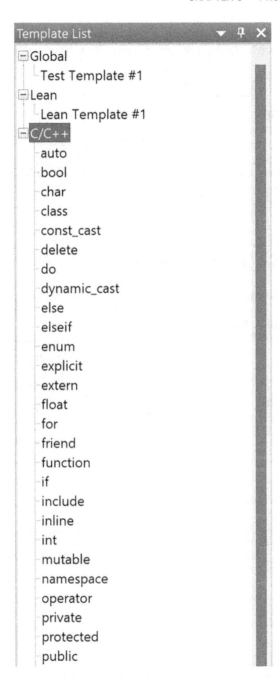

*Figure 3-11. Template List with created templates from an example
C++ source code file*

Right-clicking in the empty area or a template group of the Template List presents a context menu, which is described in Table 3-23.

Table 3-23. *Context menu for the Template List*

Context menu item	Description
Modify templates	Opens the dialog *Modify templates*
Open template file	Opens the template group's XML-based template file directly in the editor

When right-clicking on a template within the Template List, the context menu described in Table 3-24 is available.

Table 3-24. *Context menu for any template within the Template List*

Context menu item	Description
Sort alphabetically	Sorts listed templates alphabetically within active group
Move up	Moves the selected template up one position in the list
Move down	Moves the selected template down one position in the list
Delete template	Deletes the selected template from the list and the associated template file (if the template contains other templates, it will not be deleted)
Rename template	Renames the selected template
Add/modify template	Opens the dialog *Modify templates* so the selected template can be edited or new templates can be added
Insert template	Inserts the selected template into the active document

Templates are created with the dialog *Modify templates*, and text can also be selected in a file and moved via drag and drop into a template group of the Template List (the latter method is of course much faster and therefore more efficient). Newly created templates are given a generic default name that can be edited immediately.

Note   The option to create templates via drag and drop requires that the option *Disable drag & drop* is unchecked via *Advanced* ➤ *Settings* ➤ *Editor* ➤ *Miscellaneous* (Ribbon mode) or *Advanced* ➤ *Configuration* ➤ *Editor* ➤ *Miscellaneous* (Traditional menu mode) or *File* ➤ *Settings* ➤ *Editor* ➤ *Miscellaneous* (Contemporary menu mode).

We will discuss the dialog *Modify templates* in more detail in later chapters, because it is of secondary importance for this chapter – which focuses on the program navigation.

Lower Program Area

The lower program area is referred to as the Output Window area and represents the visible section, which represents output texts and lists of various UltraEdit program functions. This lower area is automatically activated as soon as the multi-window layout has been activated and can also be activated later via *Layout* ➤ *Output window* (Ribbon mode), *View* ➤ *Views/lists* ➤ *Data managers* ➤ *Output window* (Traditional menu mode), or *Layout* ➤ *Output window (Contemporary menu mode)*.

Output Window

The output is captured from user tools, the *Find in files* output, scripting output, version control (in UEStudio), and various other areas of functionality that may write messages or output.

All output sent to the Output Window will automatically scroll so that the view of the output will always be at the bottom (most recent). In addition, the user can configure this behavior by unchecking the option *Scroll output* in the Output Window context menu. Generally, any command that results in new output being written to the Output Window will result in the Output Window first being cleared before the new output is written.

Note   Whereas the number of output windows was limited in the previous versions of UltraEdit and UEStudio, today the user can create multiple new output windows by using the plus symbol at the bottom left of the output window.

Navigation within the Output Window is quite powerful:

- By double-clicking on a line containing a file name and line number, UltraEdit attempts to open the file at the line number.

- If the file name is fully qualified, the file name will be located and the number after this will be used for the line number.

- If the file name is not fully qualified, UltraEdit will attempt to determine the file name from the first word in the line that contains a period.

- UltraEdit will then attempt to open the specified file relative to the directory of the active file.

- If the file does not exist in the directory of the active file, UltraEdit will try to open the file from the project directory if this directory is specified in the project settings.

- If the file still is not located, UltraEdit will then attempt to resolve it to the setting *Set default path for relative paths*, which can be accessed via the Output Window context menu.

- By pressing Enter on a file path while the focus is in the Output Window, UltraEdit will position to the file/line while keeping focus in the Output Window.

- If the user is pressing Ctrl+Enter on a file path, UltraEdit will position to the file/line and move focus to the edit window.

Figure 3-12 shows an example of the Output Window using the *Find in Files* function of UltraEdit. What can be seen very clearly here is the color highlighting of the found positions. By default, two lines are automatically displayed before and after a search result. The search is concluded with a summary, which contains the total search hits and number of searched files. We will discuss the search functions of UltraEdit in more detail in later chapters.

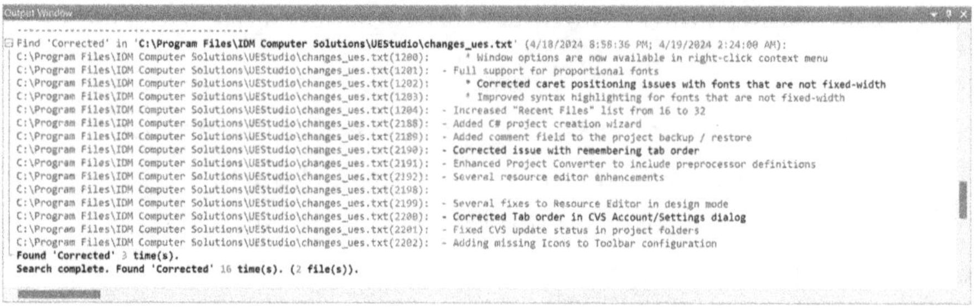

Figure 3-12. *Output Window of UltraEdit, here as an example with the function Find in Files*

Right-clicking in the Output Window presents a context menu, which is described in Table 3-25.

Table 3-25. *Context menu for the Output Window*

Context menu item	Description
Clear output	Clears all output in the output window
Copy to clipboard	Copies active line/selection to the clipboard
Copy all output to clipboard	Copies contents of active window to the clipboard
Collapse all	Collapses all foldable sections in *Find in Files* output
Expand all	Expands all foldable sections in *Find in Files* output
Next message	Moves the focus to the next item in the output window listing and opens the referenced file to the listed line
Previous message	Moves the focus to the previous item in the output window listing and opens the referenced file to the listed line

(continued)

Table 3-25. *(continued)*

Context menu item	Description
Set default path for relative paths	Opens a folder browser to allow the user to set a directory to be used for attempting to open relative paths in the output window
Go to error/warning	Opens the referenced file to the indicated line/column
Scroll output	Controls whether the output window scrolls to the last line when populated or remains at the top of the window
Allow docking	Controls whether the output window can be docked within the main application window framework
Hide output window(s)	Hides or closes the output window (depending upon its docked state)
Use spaces instead of tabs	If checked, tabs will be replaced with spaces in all text written to the output window
Show tool tips	If checked, a tooltip will be shown on hover when a line in the output window is not fully visible because it exceeds the window width

Summary

In this chapter, we have dealt with the UltraEdit program navigation and discussed the basic setting options of the user interface. This starts with the Welcome page, themes, layouts, the ribbon/menu modes, and the layout of the program interface itself.

The GUI is highly configurable and consists of the left program area, which contains a file explorer, project management, open files, and file lists. The middle edit window represents the central component for viewing and editing files. There are numerous keyboard shortcuts for this, which we will cover. The right program area contains the function list, the XML manager, and the template list, as well as the output window in the lower program area.

All UltraEdit components are supplemented by context menus that can be opened with a right mouse click. These menus are also discussed in detailed tabular form.

The next chapter deals with the GUI customization and various program options that make UltraEdit the flexible and powerful editor that we are allowed to use today as efficiently as possible.

CHAPTER 4

GUI Customization and Settings

One of the great strengths of UltraEdit (and of any editor, of course) is its versatility and flexibility, which are realized through the most detailed configuration mechanisms possible. UltraEdit takes a very complex and at the same time clear approach here, and the scope of this chapter stands in contrast to other shorter chapters. We would therefore like to point out that although this chapter describes the many possibilities and functions of UltraEdit, it can be used as a reference for the purpose of text editing, depending on the user's preference.

The various features and functions of UltraEdit can be conveniently controlled via the settings functionality. Because these options and the associated amount of details have historically become more and more varied and extensive, certain categories were used within a navigation panel arranged on the left, which is navigated through like a tree view (we will present this settings dialog in great detail below).

On the following pages, we would like to discuss the most important settings and how this setting functionality is implemented in UltraEdit. We will also discuss advanced features such as saving/restoring user configurations and the use of multiple user configurations.

© Devid Espenschied 2025
D. Espenschied, *Mastering UltraEdit*, https://doi.org/10.1007/979-8-8688-1160-9_4

Note   The author has tried to describe most of the UltraEdit options comprehensively, although new options are constantly being added and the level of detail varies. Therefore, and in any case, the online help and the UltraEdit Wiki wiki.ultraedit.com/Category:Settings are recommended in addition.

Program Configuration

The settings are opened either via *Advanced* ➤ *Settings* (Ribbon mode), via *Advanced* ➤ *Configuration* (Traditional menu mode), or via *Advanced* ➤ *Settings* (Contemporary menu mode). All three options open the *Configuration* file dialog, in which all settings are contained in a central location. Figure 4-1 shows the Configuration dialog with all categories on the left navigation panel.

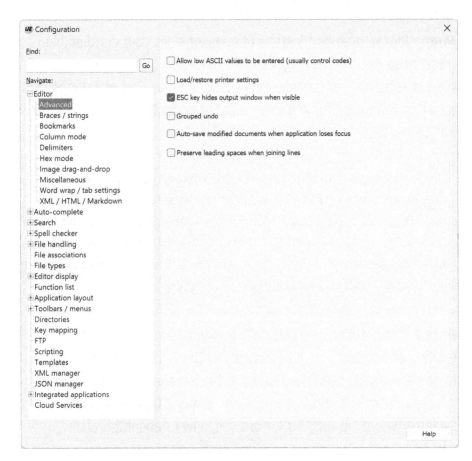

Figure 4-1. *UltraEdit Configuration dialog*

UltraEdit saves customizations such as key mappings, themes, layouts, etc., in separate files, whereby the most important INI file is called *ue. ini* and the location of this file is normally in *%APPDATA%\IDMComp\ UltraEdit*. Within the Configuration dialog in the area *Application layout ➤ Advanced*, the exact path and name are displayed in the lower area with the name *INI file location*.

Note   Please note that instead of one single INI configuration file, UltraEdit saves, for example, key mappings in a .uek file and more volatile settings (like recently opened/closed files, layout settings, and so on) in separate files in the "volatile" subdirectory in relation to the INI file location.

In that same page of the Configuration dialog, there is the option *Use registry for settings (not INI file)*. This option doesn't move the existing items to the registry but causes UltraEdit to save and retrieve all settings from the registry. After UltraEdit checks that the INI file is in use, it checks for this value before reading any other values. If this option is set, UltraEdit stores from this point on all settings in the registry.

Note 1   This option was originally implemented for the faster reading of settings from memory (rather than from INI files), therefore to achieve a faster startup. Thanks to the advancement of hardware, it is becoming less and less important. It might be useful on some systems where file read/writes are still slow or encumbered in some way.

Note 2   Please note that switching this option on/off does not result in options being transferred from one source to another, but that the options are saved in the new position from this point onward when an option is changed.

The location for saving options within the registry is *HKEY_CURRENT_USER\Software\IDM Computer Solutions\UltraEdit*.

Navigation in the Configuration Dialog

The efficient navigation within this Configuration dialog helps any user to find options quickly and maintain an overview. An additional search option for all UltraEdit settings is the Command palette, which we will discuss in more detail in Chapter 9.

The first thing to notice is the grouping of options into categories, which are displayed in the left-side navigation panel. Each category can be expanded (plus symbol) and collapsed (minus symbol). The right-side options panel contains the options contained in the selected category.

Between the left-side navigation panel and the right-side options panel is the splitter, which can be moved to the left/right by holding down the mouse button to customize the display. The same type of customization applies to the dialog border, which can be dragged in any direction to make more content visible on the screen depending on the graphic resolution.

The *Find* field at the top left and the corresponding *Go* button are useful if the user is looking for an option but doesn't know its exact name. A search keyword may help here, and the search results are displayed directly in real time in the left-side navigation panel and can be opened with a double-click.

And as in every dialog in UltraEdit, F1 opens the context-sensitive program online help with further details and explanations.

Category: Editor

The category *Editor* contains all options for the editor functionality of UltraEdit and is divided into subcategories. Figure 4-2 shows the Configuration dialog after its execution, where the Editor category and the Advanced subcategory are pre-selected by default.

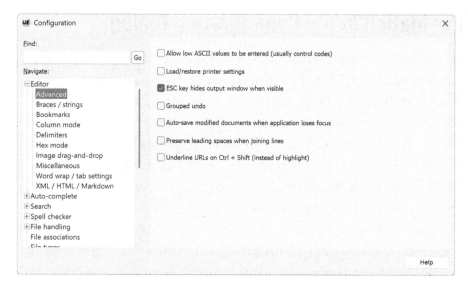

Figure 4-2. *Category Editor in the UltraEdit Configuration*

- Advanced: This category contains, for example, the permission to input "low values" such as control codes during editing (normally these would be ignored). Furthermore, printer settings can be loaded/stored, where UltraEdit tries to communicate with the printer driver when it loads and shuts down (to preserve settings). If a network printer is specified as the default printer and not available, this may cause a delay on startup while UltraEdit tries to find the printer on the network.

    More options are available including using the *ESC key to hide the output windows when visible* and a grouped undo – this means when enabled that the undo function will be executed on a word-by-word rather than character-by-character basis. The latter setting can be toggled during the editing of a document (and the undo buffer is partially created with both settings), so the undo functionality will reflect the settings in place at the time the document was created.

The Advanced Editor settings are completed with the option *Auto-Save modified documents when application loses focus*, which is quite handy, because when enabled, all modified documents will be saved when focus shifts to another application. The second option preserves leading line spaces when the join lines command is executed. And the third option *Underline URLs on Ctrl + Shift (instead of highlight)* means that pressing Ctrl+Shift will apply an underline styling to URLs instead of highlighting them. The user can click the underlined or highlighted URL to launch it in the default browser.

- Braces/strings: This category contains various options that define the handling of braces and strings. If the option *Enable auto-brace matching* is enabled and the cursor is positioned beside an open or close brace, the matching brace will automatically be highlighted. By *Brace match in comments*, the *Go to brace* and *Select to brace* functions in the Coding tab and auto-brace matching (if active) will match braces in commented text as well as in source code.

  UltraEdit contains an integrated brace auto-completion, and via this function, when an opening brace character is typed, the matching close brace character will automatically be inserted into the active document. The open and close brace characters used for this feature are specified in the wordfile associated with the active file's syntax highlighting. If the wordfile contains no open and close brace characters, or if the active file is not syntax highlighted, the default brace characters are used: {}, (), and []. If the Backspace key is pressed immediately following the auto-completion of a close brace, both the opening and the closing brace will be removed. If the user manually types the closing brace following the auto-completion of a close brace or when the caret is positioned immediately in front of a close brace, UltraEdit will detect this and skip over the closing brace without inserting a second closing brace so that multiple closing braces are not inserted. Further completion options for this auto-completion functionality can be enabled for the use within comments, strings, and plain-text files.

A string auto-completion exists in a similar way to the brace auto-completion, and when an opening string character is typed, the matching close string character will automatically be inserted into the active document. The open and close string characters used for this feature are specified in the wordfile associated with the active file's syntax highlighting. If the wordfile contains no specification for String Chars, or if the active file is not syntax highlighted, the default string characters are used: ' and ". Further completion options for this auto-completion functionality can be enabled for the use within comments and plain-text files.

- Bookmarks: Bookmarks are used in various places in UltraEdit and make it easier to find previously marked positions. Various options can be configured in this category, such as the *Prompt for name when adding bookmark*. With this option, the *Add Bookmark* dialog is presented when a bookmark is added, prompting the user to enter a name for the added bookmark. Further options exist for the display of the name when hovering over a bookmark, the highlight of the entire line rather than just the associated line number, and the column the cursor is located in at the time the line is bookmarked is stored. Jumping to a bookmark will position the cursor accordingly instead of positioned at the beginning of the line.

  The *Save Bookmarks* option allows users to save bookmarks for any file that has active bookmarks when a file is closed – if this option is disabled, UltraEdit will delete any saved bookmarks the next time the editor is closed. With the last option bookmarks will be stored and tracked independently for each split window.

- Column mode: The column mode is a powerful feature of UltraEdit and changes the operation of the editor for selecting text. This is based on the character column position of the first character selected to the column of the last character of text selected (Figure 4-3 shows Column mode with the selected word "Line").

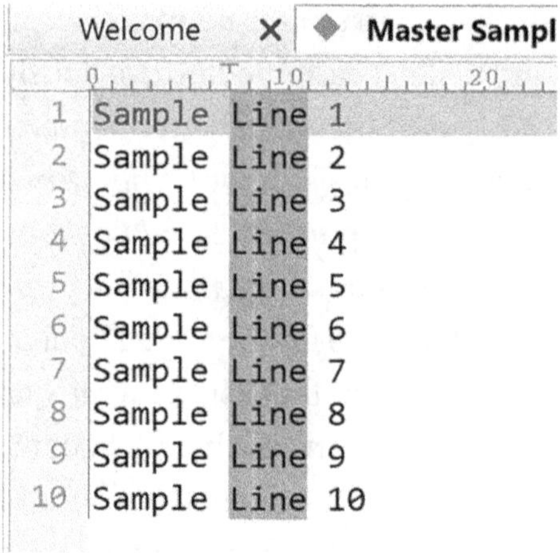

Figure 4-3. *Column mode can be activated via Alt+C*

This brings with it some powerful options, such as the prevention of *overstrike of unselected columns* and the *overstrike if UltraEdit is in overstrike mode.* The latter option means that the column operations operate either in Insert mode (as default) or Overstrike/overpaste mode based on the insert/overstrike keyboard setting. This is toggled by the Insert Key and shows up on the UltraEdit status bar. If in Overstrike mode, cut/delete operations will remove the contents but leave spaces so that column data is not shifted. Paste operations will paste over the current position data and not shift columns either.

The Column mode options are finalized with a possibility to *always enable overstrike unselected columns,* the *automatic population of sort fields inside column mode,* and the *paste into all selected columns when the clipboard contains less than 1 line.*

- Delimiters: UltraEdit allows to define a delimiter, which can be seen as the character following a file name that allows the user to add /xxx to go to a line number or column number. If this character conflicts with a file or path name, it can be modified to a character that is not likely to appear in a file or path name.

  The standard character is /.

  Furthermore, left and right delimiters can be defined for Ctrl+double-click. To describe this, we have to note that the selection of text by double-clicking the primary mouse button (usually the left button) is supported by default. Normally a single word is selected, made up of any alphanumeric character or underscore "_". If the control key is pressed at the time the primary mouse button is double-clicked, a string is selected rather than just a single word. This functionality can be very useful in selecting file names, email addresses, and so on. The characters that delimit the string are configurable with the two options for the left and right delimiters – and this function works on a single line only. The defined entries, one for the left edge of the text to be selected and one for the right edge, specify what characters should be used to stop any further text from being selected. If a space only is specified in each field, all text on either side of the cursor position will be selected until a space is encountered.

- Hex mode: The UltraEdit hex mode can be activated via Ctrl+H and toggles the active window from regular plain-text editing into hex editing mode. While the hex editing mode is typically used for binary files, these files often contain nonprintable characters and are not plain-text files. However, in some cases, hex editing is useful or necessary for plain-text files as well. When in hex mode, UltraEdit splits the screen area into three areas: *File Offset*, *Hexadecimal representation*, and *ASCII representation*. We will introduce this special editing mode in more detail later and describe the possible options here.

With the option *Open files containing hex 00's (nulls) in hex mode*, UltraEdit handles files differently. Any file containing nulls which is not detected as a UTF-16 file will be opened automatically in hex mode. If this option is disabled, then the file would be opened as a normal text file for editing. UltraEdit will respect and retain the active mode (text mode or hex mode) for the active file when reloading the file (either via Revert to Saved, File Change Detection, or File Change Polling).

The next special option *Allow editing of text files with hex 00's without converting them to spaces* means that when a file is loaded, UltraEdit checks the first 7 KB of the file and if it contains more than two Nulls (hexadecimal 00), the file is considered a binary/hex file. Nulls are not valid in an ASCII file and will be converted to spaces if the user edits the file in text mode, and this option is not enabled (by default). If the user views a hex file in text mode but makes no changes, UltraEdit will not convert the Nulls to spaces, but if the user makes changes in text mode to a hex file, the change will occur.

By enabling this option, the user overrides this conversion of Nulls (hex 00) to spaces, but it is still recommended not editing binary files in text mode. Nulls are normally considered as string terminators and are not generally valid in ASCII files. Using this setting may cause some functions not to work past the Null, although this should not affect general editing.

With the last option *Number of hex characters per line*, the user can define the number of hex characters to be shown in each line of the display. UltraEdit must be restarted once this value is changed.

- Image drag-and-drop: UltraEdit provides a functionality to add images to web files as HTML or CSS code using one of three methods:

  - By dragging and dropping the image file(s) from the Windows Explorer

  - By dragging and dropping the image file(s) from the File View (Explorer or Project pane)

  - By double-clicking the image file(s) in the File View (Explorer or Project pane)

  This feature keys off the active file's highlighting type and will only work for web-based languages (HTML, JavaScript, Perl, PHP, VBScript, XML, and CSS). The following file extensions are supported for this operation: BMP, GIF, ICO, JPEG, JPG, PNG, SVG, and TIFF. If this option is disabled, image files opened via any of the methods described above will be opened in UltraEdit in hex mode. The HTML and CSS format can also be defined, using placeholders for image format variables (e.g., $P for the file path or $S for the image size).

- Miscellaneous: Options that cannot be assigned to any other category are summarized in the Miscellaneous subcategory. This concerns the deactivation of drag and drop during editing, the lock of the Insert mode key (to avoid accidentally switching to Overstrike mode), whether the Home key goes to either the first column or the first non-space character, if the cursor is moved to the previous line when on the first position and the left key is pressed, if an arrow key to move off of a selection will dismiss the selection and move the cursor based on its current position, and if UltraEdit allows a line selection by clicking/dragging the mouse in the left margin of the edit window.

  Furthermore, an option exists to cause UltraEdit to copy/cut the active line to the active clipboard when the appropriate command is selected or the keyboard shortcut is used, if there is no selected text.

  Selected text can be automatically copied to the clipboard when a selection is made, resulting in overwriting the current contents of the active clipboard.

  The last option is related to the focus of the function list, whereby the focus will not be moved from the active document to the function list automatically when the function list is refreshed (e.g., when F8 is pressed).

- Word wrap/tab settings: The Word wrap/tab settings offer the most flexibility options, and Figure 4-4 shows an example of these options.

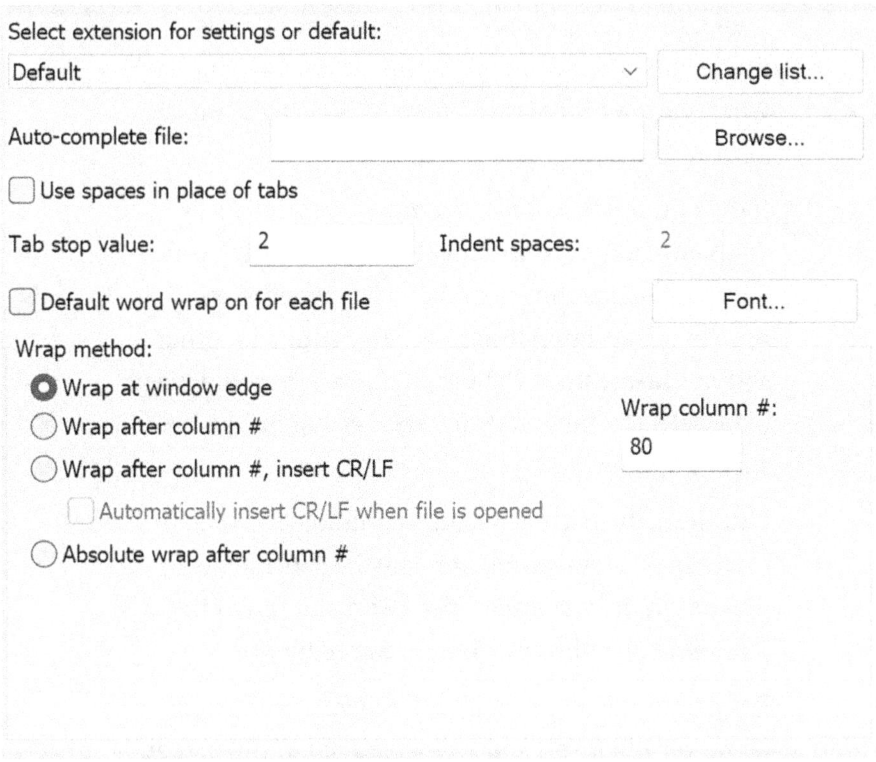

Select extension for settings or default:

| Default | ⌄ | Change list... |

Auto-complete file: Browse...

☐ Use spaces in place of tabs

Tab stop value: 2   Indent spaces: 2

☐ Default word wrap on for each file   Font...

Wrap method:
- ● Wrap at window edge
- ○ Wrap after column #
- ○ Wrap after column #, insert CR/LF
    - ☐ Automatically insert CR/LF when file is opened
- ○ Absolute wrap after column #

Wrap column #:

80

Figure 4-4. Word wrap/tab settings of the UltraEdit Configuration dialog

Via the option *Select extension for settings or default*, UltraEdit allows the tab and word wrap settings to be based on the file extension of the file. Initially the defaults will be used. To add an extension type, the user can click on *Change List* and a dialog will be displayed allowing to add or edit up to ten extension types. Users may select or add a file extension (or

91

Default) to which all settings specified on this page will be applied. The Word wrap/tab settings will change to reflect the extensions shown. The "default" settings are used for any files that do not match the user-defined extensions. Periods must not be included when specifying extensions for word wrap settings (e.g., "c cpp h" is correct, but ".c .cpp .h" is not).

If the option *Default word wrap on for each file* is enabled, then word wrap will be enabled each time a file with a matching extension is opened.Please note that if additional settings are defined for other settings (aside from Default), this option would have to be selected separately for each group to which it should apply.

If desired, the path to an auto-complete file specific to the selected file extension may be specified with the option *Auto-complete file*. Users may enter the path directly or browse to the desired file.

If the option *Use spaces in place of tabs* is enabled, UltraEdit will insert spaces instead of tab stops; then the Tab key is pressed. But setting this option will not convert tab characters in existing files.

Users may specify a font to be used for files with the currently specified extension by pressing the *Font* button and selecting the desired font.

The last set of options concerns the word wrap, which may be used to automatically wrap words to the next line at the vertical edge of the active window or at a specified column. There are four selectable modes of operation for word wrap:

- Wrap at window boundary, without inserting a hard return

- Wrap at a specified column number without inserting a hard return

- Wrap at a specified column number and insert a hard return

- Absolute wrap after column #, where the default value is 80

Two additional options specify if the file should be automatically wrapped on input or otherwise text is only wrapped as it is modified. The *Wrap column # edit field* is used for the four options where the column number is relevant in the sense of the placeholder #.

- XML/HTML/Markdown: The last subcategory contains options for XML/HTML and Markdown files. If the option *Display XML/HTML tag highlighting* is enabled, the text within matching XML/HTML elements will be highlighted using the color specified for Tags under the Editor tab in the Manage Themes dialog. The editor will determine what files are XML/HTML files based on the extensions specified in the appropriate word files.

  The option *Automatically close XML/HTML tags* controls that a close tag will automatically be inserted into the file being edited when the open tag is completed. Via *Position close tag on separate line*, the close tag will be inserted on a separate line rather than the same line as the open tag. This option is subdued if the option above is not selected.

As last option, the *Update HTML/markdown
preview as you type* defines that text typed in the
source panel will be updated in the browser view
in real time. If this is not selected, changes will not
be reflected in the browser view until the source file
is saved.

Category: Auto-complete

The category *Auto-complete* contains all options for the functionalities
Auto-complete and IntelliTips. Figure 4-5 shows the exemplary structure of
this collection of options.

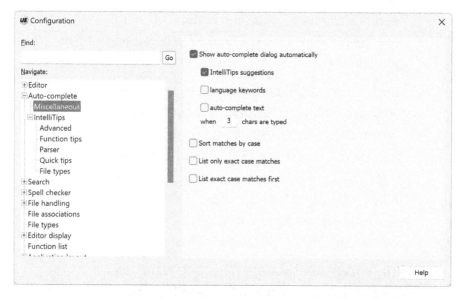

Figure 4-5. *Category Auto-complete in the UltraEdit Configuration*

- Miscellaneous: This category contains, for example, an
  option to show the auto-complete dialog automatically,
  where the auto-complete popup dialog is shown

automatically as the user types, instead of waiting for it to be invoked specifically by the user. The default setting for this behavior is not to be shown (unchecked), but if this option is in fact unchecked, the user can still access the auto-complete dialog with the keyboard shortcut Ctrl+Spacebar. Also possible is the definition of a minimum number of characters that must be typed before the auto-complete dialog is displayed.

Further additional options exist, like the *sort of matches by case*, where the auto-complete list is sorted according to case when displayed. If this option is not selected, words displayed in the auto-complete dialog are only sorted alphabetically.

The option *List only exact case matches* causes that only exact matches for the typed string will be shown in the auto-complete dialog. The order in which these items are sorted depends on the previous setting *Sort matches by case*.

For the last option *List exact case matches first*, the auto-complete dialog will promote exact matches for the typed string to the top of the auto-complete list.

- IntelliTips – Advanced: IntelliTips is a functionality within UltraEdit and UEStudio, which offers language intelligence and provides a dialog-based popup that displays class/struct data members and functions. Software developers in particular will make frequent use of this functionality and benefit from it. UltraEdit therefore divides the options into five subcategories: Advanced, Function tips, Parser, Quick tips, and File types.

In general, the user can enable or disable IntelliTips. Furthermore, the symbol list can be automatically shown, and this means the auto-complete box (including symbols) will be displayed automatically after the specified number of characters have been saved. A space can be inserted automatically after the accepted word is inserted.

The behavior of the so-called auto-complete list can be changed, if this list contains only one unique item which matches the criteria specified for typed characters. Then the item from the auto-complete list will automatically be inserted without prompting the user.

If the option *Delete "trailing" chars on auto-complete* is enabled and an auto-complete string is immediately followed by a non-matching string, the non-matching string will be deleted from the active document when the auto-completed word is selected. For example ("|" represents the cursor), the user is typing

ThisIs|Enum

and presses Enter; the auto-complete function would update the string to ThisIsVariable and the Enum portion of the active string would be deleted.

There are also options to automatically insert () when a function is typed followed by a space, and another option to change "." to "->" in any file. The latter is important for the typical "C/C++" syntax for a pointer to a structure member rather than referencing the structure/structure member directly (i.e., "struct.member").

By automatically inserting line comments at a new line, the user edits content in a commented line, and this wraps to a new line; then the new line will automatically be commented. This allows the user to write multi-line comments without stopping to insert the line comment character.

This feature can be disabled for strings occurring within comment blocks or strings (as defined by the *String Chars* setting in the associated wordfile).

By using the option *Complete with*, users may choose if options presented in the auto-complete dialog may be accepted by pressing the Tab or Enter key. If both options are disabled, a double-click will insert the auto-complete word.

- IntelliTips – Function tips: Function tips display the parameters for the function that the user called/typed. They can be shown automatically, and the redisplay is accomplished via Ctrl+Shift+Space.

The option *Use function tips data (if available) for function list* means that the built-in parser in UltraEdit/ UEStudio will be used to identify functions in the active file rather than the Function Strings defined in the wordfile. The file to be parsed must be part of the active project, and the file extension must be defined under the separate subcategory *Parser* for this to work properly. If the file type and extension aren't specified under the Parser branch, then UltraEdit/UEStudio wouldn't be able to automatically parse the functions, and the Function String definitions from the wordfile would be used.

- IntelliTips – Parser: Parsing means that a computer program breaks down text into different strings, which are recognized for further analysis – this is done here especially for the IntelliTips functionality.

  The option *Parse non-project files* means that IntelliTips will parse any loaded files even if they're not part of an active project.

  Likewise, the user can specify folders to be parsed by IntelliTips in this field when not using a project. When multiple folders are specified, they should be separated with ";".

  By *auto-parse all documents in include folders*, the folders defined with the previous option will automatically be scanned when source files are loaded for editing. The option *Auto re-parse documents when saved* defines that UltraEdit/ UEStudio will automatically re-parse the saved document for items to be provided in the IntelliTips list only if the active source file contains an include that cannot be resolved, for example:

  #include <somefile.c>

  If UltraEdit/UEStudio cannot find "somefile.c" in the active source file's parent folder, it will then search any folder paths defined under the Default include folder(s) for non-project files setting for "somefile.c".

Users may also specify a file extension to be used by default for parsing for files that are saved without an extension.

Two additional cache options allow to cache IntelliTips when closing a file, and tips generated by the IntelliTips parser will be stored between editing sessions for greater efficiency.

The usage of the option *Do not use cache for symbols* will force UltraEdit/UEStudio not to use the cache for symbols in the active project. By default, this option is not selected and should be only enabled, if very low disk space is available.

The button *Clear Cache* can be used to force to clear the cache.

- IntelliTips – Quick tips: The so-called Quick Tips display a suggestion for the word being typed, based on words previously found in the document that begin with the same characters. The first word found, scanning back from the cursor toward the top of the document, is the word that is suggested.

  The option *Show tip "x" ms* can be set in milliseconds and controls how long an IntelliTips tip will be displayed without user interaction. By using the option *Scan back "x" chars*, it can be controlled how many characters back from the current cursor position UltraEdit/UEStudio will read to populate the IntelliTips list. This is set to 100,000 characters by default, and the value of 0 characters means that Quick Tips will be disabled.

The *Complete with* option controls what keys may be used to accept the suggested word. Both Tab and Enter can be chosen here.

- IntelliTips – File types: This collection of options presents a table for defining the extensions associated with recognized parsers. Figure 4-6 shows this adaptable list.

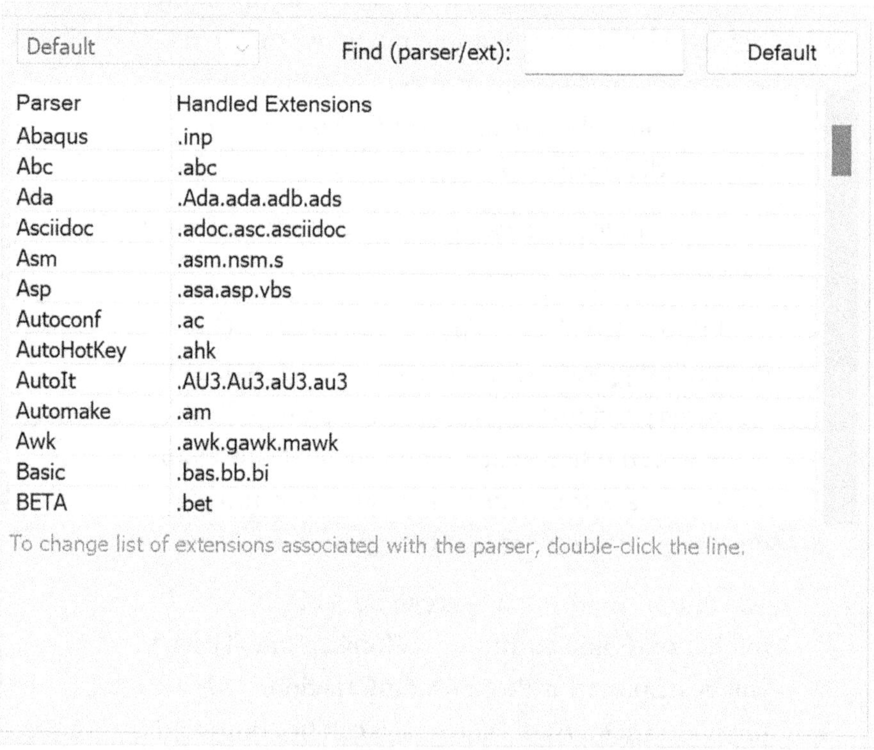

Default	∨	Find (parser/ext):	Default

Parser	Handled Extensions
Abaqus	.inp
Abc	.abc
Ada	.Ada.ada.adb.ads
Asciidoc	.adoc.asc.asciidoc
Asm	.asm.nsm.s
Asp	.asa.asp.vbs
Autoconf	.ac
AutoHotKey	.ahk
AutoIt	.AU3.Au3.aU3.au3
Automake	.am
Awk	.awk.gawk.mawk
Basic	.bas.bb.bi
BETA	.bet

To change list of extensions associated with the parser, double-click the line.

Figure 4-6. *Associated file extensions with corresponding parsers*

The *Find (Parser/Ext)* text box may be used to search for matches among the recognized Parsers or Handled Extensions. If searching for a parser, this should be typed as expected, i.e., "Fortran". If searching for a supported extension, this should be preceded by ".", i.e., ".jav". The text field is interactive in that as soon as a matching item is found, the appropriate line in the Parser table will be highlighted. The user may double-click on a parser line to modify the extensions associated with that parser. If desired, the button *Default* may be pressed to restore default extensions for all parsers.

Category: Search

The category *Search* combines all options for searching in UltraEdit. Figure 4-7 shows the exemplary structure of this collection of options.

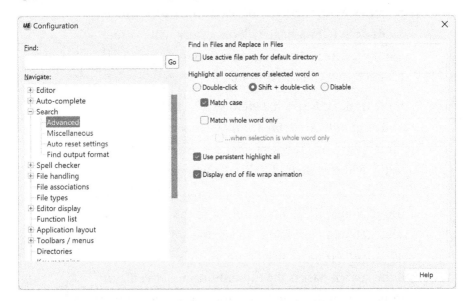

Figure 4-7. *Category Search in the UltraEdit Configuration*

- Advanced: The advanced options of the UltraEdit search allow using the active file path for the default directory, which causes UltraEdit to use the active file path for setting the *Find/Replace in Files* default directory (by default, the path from the latest search will be used).

Further options are available to control the highlight of all occurrences of the selected word. This can be achieved by double-clicking or Shift+double-clicking to select a word, and this will cause all other words in the active document that match the selected string to be highlighted as well. If the option *Match case* is selected, highlight all will only recognize strings with the exact same case as matches. With the remaining option *Match whole word only*, highlight all will only work with whole word matches. Matching strings that are part of a longer string will be ignored.

If the option *Use persistent highlight all* is enabled and *Highlight All Items Found* is selected in the Find dialog, any strings matching the search string will remain highlighted after a search is performed. Users may toggle the selection off using the *Highlight All Selected* option in the toolbar, the View tab, or by pressing the Escape key. In the last advanced option, a brief animation is showable, if the search passes the top or bottom of the file to indicate that the search is being continued from the other end of the file.

- Miscellaneous: This category contains search options that cannot be assigned to a specific category and are therefore classified as miscellaneous options.

The option *Show slim find dialog after start* determines if the slim Find dialog with Find Next and Find Previous buttons should be shown after the find command is initially started. If this is selected, the dialog is shown at the top of the screen.

The option *Continue find at end of file* determines if the search for a string is to be continued at the opposite end of the file if the string is not found. If this option is disabled, UltraEdit doesn't wrap around at the end of the file when searching for a string. The default behavior is to continue the search from the opposite end of the file when a target is not found.

For the Find dialog, there exists an option that UltraEdit automatically initializes the find/replace dialogs with the word under the cursor position, or the selected text or last find string.

Another search option concerns the scenario, if the UltraEdit function *Find next/prev* finds selected text (instead of the previous search string unless the *Regular Expressions* option is selected).

The focus can be set to the edit window after any Find operation was performed, regardless of what options are selected in the Find dialog.

Another quite long option is called *Set focus to window when going to result of lines containing string* and causes UltraEdit to set the focus to the edit window rather than the *Find String List* dialog when the result is double-clicked in the *Find String List* dialog. By default, this is set, but some users requested that focus remain on the *Find String List* dialog in this case.

Another option handles bookmarks, where a bookmark will automatically be inserted at the current cursor location when a matching string is found and moved to so that the user may return to the original cursor position.

Perl regular expressions will always be case sensitive. By enabling the option *Perl search is always case sensitive*, this will disable the *Match case* option in Find/Replace dialogs.

The last option handles special characters in Find/Replace strings, because a caret "^" (by default) has a special meaning. This setting allows a different character to be used in Find/Replace routines from the caret "^" – for example, a pipe character "|" or similar uncommon characters.

- Auto reset settings: All items selected in this category will be reset (or unselected) after a Find or Replace operation is completed – if they were selected for the last executed Search. The items that may be specified to be automatically reset are

  - Highlight all items found: This option causes all items matching the search string to be highlighted (shown as selected text) when the button *Find Next* is pressed.

- List lines containing string: This option causes UltraEdit to search for all occurrences of the string in the active document and to list them in a dialog box. By double-clicking on one of the result lines (or right-clicking and selecting Goto), UltraEdit will position to that line in the file.

- Match case: By default, the search will not be case sensitive. The option to make the search case sensitive is given. If a search has already occurred in the document, the default selection for case sensitivity is that of the previous search.

- Match whole word only: By default, the search will not be restricted to matching whole words only. This option allows the search to be restricted to whole words only. This is useful for searching for "a", or "A" without finding all words including "a". If a search has already occurred in a document, the default selection will match the previous search.

- Regular expressions: If this option is selected, the search will be executed using the regular expression type selected under the Advanced section.

- Search in column: If this option is selected, the search will be restricted to the specified start and end columns. To search an entire line, "0" and "-1" should be used.

- Use encoding: If this option is selected, the drop-down may be used to specify the encoding to be used when searching for the specified string.

There are two more options to handle the auto reset settings. If the option *Always set 'Find/Replace Where' to 'Current File' in Find/Replace dialog* is selected, the "Find/Replace Where" option in the Find/Replace dialogs will always be reset to "Current File" when the dialogs are invoked (otherwise, the option selected the last time the dialog was used will be remembered).

If the last option is selected (*Set 'Find/Replace where' to 'Selected text' if more than one line selected*), this will cause the Find and Replace dialog to default to "Selected text" for "In:" if more than one line is selected, irrespective of the above setting.

- Find output format: All options in this category allow the user to configure the format to be used to display the output of a Find in Files command. Pressing the button *Default* will restore the default options for the Find in Files output format. The following variables may be used to specify the output items described below:

```
$Dc   creation date/time for file
$Dm   time when file was modified
$P    path to file
$F    string to find
$L    line number
$S    found line
$C    number of occurrences of searched string found
$N    number of files in which search string was found
```

The options in *Output per File* control data that will be displayed for each file included in the Find in Files output:

- Header: When selected, the specified format will be used as the header for content regarding each file found containing string(s) matching the Find in Files search string.

- Found line: When selected, the specified format will be used to describe the line in which a match occurred during the Find in Files operation.

- File summary: When selected, the specified format will be used to summarize matched strings for each file included in the Find in Files output.

The options for the *Final Output* control data that will be displayed in the final line of the Find in Files output. Here the option Find Summary causes that the specified format will be used to display an overall summary of all matches in all files during the Find in Files operation.

Category: Spell Checker

The category *Spell Checker* contains all options for checking spelling errors in UltraEdit. Figure 4-8 shows the exemplary structure of this collection of options.

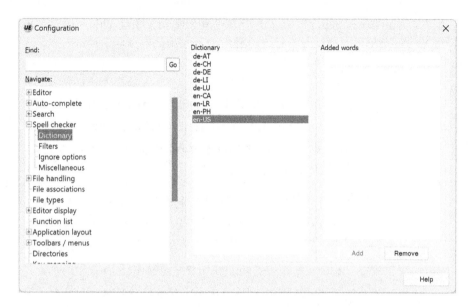

Figure 4-8. *Category Spell Checker in the UltraEdit Configuration*

- Dictionary: The dictionary is the basis for the spell checking within UltraEdit. A basic distinction is made whether Windows 8 and higher or Windows 7 is used. On all versions of Windows 8 and later, the Windows system spell checker is used for spell checking in UltraEdit. In order to add and remove languages for the spell checker in UltraEdit/UEStudio, the user would need to add or remove those languages through the section *Region and Language* of the Windows Settings. All languages installed on the system are available for selection as dictionaries in the left list called *Dictionary*.

  Should Windows 7 really still be used today, then we have to deal with the fact that this Windows version doesn't include native spell checking.

Words can be added or removed in the second column of these settings. For this, a dictionary must first be selected in the first *Dictionary* list. If a word is typed into the field *Added Words* and the button *Add* is pressed, the word will be added to the *Added Words* list. Words may be removed from the list by selecting them and pressing the button *Remove*. The *Added Words* list is maintained on a per language basis.

- Filters: This category allows the specification of filters to be used to ignore certain items in documents being checked by the spell checker. If the check box *For syntax files, only spell check* is selected, the following options are available (only one filter may be used at a time):

  - The comment option only content in line and block comments will be checked.

  - The strings option causes only content in strings (normally between ' and " characters) will be checked.

  - The comments and strings option only content in line and block comments and strings will be checked.

  - The full text option causes all text in the active file to be checked.

- Ignore options: The category *Ignore Options* allows the configuration of options to be used during spell checking operations. Options are available to ignore case, accents, all-cap words, capitalized words, words with numbers, and words with mixed case. All of these options may be toggled using the appropriate check box.

- Miscellaneous: The category *Miscellaneous* contains all spell-checking options that are not assigned to any other subcategory.

If the option *Enable spell as you type* is selected, spell checking will occur automatically as text is typed. Please note that by default, UltraEdit and UEStudio will not perform this option on any syntax-highlighted files. To change this setting and support spell check as typed for a syntax-highlighted file, the user needs to add the following to the language definition line (e.g., /L3"HTML" ...) of the wordfile:

EnableSpellasYouType

If the next option *Display suggestions on right mouse click over misspelled word* and the previous option *Enable spell as you type* are enabled, right-clicking on a word indicated as misspelled will result in a list of possible spelling options. If preferred, the additional option *Only if Ctrl is pressed* may be selected to restrict the display of these suggestions to the combination of pressing the Ctrl key along with right-clicking on a misspelled word. Users may also specify a maximum number of suggestions to be displayed using the *Display suggestions (max)* control. If this is set to "-1", then all available suggestions will be displayed.

The last option is called *Exclude from checking words shorter than (number) characters,* and it means that users may specify a minimum number of characters (from 1 to 9) required for a word to be checked for spelling errors.

Category: File Handling

The category *File handling* is one of the most complex categories, because it affects so many areas of UltraEdit. Figure 4-9 shows the exemplary structure of this collection of options.

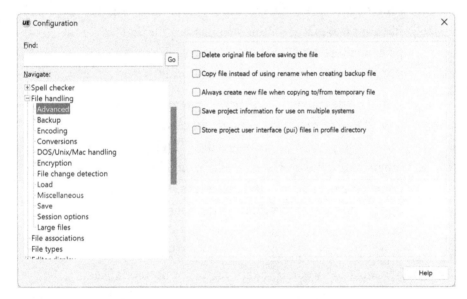

Figure 4-9. *Category File handling in the UltraEdit Configuration*

- Advanced: The option *Delete original file before saving the file* controls the circumstance; when a file is saved, the original file is overwritten with the new file. In some cases, on some servers, it's necessary to first delete the file and create a new file. Setting this option causes the file to be deleted and replaced by the new file.

  The second option *Copy file instead of using rename when creating backup file* affects how UltraEdit generates the backup file. By default, the original file is renamed to the backup file. The reason for the setting is that on some systems, if the original file is renamed to create the backup, the recreated original file does not maintain the file permissions that previously existed. Setting this causes the rename not to occur, preserving the permissions.

  When using the option *Always create new file when copying to/from temporary file* and copying to/from the temporary file to the user's file, UltraEdit doesn't create a new file and truncates the old file, but it copies the file and sets the file length. A few servers appear not to support this and do not honor the setting of the file length correctly, causing remnants of the old file to remain if the users delete a section of a file and save it. By enabling this option, it causes the file to be truncated to 0 length prior to writing the file.

  If the option *Save project information for use on multiple systems* is enabled, all project information is stored together to facilitate using project settings/workspaces on multiple systems. For example, if a project named "Project.prj" is created, the workspace information will be stored in "Project.pui", and this is saved in the same location as the .prj file so that it is accessible for all users. If this option is disabled (as per default), then the project workspace information is stored separately for each user. This allows users to share project settings with another user without the associated workspace information. In this case, if "Project.prj" is the project, the user's personal workspace information would be stored in "Project.[Workstation].[UserName].pui" so that this personal workspace would only be loaded when this user again loads the referenced project.

The option *Store project user interface (pui) files in profile directory* means when a project is created, the associated PUI file will be created in the user profile directory (%APPDATA%\IDMComp\UltraEdit) rather than the project directory.

- Backup: The option *Backup Files on Save* controls the behavior, that when a file is saved, the option to generate a backup file is provided. Three choices are available:

  - No backup: When a file is saved, the original file is overwritten and a backup file is not created.

  - Replace extension with .BAK: When the file is saved, the original file is copied or renamed to a backup file with the same file name and a ".BAK" extension in place of the existing extension. The modifications are saved to the original file name/extension.

113

- Append .BAK to the existing extension: When the file is saved, the original file is copied or renamed to a backup file with the same file name and extension, and ".BAK" is added to the file name (filename.ext.BAK). The modifications are saved to the original file name/extension.

Normally the directory used for the backup file is the same directory as the source file. The option *Default backup directory* allows all backup files to be copied to the same backup directory. If this item is left blank, the directory used will be that of the source file.

The options in *Version backup* allow users to specify settings for sequentially numbered backups of active files. The sub-option *On save* means that a backup file with a version number will be saved every time a save of an active file is executed. Via *On automatic save*, a backup file with a version number will be saved every time an automatic save of an active file is executed. The third option *On FTP save* means that a backup file with a version number will be saved every time an FTP file is modified and saved. Please note that if a *Local Backup Directory* is already specified under the Advanced tab for an FTP account, that directory will override the *Default FTP backup directory* option for files opened from that server.

In order to select the *On FTP save* item above, a local directory must be specified in the option *Default FTP backup directory*. When a file is backed up, the account name will be created as a root folder below the directory specified, and directories will be created as necessary to recreate the location of the modified file on the remote server.

The *Format* text field may be used to specify the format to be used for version backups. An example of this is *$n($c)$e,* and the following items may be defined:

- Path Variables

  ```
  $b - Default Backup Directory
  $p - File Path
  $n - File Name
  $e - File Extension
  ```

- Time/Date Variables

  ```
  $H(c,m) - Hour
  $M(c,m) - Minute
  $d(c,m) - Day
  $m(c,m) - Month
  $y (c,m) - Year
  $Y(c,m) - Year (four digits)
  c,m - Modifiers (c-file created, m-file modified)
  ```

- Miscellaneous

  ```
  $c - Counter (can also use $Xc, where X is number
       of digits)
  $u - User Name
  $s - Session (unique for running app)
  ```

The last field *Maximum number of backups* may be used to specify the maximum number of version backups to be saved for each file. A value of "-1" would indicate an infinite number of version backups.

- Encoding: The encoding options in this subsection are related to existing, pre-established encodings commonly used on computing systems. These encodings control which characters are available and how they're displayed (e.g., letters, numbers, special characters, and symbols).

  The setting *Default encoding (for new files and file open when auto-detect fails)* determines the default encoding used for new files (and for opening files when auto-detect fails). Users may select ANSI, UTF-8, or UTF-16.

  Alternatively, the setting *Default code page (for ANSI encoding)* forces UltraEdit to use a code page other than the default system code page for ANSI encoding if desired. By default, this will automatically be set to the default system code page.

  Using the option *Locale (used for sort and time/date)* means that users may configure a specific locale to be used for time/date format and for sorting files when locale-specific sorting is required.

  We continue with the next option, which is called *Automatically detect encoding (and code page, if applicable)*. It forces UltraEdit to evaluate if the content of the active file should be displayed with a code page other than the default code page. Once the appropriate code page is determined, UltraEdit will ask Windows to provide an appropriate font to be used to display content from that code page.

The next sub-option *Prompt to accept code page* is only active when the parent option *Automatically detect encoding* is enabled. If this option is selected and UltraEdit detects that a new code page is required, a dialog will be displayed where the user may select the code page to be used for the active document. If this option is disabled, but the parent option *Automatically detect encoding* is enabled, the highest rated matching code page will automatically be used.

The last encoding option is called *When converting from Unicode to ANSI always use default code page*, and if it's enabled, the default code page (specified above) will be used for the conversion when a file is converted from Unicode to ANSI. If this option is disabled and a file is converted from Unicode to ANSI, a dialog will be presented for the user to select the code page to use for the ANSI conversion.

- Conversions: The category Conversions summarizes some settings that relate to conversion between different encodings and operating systems.

The setting *Use IBM-500 standard for EBCDIC conversion* forces UltraEdit to use the IBM-500 standard for EBCDIC conversion. The default conversion did come from published EBCDIC tables but does not provide a direct one-to-one comparison.

The setting *Do not convert returns (CR/LF) during EBCDIC conversion* overrides the conversion of EBCDIC returns when converting files to ASCII format. The EBCDIC table does call for conversion of hard returns (CR/LF), but some users requested that this not occur.

The line ending after a paste process is affected with the option *On paste convert line ending to destination type (Unix/Mac/DOS).* If enabled, UltraEdit will check the format of the destination document when pasting from the clipboard and modify the line terminators of the clipboard content if necessary to match the format of the destination file.

The last conversion option is quite long with its name and is called *Prompt to convert active file to UTF-8 on paste if encoding of clipboard content doesn't match.* If enabled and the active file is not a UTF-8 or Unicode file, but the clipboard content is UTF-8 or Unicode, UltraEdit will prompt the user to convert the file to UTF-8 format before pasting the clipboard content. If the user selects "Yes", then the file is immediately converted and the clipboard contents are inserted. On the other hand, if the user selects "No", then no conversion occurs and the clipboard contents are inserted. Please note that declining the conversion could lead to certain Unicode/UTF-8 characters being corrupted.

- DOS/Unix/Mac handling: This category concerns all files that originate from other operating systems such as DOS, Unix, and Mac and must be handled accordingly by UltraEdit.

  The setting *Default file type for new files* allows the platforms DOS, Unix, and Mac and determines the default file type for new files created within UltraEdit. DOS files are the default option, but alternatively a default of Unix or Mac file types may also be selected.

  Three options for the *Unix/Mac file detection/ conversion* allow the user to determine if UltraEdit should automatically detect and convert Unix/ Mac files to DOS format when they are opened. Optionally the user may select to be prompted each time a Unix/Mac file is detected before it is converted. If no detection/conversion is desired, this may be disabled. Here the following three options exist:

  - Never prompt to convert files to DOS format.

  - Prompt to convert if file is not DOS format.

  - Automatically convert to DOS format.

  The option *Only recognize DOS terminated lines (CR/LF) as new lines for editing* causes UltraEdit to only recognize DOS terminated lines (CR/ LF) as new lines for editing. By default, UltraEdit automatically recognizes Unix/Mac terminated files for display purposes. If this feature is used with a file that has mixed line terminators (and they must be maintained), it should be used without enabling automatic conversion to DOS format (above). If automatic conversion is used when editing such files, any occurrences of CR or LF only line terminators would be converted automatically to CR/LF.

The setting *Save file as input format (Unix/Mac/DOS)* instructs the editor to automatically save the file as the original format (Unix/Mac) when saved, unless it was manually converted after opening.

And the last option *Status bar shows original line terminator format (on disk)* means that if enabled and the opened file is automatically converted to DOS format when opened, the status bar will still indicate the file's original format (Unix or Mac) when the file is loaded.

- Encryption: This category contains various options that affect UltraEdit's file encryption. One or more files can be encrypted and decrypted again using an Advanced Encryption Standard (AES) algorithm.

  The setting *Delete original file(s) after encrypting* determines if the original plain-text file should be deleted automatically after it is successfully encrypted. For backup files, the option *Delete backup file(s) after encrypting* causes that backups of the original plain-text file should be deleted automatically after it is successfully encrypted.

If the option *Replace encrypted/decrypted file if it exists* is enabled, any files that already exist in the specified path with names and extensions matching the files selected for encryption/decryption would automatically be overwritten.

The last encryption option *Automatically re-encrypt file on close* means that files that are decrypted prior to editing will automatically be re-encrypted when saved and closed. This option will respect other encryption options set in the program configuration as well which pertain to deletion/overwriting of files after encryption.

- File change detection: All options collected in this category control the behavior of UltraEdit when the active file is updated by another user (in the case of a file being edited by more than one user at a time) or an external process (i.e., an application or log file, for example).

The *File change detection* can be selected with three options (*Disable, Prompt for update when files change*, and *Automatically update changed files*), and generally UltraEdit detects any changes to a file that is loaded and is changed outside of itself. By default, the second option *Prompt for update when files change* is selected, and when the changes are detected, UltraEdit will prompt the user with the option to reload the file (in which case any unsaved changes to the file in UltraEdit will be lost). The user may choose to reload the file or ignore the changes.

Optionally UltraEdit provides the ability to ignore any file changes by setting the first *Disable* option. In this case, UltraEdit will not detect or prompt for any file changes. If preferred, UltraEdit provides the ability to automatically update the loaded files with any changes that have been made outside of UltraEdit by setting the third option *Automatically Update Changed Files.* In this case, the file will be loaded, and any unsaved changes made within UltraEdit will be overwritten automatically without prompting.

The longer option *When a file is detected as changed and reloaded, make it active* instructs UltraEdit to make any file it detects as changed and reloads to be the active file. The default setting is not to make the file active.

By using the option *Ignore file changes if the file was deleted*, this instructs UltraEdit not to notify the user when an opened file has been detected as changed. If this is not set (default), UltraEdit will notify the user that a file has been deleted if the file change detection is enabled.

Another very interesting option is called *Check files for changes on application focus change*, and if enabled, files will only be checked for changes when UltraEdit receives the focus (when switching from another application or from a dialog within UltraEdit) rather than checking automatically at predefined intervals. This option was provided to help with performance, for example, if files are opened from a network drive with a high degree of latency. This prevents UltraEdit from becoming unresponsive while it waits for the network to reload the file.

If the option *Check active file only* is enabled, only the active file will be checked for changes when file change detection is triggered. This can improve the performance for users with many files open at the same time.

The option *Poll for file changes at forced interval in seconds (0 disables)* defines the interval in seconds at which UltraEdit checks for changes to files for which polling has been activated using the *Toggle file change polling* command in the *File change polling* drop-down in the View tab (Ribbon mode) and the View menu (Contemporary and Traditional menu modes). If this is set to "0", this feature is disabled.

The last File Change Detection option is quite long and is called *When a file marked for polling is detected as changed scroll to the last line in the file (used for tailing log files)*. This setting forces UltraEdit to scroll such that the last line in a polled file is always visible in the edit window when the file is active. This is similar to the Unix tail command.

- Load: This category contains all the options for loading files, which is part of the daily business of a text editor and can be configured in more detail here.

The first option is called *Instead of using last-opened file for default file open directory*, and if this option is disabled, the options below will be subdued and the directory of the last opened file will be used as the default directory for file open. If the option is enabled, it can be chosen between two additional options. The first one is called *Use default directory from shortcut on initial file open*, and if set, the normal behavior is overridden and the directory the application is launched from is used as the default File Open directory. The second is called *Use active file directory for file open dialog default*, and if set, the normal behavior is overridden and active file's directory is used as the default File Open directory.

Please note that only one of the two items described above can be selected.

The setting *Open link (.lnk) files, not the file the link points to* causes UltraEdit to open the link for modification. The default setting (not setting this option) causes UltraEdit to expand the link to open the root file.

The Read Only command toggles the state of the read-only status of the file. If the read-only status is set, the file cannot be modified. If the option *Open files as read-only by default* is enabled, files will automatically be opened as read-only. This does not change the status of the file itself, just the ability to modify it within UltraEdit.

By using the last option *Remember the read-only setting when reloading a file currently open*, it causes UltraEdit to maintain the Read-Only status of a file when this file is reloaded. By default, when a file is reloaded, the status of Read-Only does revert to the status of the underlying file. This is because a lot of users use this feature with version control systems and the only thing that changes is the Read-Only status and the users want/expect the status within the editor to change also.

- Miscellaneous: This category contains all options that cannot be assigned to any other category.

  File attributes can be affected using the option *Change file attribute when toggling read-only for active file*, which instructs UltraEdit to change the read-only status of the file when the command for read-only is toggled. The default setting (disabled) allows the user to change UltraEdit's state, preventing or allowing modification of the file, but causes no change to the actual file status when the read-only status is changed from the ribbon or the menu.

  The option *Lock file for write while editing* causes UltraEdit to keep the lock on any file that is opened. Additionally, if the file is already locked, it allows for open by read-only in this case prompting the user with a dialog box to confirm the open as read-only. This feature prevents modification of a file from outside of the edit session, preventing loss of changes made.

Open files can be handled with the option *Close all files when opening or switching projects*, which means that when enabled, all currently open files will be closed without a warning prompt when opening, closing, or switching projects. If this is disabled, the user will be prompted as to whether or not the open files should be closed.

If a certain file is specified on the command line and this file doesn't exist, UltraEdit would normally show an error message. Here the option *Create new file if file specified on command line does not exist* changes this behavior and creates a new file with the specified file name. The default setting is to create the new file.

The setting *Create new Edit file when opening with no other files* instructs UltraEdit to create a new empty document (Edit1) file when it starts up if no other files are being opened.

Via the last miscellaneous option *Create new Edit file on last file close*, a new blank edit file will automatically be created when the last open file is closed.

- Save: In contrast to loading files, this category contains all the options for saving files.

  The first option *Write UTF-8 BOM header to all UTF-8 files when saved* instructs UltraEdit to write the UTF-8 BOM (byte order mark) to all files when they're saved. If this option is disabled, the BOM will not be written to the file when it is written to the disk. This will not remove a BOM that already exists in the file.

One of the options is called *Write UTF-8 BOM on new files created within this program (if above is not set)* and instructs UltraEdit to write the UTF-8 BOM only to new files created within UltraEdit when they are saved. If this option is disabled, the BOM will not be written to the file when it is written to the disk. This will not remove a BOM that already exists in the file.

By using the option *Trim trailing spaces on file save*, it causes UltraEdit to automatically remove the trailing white space (spaces/tabs) from the end of every line in the file and positions back to the original cursor position when it is complete each time a file is saved. The functionality of *Trim Trailing Spaces* is such that it does require a newline to operate on a given line of text. If the last line of text in the file is terminated with a hard return, *Trim Trailing Spaces* will work on that line as well.

The option *Remember last directory specified for Save As for session* means that a Save As operation or saving a new, unsaved file (i.e., "Edit1") will default to the last directory specified for a Save As operation. If this option is disabled (or if a directory has not yet been specified), a Save As operation for saving a new, unsaved file will default to the directory the last file was opened from using the Open command in the current or previous editing session. The Save As dialog always opens in the directory of the named file when working with a file that has already been saved.

The encoding in the Save As dialog can be affected by using the option *Always set Encoding to "Default" in Save As dialog.* If enabled, the Encoding drop-down in the Save As dialog will always be set to "Default" when the Save As dialog is invoked. If this option is disabled, the Save As dialog will remember the last option selected when the Save As dialog is invoked.

Similar to other powerful text editing applications, UltraEdit naturally has an automatic save function. The option *Automatic Save* is provided to automatically save all open files at the desired interval. The interval is configurable in minutes. If the interval is set to zero (0), no automatic save is performed.

In this context, there are two other options. If *Do not auto-save unnamed (new) files* is selected, the automatic save will ignore files that do not have a name (i.e., files that were created with the New command). This stops the Save As dialog from appearing if an unnamed file exists and has been modified.

If *Do not auto-save FTP files* is selected, the automatic save will ignore modified FTP files that are open for edit.

If a file is saved due to the automatic save command, a .BAK file is only created for the first save of the session. For subsequent saves with this feature, the .BAK file is not created or overwritten.

- Session options: All options that are categorized in this session category are grouped together here.

If the option *Reload files previously open on startup* is enabled, UltraEdit saves information about the open files when UltraEdit is closed. This information is used to automatically reload the files that were open the next time UltraEdit is started. And it allows easy reloading of a set of files that are edited on a regular basis. If UltraEdit is invoked automatically for printing, the files are not reopened.

The option *Remember and reload unsaved changes to saved files* is subdued if the option *Reload files previously open on startup* is disabled. If this option is enabled, and the user closes UltraEdit with unsaved changes in previously saved files, no prompt will be shown, and those files will be reloaded in the same state (changes unsaved) the next time UltraEdit is launched. If this option is disabled, the user will be prompted to save changes prior to closing UltraEdit.

In connection with this is the additional option *Remember and reload unsaved changes to unsaved "Edit" files*, which is also subdued if the option *Reload files previously open on startup* is disabled. If this option is enabled, and the user closes UltraEdit with unsaved changes in unnamed "Edit" files, no prompt will be shown, and those files will be reloaded in the same state (changes unsaved) the next time UltraEdit is launched. If this option is disabled, the user will be prompted to save changes prior to closing UltraEdit unless the option *When closing application prompt to save unsaved "Edit" files* is disabled.

We continue with session options, and they are related to the handling of already-opened FTP files and whether they should be reloaded between sessions. The option *Reload FTP files when reloading a project or last open files* determines if UltraEdit should reload FTP files when it reloads files for a project/workspace. Typically, FTP files are not reloaded automatically due to the potential time delay in connecting and loading the files. Enabling this option will ensure FTP files are treated as normal files in this regard.

The second FTP option is called *Remember and reload unsaved changes to FTP files* and is subdued if the option *Reload FTP files when reloading a project or last open files* is disabled. If this option is selected, and the user closes UltraEdit with unsaved changes in previously saved remote files, no prompt will be shown, and those files will be reloaded in the same state (changes unsaved) the next time UltraEdit is launched. If this option is disabled, the user will be prompted to save changes prior to closing UltraEdit.

A very powerful Explorer option is hidden in the inconspicuous setting called *Open from Explorer also opens files list.* When this option is enabled and a file is selected in the Windows Explorer to be opened in UltraEdit, the last-used workspace (and all associated files) is reloaded when the file selected in the Windows Explorer is loaded.

The last option *Discard unsaved "Edit" files with no prompt on application close* is subdued if the option *Remember and reload unsaved changes to unsaved "Edit" files* is selected. If this option is enabled, no prompt to save changes will be shown when closing UltraEdit with unsaved changes in "Edit" files. If disabled, the user will be prompted to save changes before UltraEdit is closed.

- Large files: A great strength of UltraEdit is the stable and powerful handling and processing of extremely large files, and this last category *Large files* in the section *File handling* summarizes all the associated options (please see Figure 4-10). We will discuss more details on processing large files in a later chapter.

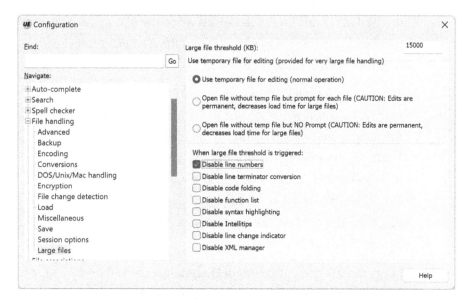

Figure 4-10. *UltraEdit Configuration for the handling of large files*

The first option is extremely important because it defines the threshold value from which a file is categorized as a large file. The *Large file threshold (KB)* field is provided to allow the user to specify files that are equal or larger than this value to be loaded without the creation of the temporary file. Files smaller than this would be loaded normally, creating a temporary file. Setting the value to zero means that all files would be loaded without the creation of the temporary file. The *Large file threshold (KB)* field is only applicable if the option to open files without the temporary file is set.

The option *Use of temporary file for editing (Provided for very large file handling)* is divided into three sub-options:

- Use temporary file for editing (normal operation).

- Open file without temp file but prompt for each file (Caution: edits are permanent, decreases load time for large files).

- Open file without temp file but no prompt (Caution: edits are permanent, decreases load time for large files).

In addition, there are various options that can be disabled for editing large files, mainly to improve performance:

- Disable line numbers.

- Disable line terminator conversion.

- Disable code folding.

- Disable function list.

- Disable syntax highlighting.

- Disable IntelliTips.

- Disable line change indicator.

- Disable XML manager.

Category: File Associations

The category *File associations* contains all options for file associations in combination with UltraEdit, and Figure 4-11 shows the exemplary structure of these settings.

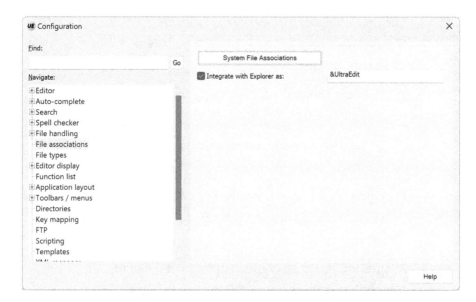

Figure 4-11. *Category File associations in the UltraEdit Configuration*

Clicking the button *System File Associations* opens the Windows interface for setting file associations for applications. In previous UltraEdit versions, file associations could be set within UltraEdit itself, but with changes introduced in Windows 8, this is no longer the recommended method of setting file associations.

If the option *Integrate with Explorer as* is enabled, several UltraEdit options are added to the context (right-click) menu in the Windows File Explorer, allowing users to open either files or folders in UltraEdit.

Users may right-click on a file and select UltraEdit from the context menu to open the selected file for editing. If the option *Open from Explorer also opens file list* is selected under the category *File handling ➤ Advanced*, the last used workspace (and all associated files) is reloaded along with the selected file.

If the user right-clicks on a folder, the user may select *Open folder in UltraEdit* from the context menu. When this option is disabled, the following will occur:

- The File View will be opened (if not already visible) with the selected folder set as the root in the *Explorer* pane.

- While the folder is "open" in UltraEdit, the following will happen:

  - The first time *Find in Files* is opened in this session, the *Directory* field will default to the selected folder.

  - The first time the *File Open* dialog is opened in this session, it will default to the selected folder.

- Users may close the open folder by double-clicking on the *Close folder* item shown directly beneath the folder root.

Category: File Types

The category *File types* contains the list of file types that appear in the *File Open* and *File Save As* dialog boxes, and Figure 4-12 shows the exemplary structure of these settings.

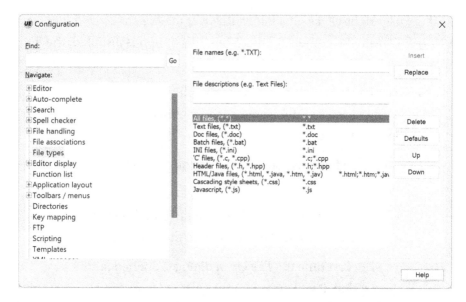

Figure 4-12. *Category File types in the UltraEdit Configuration*

Up to ten file types may be configured here. These file types will be shown in the file operation dialog boxes in the same order they are shown on this page.

Each configured file type consists of a file name and a file description. The file name may (and probably does) include wildcard characters and may include multiple file extensions each separated by a semicolon ";" (i.e., "*.c;*.cpp"). The file description is a text field describing the file types.

There are various buttons on the right side that can be used to control the entries:

- Insert: Inserts the content of the file names and file description fields to a new entry

- Replace: Replaces the file names or file descriptions with the current content of the upper edit fields

- Delete: Deletes the selected file type without any further confirmation

- Defaults: Resets the file types to the initial settings

- Up: Moves the selected file type one entry upward

- Down: Moves the selected file type one entry downward

From the basic navigation, the user selects an entry in the lower list of file types, whereupon the edit fields *File names* and *File descriptions* at the top are filled with its content. A change in the edit fields in turn causes the list below to be adjusted.

Category: Editor Display

Comparable to the *File handling* category, this *Editor display* category is one of the most complex categories, because it covers many areas of UltraEdit's core functionality, namely, the editor engine. Figure 4-13 shows the exemplary structure of this collection of options.

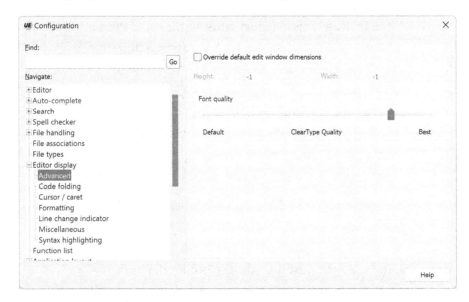

Figure 4-13. *Category Editor display in the UltraEdit Configuration*

- Advanced: This category with the advanced options contains the setting *Override default edit window dimensions*. When a new document is created, it is automatically sized to fit the dimensions of UltraEdit. This option overrides this auto sizing with specific values. If the dimensions of UltraEdit are smaller than the specified height and width, the new document will be created with the old auto sizing method.

  With the lower *Font Quality* section, the user may set the quality level Windows will use to render fonts in UltraEdit. Information regarding the quality selected is displayed as the slider is moved. All options are available on a scale from Default to Best: *Default Quality, Draft Quality, Proof Quality, Non Antialiased Quality, Antialiased Quality, ClearType Quality,* and *Natural Quality*.

- Code folding: This category summarizes all options for code folding, which basically refers to a function in editors and modern Integrated Development Environments (IDE) for grouping logically related source code sections such as classes or methods in so-called folds, allowing them to be visually collapsed within the editor for easier browsing, more targeted focus, or quickly determining scope of a code block.

  If the option *Save folded lines* is enabled, information regarding folded lines will be stored when a file is closed so that it will be opened in the same state the next time the file is edited. If this option is disabled, all lines will be unfolded the next time a file is loaded regardless of their fold state at the time a file is closed.

One of the most important options in this area is *Enable show/hide lines and code folding*, and this permits the hiding/showing of selected text and folding/expanding of code blocks. If this is disabled, the folding gutter will not be visible in the edit window and folding is disabled. If a file is opened that exceeds the threshold specified for using temporary files under the category *File handling* ➤ *Large files/Temporary files*, and the option is set to open without a temporary file in this case, code folding will not be displayed. For large files with complex folding structures, there may be a delay in displaying code folding lines as the folding algorithms require additional time to process and calculate large data sets.

Another quite powerful option is called *Enable show/hide lines in non-syntax-highlighted files (above must also be set)*, and this permits text to be hidden in non-syntax-highlighted files and expanded/collapsed using the View tab commands (Ribbon mode) and the View menu commands (both Contemporary and Traditional menu modes) of UltraEdit. If this is disabled, the folding gutter will not be visible in the edit window in non-syntax-highlighted files and folding is disabled.

If the option *Show last line of fold in syntax highlighted files* is enabled, the last line of a folded section will be displayed in files with syntax highlighting. Should this option be deactivated in return, only the initial line of a folded section will be displayed.

Should the option *Automatically unfold hidden areas on Find and Goto* be enabled and a Find or Goto command positions the cursor within folded text, that folded level will be unfolded automatically to correctly display the searched text in context.

By using the setting *Detect XHTML from DTD on file load*, UltraEdit will scan files for a DOCTYPE declaration. If a DTD for XHTML 1.0 Strict or XHTML 1.1 is specified, the rules for elements associated with this document type will be respected for code folding and indentation.

Graphical lines are a useful support to make code-folded sections more visible, and if the option *Draw graphical lines* is enabled and *Enable show/hide lines and code folding* is selected above, lines are drawn in the folding gutter to the right of the line numbers to indicate where folding nodes begin and end.

Draw indent lines can be understood as a supplementary option, and if enabled and *Enable show/hide lines and code folding* is selected above, lines are drawn within the active file from the first indented line of a fold block to the last indented line of a fold block to indicate where folded sections begin and end.

- Cursor/caret: As base option, the *Normal Cursor/Caret type* can be chosen, and this represents the type of the cursor/caret that will normally be displayed in the editor – here both options *Vertical bar* and *Underscore cursor* exist.

The same applies to the *Overstrike Cursor/Caret type*, and this option represents how the type of the cursor/caret will be affected by *Overstrike mode* settings within UltraEdit. Possible options are

- Block caret for Overstrike mode, normal caret for Insert mode

- Inverted – Normal caret for Overstrike mode, block caret for insert

- Block caret disabled, always use normal caret

By using the option *Allow positioning beyond line end* this allows the cursor to be positioned beyond the end of text in a line.

If the option *Underscore is word stop for Ctrl Left/ Right arrow* is enabled, the cursor will stop at occurrences of "_" in text when Ctrl+Left/Right arrow is used for navigation. The default is for this option not to be selected. The setting chosen for this option can affect the functionality of macros/scripts that include navigation operations.

Another quite handy option for the cursor is *CamelCase naming stops for Ctrl left/right arrow*, and if selected, the cursor will stop at uppercase letters in mixed case words when Ctrl+Left/Right arrow is used for navigation.

The last cursor/caret option concerns multi-caret editing in UltraEdit, which is a powerful editing function that we will discuss in more detail later. Generally, users may set multiple carets in the active file by holding the Ctrl key while clicking with the left mouse button. At this point, the functionality can be switched on and off using the option *Enable multi-caret editing.*

- Formatting: The term formatting or layout plays an important role in the field of editors because it is used to give an existing text a certain shape (e.g., line length, page break, character sets used, etc.).

The *Auto indent new lines* option toggles the state of automatic line indentation. When automatic line indentation is enabled, UltraEdit automatically indents a line to match the indentation of the previous line. The indentation is performed by inserting spaces or tabs into the document, depending on the Tab settings. Additionally, language-specific indenting and out-denting are supported. This provides for additional indenting after a certain character/string to indent a block of code and out-denting after a closing character/ string. This option is only active in Insert mode, not in Overstrike mode. Please note that this functionality is specified in the syntax highlighting wordfile, not here in the settings panel.

By using the option *Auto indent wrapped lines,* UltraEdit automatically indents wrapped lines to match the indentation of the previous line.

With *Break on hyphen (-) when converting/ reformatting paragraphs,* UltraEdit determines if it should break words at hyphens when reformatting a line. The default setting is to break lines at hyphens. If this setting is disabled, UltraEdit will not break the line when a hyphen is encountered.

One of the longer options is called *Reformat paragraph after paste when wrap settings set to add hard returns at specific column number* and causes UltraEdit to automatically reformat a paragraph after a paste command if the *Word Wrap* settings are set to wrap at a specific column number with the insertion of hard returns (CR/LF). This is the default behavior, and disabling this option will disable this feature.

The last formatting option is *Do not convert spaces and tabs inside comments and strings*, and if enabled, spaces and tabs inside comments and strings (as defined in the associated wordfile) will not be converted by formatting operations.

- Line change indicator: The line change indicator is a feature by which UltraEdit provides a visual indicator in the margin of the editor to show that text in a line has been changed (or a new line has been inserted) since the last save to disk. The various options for this are summarized in this subcategory.

  Within the text field *Width of Line Change Indicator in pixels*, the user can specify the width of the Line Change Indicator in pixels. Values may be set between 1 and 9.

If the option *Enable line change indicator (LCI)* is enabled, modified lines will be indicated with a special-colored shading between the line numbers and the first character on the line. The colors used to indicate saved and unsaved changes to a file within an editing session are configured under the *Editor* tab in the *Manage Themes* dialog. If the undo buffer is cleared during an editing session, the line change indicators would be reset as well. If a file is opened that exceeds the threshold specified for using temporary files under the *Temporary Files* branch in the *File Handling* section of configuration, and the option is set to open without a temporary file in this case, the line change indicator will not be displayed.

This setting is a global toggle for the function. If users wish to toggle this option on/off on a file-by-file basis, this may be done using the option in the View tab (Ribbon mode) or the View menu (Contemporary and Traditional menu modes). If files are open for editing when this option is changed, they would need to be reloaded or the *Line Change Indicator* setting would need to be toggled in the View tab or View menu to affect these files.

The option *Hide LCI by default on file open* can only be selected if the option above is selected. When this is enabled and changes are made to a file, the changes are tracked, but the LCI is not immediately shown for modified lines. If the user wishes to see which lines have been modified, they can click the *Line change indicator* button in the *View* tab

(Ribbon mode) or the View menu (Contemporary and Traditional menu modes) to toggle visibility of the LCI.

The next option *Treat saved LCIs as changed lines* requires a more detailed explanation. If the user makes changes to a file but doesn't save those changes, they can go to the View tab (Ribbon mode) or the View menu (Contemporary and Traditional menu modes) and click "*Hide/show*" and select "*Hide unchanged lines*" – this will cause UltraEdit to filter and hide all lines that don't currently have unsaved changes. When the user makes a change in a file, UltraEdit tracks those changes during the editing session. Unsaved changes are marked with a red vertical line at the beginning of the edited line. If the user saves the changes, by default, that changes to a green vertical line. If the option *Treat saved LCIs as changed lines* is selected, then even if they saved the changes during the active editing session, but the lines do have an LCI (Line Change Indicator) marking, then those lines (as well as lines with unsaved changes) will be considered changed lines for the purpose of the filtering discussed above.

- Miscellaneous: This subcategory contains all settings that cannot be assigned to any other category, and the list is correspondingly extensive (please see Figure 4-14).

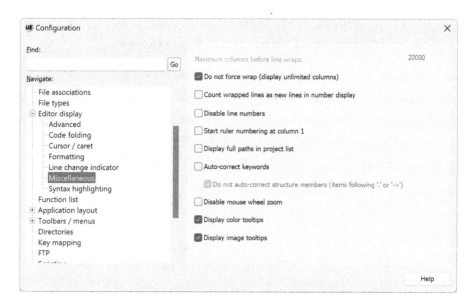

Figure 4-14. *Various settings for the subcategory Editor display* ➤ *Miscellaneous*

The option *Maximum columns before line wraps* sets the maximum columns allowed within UltraEdit before it wraps the line (soft wrap). The default is 4096 columns, but a maximum of 20000 is allowed. Please note that this behavior can be overridden with the option *Do not force wrap.*The term "wrap" defines the wrapping of a line or word, which takes place according to certain criteria. If the option *Do not force wrap (display unlimited columns)* is enabled, there is no limit to the number of characters that can be displayed on a single line. Selecting this option will subdue the option above. By using the next option *Count wrapped lines as new lines in number display*, this causes UltraEdit to show wrapped lines with different line numbers (by default disabled). While we are talking about line numbers, the next option *Disable line numbers* could be interesting, because if enabled, line numbers will not be displayed in UltraEdit and the *Line numbers* option will be subdued in the View tab (Ribbon mode) or the View menu (Contemporary and Traditional menu modes).

The ruler is a useful tool for any kind of orientation during the editor navigation and is used in the upper editor area. This ruler normally starts with the initial value 0 but can be changed to 1 if the option *Start ruler numbering at column 1* is enabled.

For a better control inside the project list, the option *Display full paths in project list* can be used, and if enabled, the list of recent projects will display the full paths for projects in the *Recent* drop-down under the Project tab (Ribbon mode), the Project menu (Contemporary menu mode), or the File menu (Traditional menu mode). If this option is disabled, the project paths may be shortened with an ellipsis.

Within UltraEdit, there is a kind of auto-correction that is applied to certain keywords. The option *Auto-correct keywords* switches the state of the auto-correct feature, and if enabled, keywords detected will be corrected to match their case in the active wordfile. For example, "javaarray" would automatically be changed to "JavaArray" for JavaScript files.

By using the option *Do not auto-correct structure members (items following "." or "->")*, this causes UltraEdit not to auto-correct keywords following a "." or "->". This was configured as the default due to issues faced particularly by Java programmers using Auto Complete. If this setting is disabled, keywords following these items would be auto corrected.

Another function is called "mouse wheel zoom" and means that the font size can be increased/decreased by using Ctrl+mouse scroll. This function can be disabled with the option *Disable mouse wheel zoom*.

So-called color tooltips are helpful, because a color swatch will be displayed reflecting the specified color when the cursor hovers over a color specification in CSS, HTML, JavaScript, Perl, PHP, Python, and Ruby files. If the user holds down the Ctrl key and clicks on the color swatch, a color picker is displayed, and users may use this to specify a different color. Pressing OK in the color picker after specifying a different color will insert the appropriate values into the active source document. With the option *Display color tooltips*, those color tooltips can be disabled, if, for example, they are perceived as disturbing.

The last miscellaneous option is called *Display image tooltips*, and if selected, a preview will be displayed of an image when the cursor hovers over its reference in the file being edited. Supported image types include BMP, GIF, JPE, JPEG, JPG, PNG, and TIFF. These will be displayed for CSS, HTML, JavaScript, JSON, Markdown, PHP, Perl, Python, and Ruby files.

- Syntax highlighting: Syntax highlighting is a powerful function of text editors and Integrated Development Environments (IDE) and the ability to recognize predefined words and display them in different colors. This is particularly useful for programmers and can also be useful to other users who may want certain words in a document to show up in a different color. Support for many languages or word sets that may be recognized is provided. We will describe this powerful function in more detail in a later chapter.

The first edit field contains the *Full directory path for wordfiles*, and UltraEdit reads configuration files (the default file extension is "*.UEW") from this directory to configure the syntax highlighting. These files are read each time the editor starts up, and each file may be up to 372 KB in size.

In general, syntax highlighting can be enabled or disabled with the option *Enable syntax coloring*.

The drop-down field *Installed wordfiles* is populated with the list of language wordfiles on the current system, and the user can open a language's associated wordfile by clicking the button *Open*.

The option *Highlight new file as* allows the user to set the default highlighting for new files when they're created within UltraEdit. If this is enabled, the highlighting type previously specified is used until the user saves the file with an extension for a different language type.

Inside of selections, the syntax coloring can be disabled with the option *Disable syntax coloring in selections.*

The last option is a button called *Add/remove languages.* This button opens the *Add syntax highlighting languages* dialog where the user can easily add and remove syntax highlighting languages.

Category: Function List

The category Function list provides access to the *Modify Groups* dialog, which is used to define the groups and subgroups that populate the hierarchical function list for a given language. Figure 4-15 shows the exemplary structure of these settings.

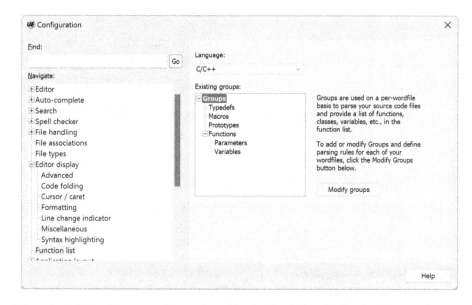

Figure 4-15. *Category Function list in the UltraEdit Configuration*

If the active file is highlighted, the *Language* drop-down will default to the language appropriate to the active file. This drop-down list includes, for example, the languages Batch, C#, CSS, C/C++, HTML, Java, JavaScript, JSON, Markdown, MySQL 5.1, Perl, PHP, PowerShell, Python, Ruby, Unix shell scripts, VBScript ASP, Visual Basic, UltraEdit Wordfiles, and XML.

The tree field *Existing groups* will display the groups and subgroups currently defined for the selected language. Different languages may be selected with the *Language* drop-down, and the *Existing groups* tree will be updated accordingly.

If the button *Modify Groups* is pressed, the *Modify Groups* dialog will be shown (please see Figure 4-16) so that users can define groups and subgroups for the selected language.

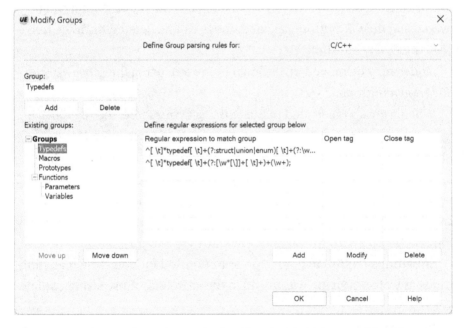

Figure 4-16. *Modify Groups dialog for the definition of (sub)groups according to the selected language*

The *Modify Groups* dialog is used to define parsing rules which define groups and subgroups for syntax highlighting languages used in UltraEdit. These groups and subgroups determine how the hierarchical function list will be populated for a given language.

By default, the drop-down called *Define Group parsing rules for* will be set to the appropriate language for the active file. If the user wishes to modify parsing rules for a different language, it may be selected.

The text field called *Group* is used to define new names for groups/ subgroups that would be added to the hierarchical tree using the *Add* button. Any group/subgroup which is added will be inserted into the tree under the node currently selected in the tree displayed in the *Existing Groups* control. If a previously defined group is selected in the *Existing Groups* control, its name may be modified, and the modification can be saved using the *OK* button. Selected nodes can be deleted from the tree using the *Delete* button.

Nodes may be moved up or down in the tree using the *Move up* and *Move down* buttons.

When a group is selected in the *Existing Groups* tree, the regular expression(s) associated with that group needs to be specified in the list labeled *Define regular expressions for selected Group below*. Multiple expressions may be defined for each group/subgroup, but each added expression will affect the time required to parse documents. Groups (e.g., Functions and Classes) would not need to have a scope defined, and they would be scanned for throughout the entire document.

Subgroups require regular expression(s) used for detecting matching strings as well as a scope within which the search for those strings will be executed.

Below the control element for the regular expressions, there are three buttons for editing the entries:

- Add: A field in the regular expressions table will be activated for editing. Users may define a new regular expression string here.

- Modify: Allows the modification of an existing and selected expression.

- Delete: Allows the deletion of an existing and selected expression, for example, if a particular expression is no longer required.

Category: Application Layout

The category Application layout is also one very complex category, because it makes the layout of UltraEdit configurable, which in turn has a major influence on the workflow. Figure 4-17 shows the exemplary structure of this collection of options.

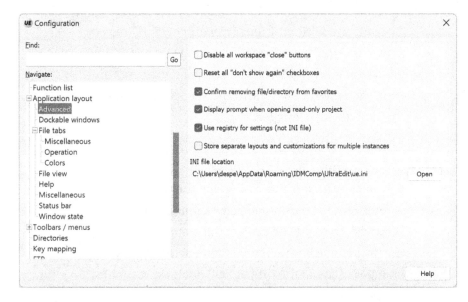

Figure 4-17. *Category Application layout in the UltraEdit Configuration*

- Advanced: This section contains advanced options which concern mostly the storage of the program configuration. The *Disable all Workspace "Close" buttons* option toggles the state of close buttons for peripheral windows (File Tree View, ASCII Table, Function List, Macro List, Tag List, Template List, Clipboard History, Script List, Bookmark List, Output Window, and SSH/Telnet Console).

  If the option *Reset all "Don't Show Again" checkboxes* is enabled, all dialogs with a "Don't show this window again" option are reset to an unchecked state so they will be visible the next time the associated option is invoked.

  By using the option *Confirm removing File/Directory from Favorites*, a confirmation dialog will be shown whenever a file or directory is selected for removal from the *Favorites* list shown under the *Lists* tab in the Workspace Manager.

  With the option *Display prompt opening read-only project*, a confirmation dialog will be shown when a project is loaded, indicating that the project file is read-only. The user will be prompted to decide if they wish to make the project file writable or not. If the project file is not changed to be writable, then changes made to the project will not be saved when the project is closed.

  By default, the UltraEdit configuration is saved in an INI configuration file, and with the option *Use Registry for settings (not INI file) - This will NOT move the existing items to the registry*, this storage target is redirected to the Windows registry. After UltraEdit determines the INI file in use, it checks for this value before reading any other values. If this is enabled, UltraEdit stores all settings in the registry. When this option is selected, existing settings are not copied from the INI file to the registry. In turn, this means that if this option is unchecked, options stored in the registry are not moved to the INI file. Please note that if this option is selected, the options to *Import settings* and *Export settings* in the *Backup settings* drop-down in the Advanced tab (Ribbon mode) or the Advanced menu (Contemporary and Traditional menu modes) will not work.

The last option of this advanced settings is called *Store windows/menu/toolbars placements and configurations for multiple instances of application*, and if enabled and a second instance of UltraEdit is open and window sizes/positions or menu/toolbar configurations are changed, the next time a second instance of UltraEdit is opened, it will use the separately saved sizes and positions.

The lower block is called the *INI file location* and displays the full path to the INI file being used by the current instance of UltraEdit. This text may not be edited by the user but is provided to facilitate locating the INI file when necessary. The *Open* button to the right opens Windows Explorer and selects this file.

- Dockable windows: This category contains options for dockable windows, because UltraEdit works a lot with window navigation in its operating concept.

  The first edit field is called *Time-out before Auto-hide (in ms)* and is used to specify the number of milliseconds of delay that will pass before an auto-hide occurs when a child window which is configured to auto-hide loses focus.

  The second option is represented with a slider called *Auto-hide scrolling* and can be used to adjust the speed used to close a child window when set to auto-hide. If the slider is moved as close as possible to *Disabled*, the scrolling will be very fast. As the slider is adjusted more toward *Smooth*, the scrolling will seem to slide out of the edit window space more gradually.

- File tabs: This category contains options for file tabs, which are quite often used in UltraEdit, for example, for editing multiple files together with the associated navigation.

  - Miscellaneous: This subsection contains all settings, which can't be sorted into the other categories.

    If the option *Double-click tab will close file* is enabled, double-clicking on an open file tab will close the associated file. This option is selected by default.

The next option is also quite useful in connection with mouse operation and is called *Middle-button-click will close file*. When enabled, clicking the middle mouse button on an open file tab will close the associated file – this option is selected by default.

By using the option *MDI close button closes active file (not file tabs)*, the active file is closed by pressing the MDI close button instead of the file tab.

The mouse wheel has a further meaning with the option *Scroll tabs with mouse wheel*, because if enabled, file tabs can be scrolled by positioning the cursor above the open file tabs and scrolling the mouse wheel.

Using the option *After current tab is closed, move to*, users may select which file tab focus should shift to when the current tab is closed.

Sort tabs on file open means that file tabs will automatically be sorted as each file is opened. Files may be sorted by name, by extension, by path, or by modification date. Sorting options are also accessible under *File tabs ➤ Sort tabs by* in the file tab context menu.

If the option *Display status icons* is enabled, icons will be displayed in file tabs to indicate the status of the related file. Icons are included for the meaning of *New file (unsaved)*, *Local modified file (unsaved)*, *Local modified file (saved)*, *Modified FTP file (unsaved)*, *Modified FTP file (saved)*, and *Read only file*. If no icon is displayed, this means that the file has not been modified since it was opened.

- Operation: The operation of the file tabs is configured in the section of the same name.

If the option *Dockable tabs* is enabled, the file tabs will be displayed in a dockable control that may be moved outside of the main GUI and arranged and resized as desired. If this option is not selected, files cannot be cascaded or tiled using the relevant Window menu commands.

The *Types* option defines the way in which the file tabs are displayed and handled. There are three possibilities here:

- Single line – scrollable: File tabs will be displayed in a single row. When the file tabs for the number of files opened exceed what can be displayed on a single line, left and right scroll arrows will be displayed at opposite ends of the tab row.

- Single line – drop down file list: File tabs will be displayed in a single row. In this mode, a list of currently open files may be accessed by clicking on the down arrow at the end of the tab row.

- Multiline: The number of lines used to display file tabs for the open files will automatically expand and contract as necessary based on the number of open files.

The *Close Tab* button is used to close a file tab, and users may select one of four options related to the display of an "x" close button for file tabs:

- None: A close button is not displayed.

- On tab bar: "x" will be displayed at the end of the file tab row, and users may click on this to close the active file. The *On tab bar* option is subdued unless the *Single line - drop down file list* file tab type is selected above.

- On active tab: "x" will be displayed on the active file tab.

- On all tabs: "x" will be displayed on all file tabs.

- Colors: This category contains all color options for the file tabs (see also Figure 4-18).

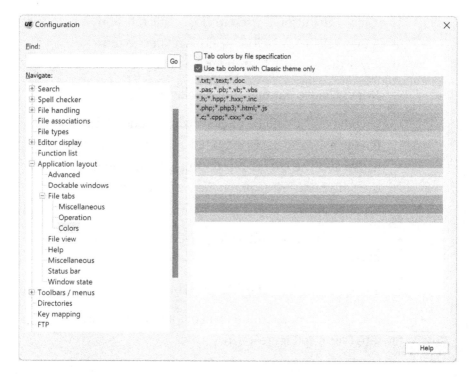

Figure 4-18. *Color options for File tabs based on the Application layout*

If the option *Tab colors by file specification* is enabled, the background color of file tabs will be changed to indicate the file type. Users may assign file types to the colors available in the table by double-clicking on a color line and adding an extension (i.e., "*.html"). Additional extensions should be listed immediately following the preceding extension and a semicolon ";" (i.e., "*.php;*.php3;*.html;*.js"). If preferred, users may specify colors for individual files rather than extensions, i.e., "ResolveLine.cpp".

By using the option *Use tab colors with Classic theme only*, selecting the option above will have no effect unless the Classic theme is active.

- File view: This category contains options for viewing files in UltraEdit.

  If the option *Show volume labels in Explorer view* is enabled, volume labels rather than just drive letters will be displayed under the *Explorer* tab in the File Tree View.

  By using *Network drive label format*, the format defined in this field will determine how the volume label is displayed under the *Explorer* tab in the File Tree View.

  Show registered file type icons in Explorer view means that system registered icons will be used under the *Explorer* tab in the File Tree View rather than generic file type icons.

  Empty folders can be specially handled with the option *Scan for empty folders in Explorer view*, whereby UltraEdit will detect empty folders in the *Explorer* view in the File Tree View. Those folders determined to be empty will not have a "+" shown beside them (indicating that they may be expanded). If this option is not selected, the "+" may or may not be accurate but will not be updated until the editor attempts to update/expand the selected folder.

When the mouse hovers over a drive in the *Explorer* view, the editor attempts to get the latest information about that drive and display it. By using the option *Cache volume info in Explorer view*, drive information is cached, and the drive is not accessed so often.

With the option *Activate file in Open file list on single click*, a single click in the Open file list in the File Tree View will cause the referenced file to become the active file in UltraEdit. By default, this option is not selected, and a double-click is required.

The UltraEdit explorer is a handy tool to navigate through drives, partitions, and directories, and with the option *Resolve Link files and directories in Explorer view when opened*, linked files will be opened when the lnk file is clicked on in the Explorer view, and the Explorer view will navigate to the linked directory when the lnk directory is clicked on in Explorer.

The last option is called *Show Network browser in Explorer view* and means that a *Network* node is shown in the display tree in the *Explorer* pane of the File Tree View. When this node is expanded, a listing of the members of the network to which the system is currently connected is displayed. Users may navigate this tree and access remote servers without mapping drives. Paths for files opened via this method will be accessed/referenced using Universal Naming Convention (UNC) format.

- Help: This *Help* subcategory contains probably the only option for the UltraEdit help.

  Show CHM user help files always on top allows users to force UltraEdit to always show user-defined CHM help files as the top-level window when opened.

- Miscellaneous: Once again, options in this category cannot be assigned to any other category and are collected here.

  The setting *Display file name only in document title* allows the user to specify that UltraEdit should only display the file name only and not the path in the title bar for the editing window. If this is disabled, the file name and path will be displayed (default). On the contrary, if enabled, only the file name will be displayed.

  An instance is a separate program execution of UltraEdit, and when the option *Files selected in Explorer will open in a new single instance* is enabled and multiple files are selected at once in Windows Explorer, and UltraEdit is selected from the context menu, all selected files will be opened in a single new instance. If this option is disabled, each file selected may be opened in a separate instance.

  The *Allow multiple instances* option determines if another instance of UltraEdit is opened if UltraEdit is invoked when an instance is already active. If this option is enabled, a new instance is opened each time UltraEdit is invoked. If this option is disabled, only a single instance of UltraEdit is opened, and any additional requests result in the first instance becoming active with the new file loaded in addition to any files already open.

In some cases, it may be necessary to select the long option *Maintain separate process for each file opened from external application* to support opening multiple files in a single instance of UltraEdit from an external application. If this option is enabled, each open file will have a separate process in the Windows Task Manager until the file is closed or UltraEdit is closed. This option cannot be selected if the option *Allow multiple instances* is enabled.

By using *Start application title with file name*, the path of the active file will be shown in the title bar before the name of the application. If this is disabled, the application name will be displayed before the active file path.

Automatically check for updates means that UltraEdit will automatically check for the availability of updates every 30 days. This is a very helpful and powerful feature to stay up to date and receive the latest features and security updates.

When ESC exits full screen mode is enabled, pressing the Escape (ESC) key will cause the full screen mode to exit.

- Status bar: The status bar is located in the lower editor area and contains helpful status values for editor processing.

The only option in this subcategory is called *Use basic status bar*, and if enabled, the status bar will provide a display of information related to the active file without any interactive controls. If this option is disabled, the status bar will include an *Encoding Type* control and a *Highlighting Type* control as well as interactive toggles for *Read Only/Write* status and *Insert/Overstrike* status.

- Window state: The Windows status describes whether a window in UltraEdit is minimized or maximized.

  If the option *Minimize on last file close* is enabled, UltraEdit will minimize when all open files are closed.

  By using *Minimize on system tray (not taskbar)*, UltraEdit will minimize to the system tray and not to the taskbar.

  The last option is called *Always open editor maximized*, and this setting determines if UltraEdit should always open its main window in a maximized state. The default is for the previous settings to be remembered. If this setting is checked, UltraEdit will open the main window in a maximized state.

Category: Toolbars/Menus

Depending on the used layout, UltraEdit is controlled via menus and toolbars, and many functions are made accessible via these. This category therefore contains the corresponding options, and Figure 4-19 shows the exemplary structure of this collection of options.

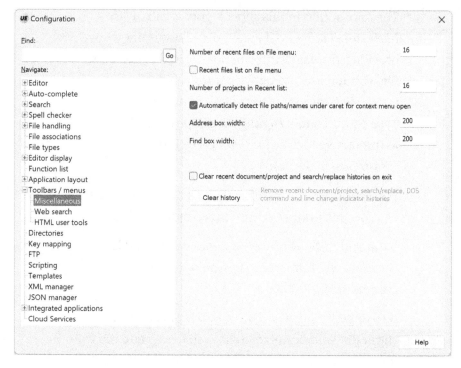

Figure 4-19.   *Category Toolbars/menus in the UltraEdit Configuration*

- Miscellaneous: This subsection contains various uncategorized options that are summarized here.

  The option *Number of recent files on file menu* sets the number of recent files that appear on the Application menu for quick opening of files.

  Recent files and their display can be handled with the option *Recent files list on file menu*. It configures the recent file list to appear on the File menu rather than as a submenu of the File menu. If this option is disabled, the recent file list appears as a submenu of the File menu. By changing this option, UltraEdit will have to be shut down and restarted for the change to take effect.

By using the quite long option *Automatically detect file paths/names under caret for context menu open*, users may right-click on file paths/URLs in open files and an option to open the referenced file/URL will be shown at the top of the context menu.

The setting *Address box width* configures the width of the *Open address bar* control when added to a toolbar. In addition to this, *Find box width* configures the width of the Search string to find control when added to a toolbar.

If data protection and the associated history of the last opened files play a special role, the option *Clear recent document/project and search/replace histories on exit* could be interesting. If enabled, the Recent Files list and Recent Projects lists, the stored search/replace strings, the last used DOS commands, and the line change indicator information for edited files will automatically be cleared upon exit.

The last option is an action button called *Clear History*. When pressed, the Recent Files list and Recent Projects lists and any stored search/replace strings are immediately cleared. This button will also clear line change indicator histories stored in the INI file.

- Web search: This subsection provides an interface where users may customize the search strings used when a search for text selected in UltraEdit is executed using the commands in the *Search* group in the *Coding* tab.

  Through this interface, users may localize (if desired) the portal through which their search is executed. For example, a user located in Germany may wish to search on "www.google.de" rather than the US portal – "www.google.com". This may be accomplished by changing the "Google" search string to

  http://www.google.de/search?q=$K

  In all cases, the "$K" represents the string selected in UltraEdit at the time the search is executed. If desired, the default search strings may be reinstated for each option by pressing the associated *Default* button and by closing the Configuration dialog, which means that all changes are applied.

- HTML user tools: This subsection provides an interface where users may customize the HTML text inserted when HTML buttons are selected in the HTML toolbar.

  When a button is selected from the toolbar row, the text associated with this button will be displayed in the edit window, and users may modify this text and save it to customize what is inserted by pressing the selected HTML button. By default, the HTML option will be selected in the *Predefined* section, and the default buttons will insert text conforming to the HTML 4 standard. If the XHTML option is selected, the default buttons will insert text conforming to the XHTML standard.

Users may specify where the cursor should be presented when an element is inserted into the active document by using "|" in the text area, as is supported for templates. For example, typing "<td>|</td>" would present the cursor or any currently selected text between the specified HTML elements. "\n" should be used in the template text to represent a new line. If a tab is desired, users should copy an actual tab character to the Windows clipboard prior to opening the HTML toolbar configuration dialog and paste the actual tab character into the template text.

When custom tags are associated with generic "HTML user command" buttons, the tooltip text will help to clarify what the button does when it is clicked. If a customized button is added to the Ribbon, it will first be added with its generic name, for example, "HTML user cmd 01". The user may select this in the *Customize* dialog and click the *Rename* button to specify a more descriptive name.

Category: Directories

This category allows the default directories used by UltraEdit to be configured, and Figure 4-20 shows the exemplary structure of this collection of options.

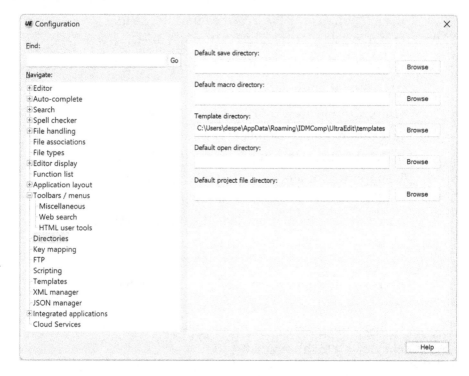

Figure 4-20. *Category Directories in the UltraEdit Configuration*

The following directories can be configured, and in addition, a *Browse* button appears behind each directory edit field, which can be used to conveniently select the corresponding directory:

- Default save directory: Sets the default directory for saving files with the *Save as* command

- Macro default directory: Sets the default directory for loading and saving macros

- Template directory: Sets the directory for template storage

- Default open directory: Sets the default directory for opening files with the *Open* command if no files are opened for editing (otherwise, the active file's directory is used)

- Default project file directory: Sets the default directory for creating new projects with the *New project* command

Category: Key Mapping

This category allows the user to reassign the default key mapping provided by UltraEdit to suit their particular needs, and Figure 4-21 shows the exemplary structure of this collection of options.

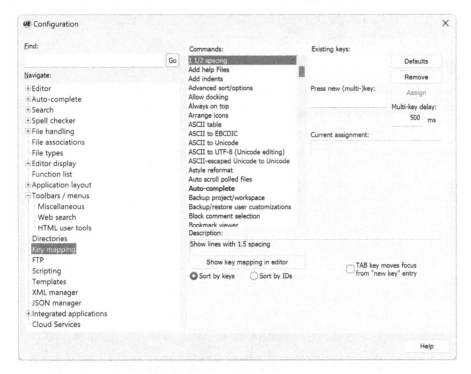

Figure 4-21. *Category Key mapping in the UltraEdit Configuration*

171

This dialog shows a list of commands within UltraEdit that may be mapped by the user to a key combination of their choice. Clicking on any of the commands will show the existing key assignment (if any) and the command description below the list. Commands will be sorted alphabetically.

To add or change a command key assignment:

- Select the command you wished to modify from the Commands list.

- Click the mouse in the *Press New (Multi-)Key* entry window area, or press Tab to give it focus.

- Type the new key assignment just as the user would if they were invoking the command – this key combination will be captured and displayed. Users may use up to three keys (i.e., "Ctrl+Shift+T") for multi-key assignments in each field.

- Click the *Assign* button and the new key will be assigned to the command. If an existing key is assigned, the user will be asked if they wish to delete it and replace with the new assignment.

Users may use both text fields under *Press new (multi-)key* to define so-called chords. For example:

Ctrl + R

M

could be used to toggle a bookmark when "Ctrl + R, and M" are pressed in quick succession.

The *Multi-key delay* value may be set to allow the user time to enter multi-key keyboard shortcuts rather than having the first portion of a multi-key keyboard shortcut processed on its own.

To remove a key assignment:

- Select the command that needs to be modified from the *Commands* list

- Select the existing key assignment from the *Existing keys* list

- Click the *Remove* button and the key assignment will be removed

To reset the key assignments to the default:

- Click the *Defaults* button and the key assignments will be reset to the defaults. The user will be prompted to confirm the action.

The file containing user keyboard mappings is stored (and searched for when UltraEdit starts up) in the same directory as the INI file. The file name is the same as the INI with the .UEK extension, i.e., UE.UEK or UES. UEK. The corresponding button *Show key mapping in editor* creates a listing of all currently configured keyboard shortcuts for use with UltraEdit and writes them to a file with the format "[Editor Name].shortcuts". This includes standard keyboard shortcuts, menu shortcuts, and macro hotkeys.

If the option *TAB Key moves focus from "New Key" entry* is enabled, pressing the Tab key while focus is on the entry field *Press new (multi-) key* will move focus out of this field rather than including "TAB" in the mapping for the selected command.

The last options are sorting options and called *Sort by keys* and *Sort by IDs*. If *Sort by keys* is selected, this list will be sorted based on the shortcut keys for each function. In contrast to this, when *Sort by IDs* is selected, this list will be sorted based on the command names. If desired, this list may be printed for reference.

Category: FTP

As UltraEdit has an integrated FTP functionality, for example, to edit files from an FTP server, this category summarizes the associated options. Figure 4-22 shows the exemplary structure of this collection of options.

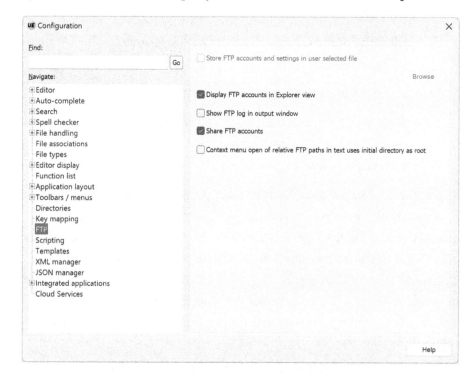

Figure 4-22. *Category FTP in the UltraEdit Configuration*

The first option is called *Store FTP accounts and settings in user selected file* and may be used to allow the user to specify a file which will be used to store FTP account options. The user may define this directly in the provided text box or browse to select a file that already exists. If this option is not selected, FTP account information will be stored in the FTPDataU.ini file under %APPDATA%\IDMComp\UltraEdit. If the later described option *Share FTP Accounts* is enabled, then the FTP account info is stored under %APPDATA%\IDMComp\Common\FTP Accounts.

The display of the FTP accounts can be controlled with the option *Display FTP accounts in Explorer view*. When enabled, FTP accounts will be shown in the *File Tree View/Workspace Manager* under the *Explorer* tab. The root of the account will be listed as a top-level directory and may be expanded to show files/folders under this account.

By using the option *Show FTP log in output window*, an FTP log showing all commands sent to and data received from the FTP server will be displayed in the output window. This can provide helpful diagnostic information, and the contents of this window may be copied using the clipboard.

With *Share FTP Accounts*, the option *Store FTP accounts and settings in user selected file* will automatically become subdued. When this option is selected, FTP account information is written to a new file IdmFTPAccountsU.txt created under %APPDATA%\IDMComp\Common\ FTP Accounts. This will allow UltraEdit, UEStudio, and UltraCompare to access FTP account information maintained in a common file rather than storing this information separately for each application.

The last and at the same time longest option is called *Context menu open of relative FTP paths in text uses Initial Directory as root*. When enabled and an *Initial Directory* is defined for an account under the *General* tab in the *FTP Account Manager*, when a partial path is right-clicked in a file opened via FTP, UltraEdit will use the path defined for the *Initial Directory* as the root or base path for opening the relative path referenced in the active file.

Category: Scripting

Another great strength of UltraEdit is the scripting functionality, and there are quite few options for this in this category. Figure 4-23 shows the exemplary display of those options.

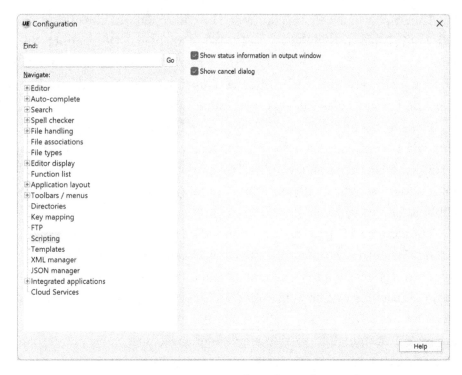

Figure 4-23. *Category Scripting in the UltraEdit Configuration*

The first option is called *Show status information in output window*, and if selected, all status information including script name, whether the script succeeded or failed, and error information is printed to the output window. If the output window is closed but this option is selected or if the *showOutput* property is true (which it is by default), then data is still written to the output window, but the output window is not automatically displayed.

By using the second option *Show cancel dialog*, a cancel dialog will be displayed when scripts are run.

Category: Templates

Templates are a powerful function during text processing, and UltraEdit offers various configuration options for this. A template is predefined text that is stored and can be recalled later to insert into a file. Figure 4-24 shows the exemplary structure of this collection of options.

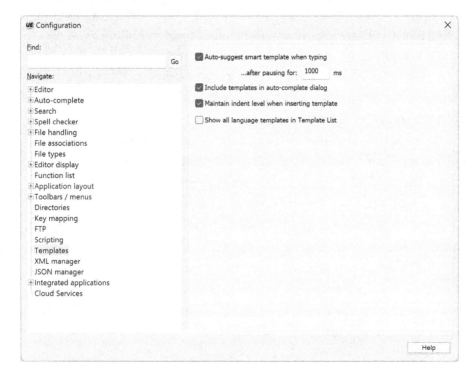

Figure 4-24.   *Category Templates in the UltraEdit Configuration*

With the first option *Auto-suggest smart template when typing*, UltraEdit will auto-suggest a template based on what the user has typed into the active file. The template name must match the word that has been typed into the active file in order for UltraEdit to auto-suggest a template. There are two ways to insert a suggested template:

- Let UltraEdit suggest the template based on what was just typed, then press Tab to insert it.

- Press Ctrl+Space to invoke the auto-complete dialog and choose a template from here.

The option ...*after pausing for* is also important in this context, because it allows the user to specify the delay in milliseconds that must occur after typing a word in a file before UltraEdit auto-suggests a template. This setting is disabled if the option above is unchecked.

By using *Include templates in auto-complete dialog*, templates matching the string typed into the active file will be displayed at the top of the auto-complete dialog.

When *Maintain indent level when inserting template* is selected, the current indentation level of the active document will be respected, and auto-indent will adjust accordingly when a template is inserted into a document. If this option is not selected, insertion of the selected template will begin at the current caret position but will not respect indentation on subsequent lines of the inserted template.

The Template List contains all templates and was already described in Chapter 3. By using *Show all language templates in Template List*, all language templates will be accessible in the Template List regardless of the type of file currently loaded for editing.

Category: XML Manager

The XML manager was also described in Chapter 3 and provides a parsed, visual, tree-style representation of the active XML file with options for modifying the XML structure. In this category, all available options are bundled, and Figure 4-25 shows the exemplary structure of those settings.

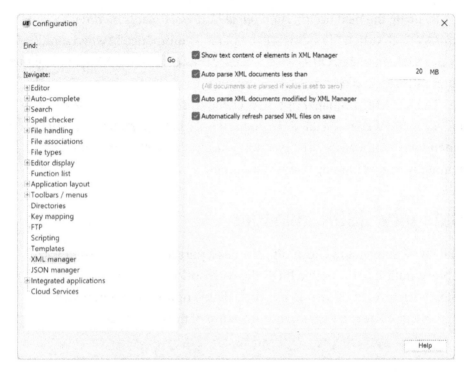

Figure 4-25. *Category XML manager in the UltraEdit Configuration*

If the option *Show text content of elements in XML Manager* is enabled, it may slow down the parser, and there may be a noticeable increase in the amount of memory used when large files are parsed.

The auto parse feature automatically parses XML files, but depending on the file size especially at larger files, the performance decreases. Here the option *Auto parse XML documents less than (value specified) MB* allows a handy threshold value definition, and if enabled, all XML documents smaller than the specified value will be parsed automatically when loaded. Otherwise, the user may click in the XML manager to manually trigger parsing of any document. Users may also right-click in the XML manager and select the *Parse Document* option from the context menu. Any extensions defined in wordfiles that include the XML_LANG or XSL_LANG language markers will be recognized for parsing by the XML manager.

By using the next option *Auto parse XML documents modified by XML Manager*, all XML documents will be parsed automatically when modified by the XML manager. Otherwise, the user may click in the XML manager to manually trigger parsing of any document.

The last XML manager option is called *Auto parse XML documents on file save*, and if enabled, all XML documents will be parsed automatically when saved. Otherwise, the user may click in the XML manager to manually trigger parsing of any document.

Category: JSON Manager

The JSON manager in UltraEdit provides a parsed, visual, tree-style representation of the active JSON file with options for modifying the JSON structure. In this category, all available options are bundled, and Figure 4-26 shows the exemplary structure of those settings.

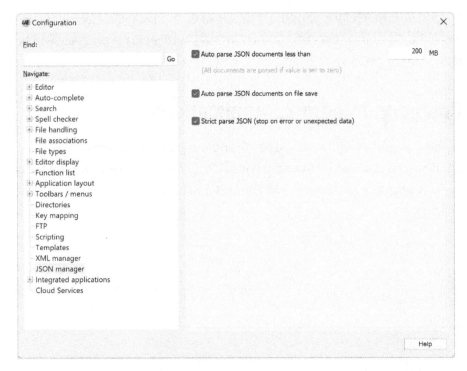

Figure 4-26. *Category JSON manager in the UltraEdit Configuration*

The first option is a threshold value definition and called *Auto parse JSON documents less than (value specified) MB*. If enabled, all JSON documents smaller than the specified value will be parsed automatically when loaded. Otherwise, the user may click in the JSON manager to manually trigger parsing of any document. Users may also right-click in the JSON manager and select the Parse Document option from the context menu.

If the option *Auto parse JSON documents on file save* is selected, all JSON documents will be parsed automatically when saved. Otherwise, the user may click in the JSON manager to manually trigger parsing of any document.

Strict parse JSON means that parsing of the active JSON document will stop when a syntactical error is encountered, and an error message will be shown in the JSON manager.

Category: Integrated Applications

In this category, various subcategories define paths for external applications that can be integrated into UltraEdit. This primarily concerns various scripting languages, and Figure 4-27 shows an example of these options.

Figure 4-27. *Category Integrated applications in the UltraEdit Configuration*

- JavaScript Lint: The field *Full path for JavaScript Lint configuration file* is by default populated with the path to a configuration file with default settings. If desired, the user may create a custom configuration file in another location and specify the path to that file here. Pressing the *Open* button will open the specified file for editing.

- Python: The field *Full path to the Python executable* is by default populated with the path to the pythonw.exe. Pressing the *Browse* button will open a dialog that may be used to browse to the location of the pythonw.exe.

- PHP: The field *Full path to the PHP executable* is by default populated with the path to the PHP.exe. Pressing the *Browse* button will open a dialog that may be used to browse to the location of the PHP.exe.

- Ruby: The field *Full path to the RUBY executable* is by default populated with the path to the ruby.exe. Pressing the *Browse* button will open a dialog that may be used to browse to the location of the ruby.exe.

Category: Cloud Services

In this category, the UltraEdit's Cloud Services are configured, which are a subscription-only service that allows settings and files to be shared between systems. Figure 4-28 shows the exemplary structure of these settings.

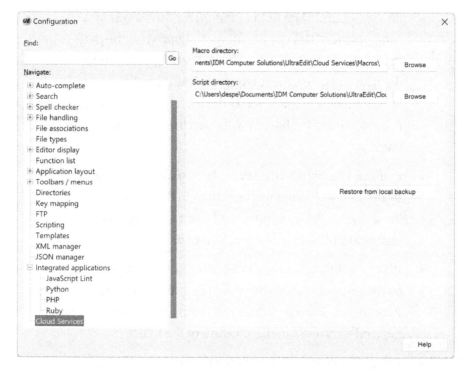

Figure 4-28. *Category Cloud Services in the UltraEdit Configuration*

By default, the fields *Macro directory* and *Script directory* are populated with the path to the directory Cloud Services will check when sharing macros or scripts with other systems. Any macros and scripts will only be synced if they are saved in these directories.

If macros/scripts are not saved in the specified directories, they will not be detected when data is shared with other systems. Pressing the *Browse* button will open a dialog that may be used to browse to the folder the user wishes to specify for this purpose.

Backup/Restore User Customizations

A great strength of UltraEdit is its flexibility and configurability, and the scope of this chapter shows impressively how complex this matter actually is. One aspect has been neglected in the time spent on UltraEdit's configuration – what happens if the user wants to use UltraEdit on a different computer or move the computer to a different system in the course of the valid license?

UltraEdit offers an option for this which can save and restore user customizations. The option can be opened either via *Advanced* ➤ *Backup settings* (Ribbon mode), via *Advanced* ➤ *Backup/restore user customizations* (Traditional menu mode), or via *Advanced* ➤ *Backup settings* (Contemporary menu mode). All three options open the *Backup/ Restore User Customizations* dialog, in which the *Backup* and *Restore* tabs are located at the top. Figure 4-29 shows the dialog with the selected *Backup* tab.

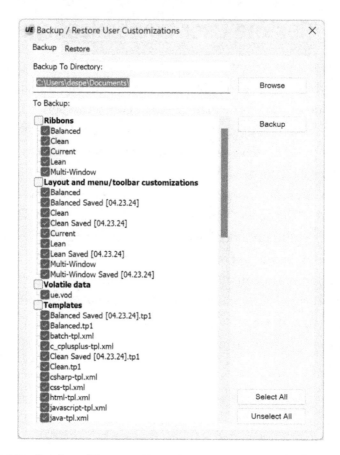

Figure 4-29. *Backup/Restore User Customizations dialog*

This dialog can be resized, which is particularly helpful for the many listed backup areas.

Basically, the tabs at the top are used to select whether the settings are to be backed up or restored. When backing up, the topics are categorized into groups and individual entries or complete groups can be selected or deselected:

- Ribbons: All ribbon styles as well as the current ribbon configuration

- Layout and menu/toolbar customizations: The main menu and pop-up menus as well as the main toolbar and icons along with any custom toolbars

- Volatile data: Mainly defines the file *ue.vod*, which contains a history of many UltraEdit functions (e.g., recently opened files or entered search terms)

- Templates: Contains all templates

- Wordfiles: Contains all wordfiles

- Others: All other backup sources such as the configuration file *ue.ini* and the keyboard shortcuts in the file *ue.shortcuts.txt*

The buttons *Select All* and *Unselect All* allow to quickly and completely select/deselect all entries.

Before the process is started, the backup directory must be defined in the upper edit field called *Backup To Directory*. This can either be entered manually or with a convenient selection dialog via the *Browse* button.

Finally, the process is started via the *Backup* button, and a status window with the success or failure is displayed directly after the backup process. Figure 4-30 shows an example of this status window.

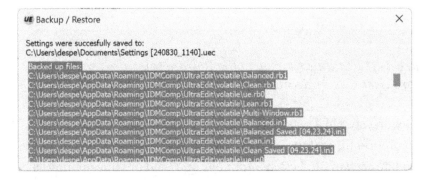

Figure 4-30. *Backup status window*

On the one hand, this status window shows the saved files below to the summarized success result and that the configuration was saved in a file with the extension "uec" (which stands for UltraEdit Configuration). The file name also contains a date and time stamp, which is quite useful if the user is working with different configuration backups and can therefore differentiate between them.

Now that we have discussed the backup process, the next step is to restore a previously created backup. To do this, the user needs to open the same dialog on the target system and switch to the *Restore* tab at the top. Figure 4-31 shows this dialog in its standard view.

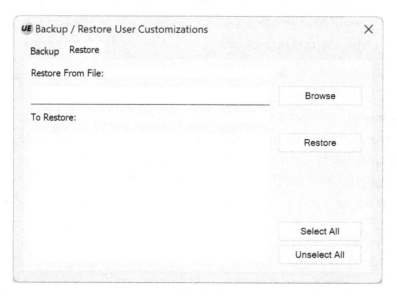

Figure 4-31. *Standard view of the Restore tab from theBackup/ Restore User Customizations dialog*

The first step in a restore process is to select an UltraEdit Backup Configuration file (extension "uec"), whereby the file name is either entered directly in the *Restore From File* edit field or conveniently selected using the *Browse* button.

Immediately after the selection, UltraEdit analyzes the backup configuration and lists the contained areas in the *To Restore* list. Figure 4-32 shows an example of this analysis.

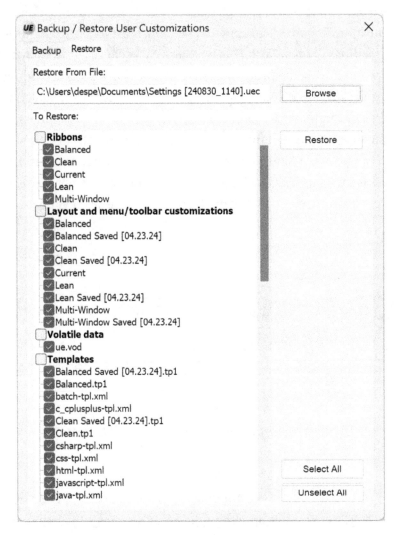

Figure 4-32. *Restorable elements inside the Restore tab from theBackup/Restore User Customizations dialog*

Just as in the *Backup* tab, the areas to be restored can be selected individually, and the buttons *Select All* and *Unselect All* enable a quick and complete selection/deselection.

The restore process is then started with the *Restore* button, after which the following message appears: *You must restart UltraEdit for the updated settings to take effect.* This is necessary because UltraEdit reads its configuration during the program start and configures itself accordingly. As the configuration has changed, this process is necessary again and results in a program restart. Unfortunately, this is only a status message, which means that the user must restart UltraEdit manually and then the restored program configuration is activated. Immediately after restarting UltraEdit, a status message appears again to indicate whether the restore was successful and which files could be restored (see also Figure 4-33).

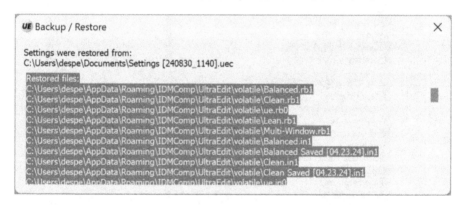

Figure 4-33. *Restore status window after UltraEdit restart*

Tip   Even if the user is not planning to move the computer or wants to use UltraEdit on another computer, it can be useful to back up the program configuration if UltraEdit configurations have been set up carefully. The configuration file is relatively small compared to the time required by most users to fine-tune UltraEdit.

Use of Multiple UltraEdit Configurations

This is a less common but very helpful advanced function that allows users to start UltraEdit with a separate, multiple program configurations. However, using this function means that UltraEdit saves configuration files in different locations as specified by the user. The user should take care to understand what the configuration files are and where they are stored on the system when using this functionality.

Basically, the command-line parameter */i* is used, to which the path and file name of a specific INI configuration file are passed directly after an equal sign.

Here are some examples of the call:

- /i=c:\Windows\ue.ini

- /i=c:\Users\Public\Desktop\ue.ini

- /i="f:\USB Stick\UltraEdit\ue.ini"

The file name must follow the */i=* immediately, and it can be a long name with spaces, in which case it must be in quotes.

Since UltraEdit will rarely be started from the command line, a batch file or PowerShell script that executes the call and is located in an easily accessible location (or makes the link to it easy to call) is a good choice.

Summary

In this chapter, we have dealt extensively with the many UltraEdit options and discussed them in detail. The chapter may seem very complex, but it can also be used as a reference to look up certain functions or to get an overview of the program functionality.

In the next chapters, we will therefore go into more detail about the editor functionality and file processing, which are among the core functions of UltraEdit.

CHAPTER 5

Window Arrangement

In this chapter, we will focus on the different types of window organization, because UltraEdit can in principle be used to edit countless files simultaneously. The way in which the user organizes files determines whether they can manage them, keep an overview, and maintain their own productivity.

UltraEdit offers various display options for this and even with ever larger monitors (including 4K and 8K), more and more content can be displayed, and UltraEdit tries to play its part in this.

Basically, one area in UltraEdit reflects all associated functions, and this is the Window tab (Ribbon mode) or Window menu (Contemporary and Traditional menu modes). Compared to the Ribbon mode, both menu modes do have the advantage that several files are integrated directly into the menu and can therefore be selected.

Duplicate Window

The duplicate function is often useful if the user wants to display different parts or views of the same document at the same time.

The function can be launched via the *Window* tab ➤ *Duplicate window* (Ribbon mode) or the *Window* menu ➤ *Duplicate window* (Contemporary and Traditional menu modes).

The currently focused file always serves as the basis, and the duplicate function always opens a new duplicate window with the same content as the current window. If, for example, a file with the name *Testfile.txt* exists

D. Espenschied, *Mastering UltraEdit*, https://doi.org/10.1007/979-8-8688-1160-9_5

and the duplicate function is called, UltraEdit mirrors the file content in an additional file. The original file name is extended by a consecutive number, which is displayed after the file name separated by a colon. As a result, our new two file names are named *Testfile.txt:1* and *Testfile.txt:2*, as can be seen in Figure 5-1.

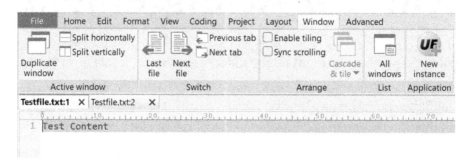

Figure 5-1. *Example of a duplicated file*

If the user changes the contents in one window, all other windows containing the same document reflect those changes. By opening a duplicate window, it becomes the active window and is displayed on top of all other open windows.

With duplicated windows, the user can then grab the file tab and pull it out to create a side-by-side view of the same file. The same is achievable with the *Split window* function, but the duplicate window function is more interesting and a bit more dynamic.

Split Window

Split window is a feature that is similar to duplicate window, but unlike duplicate window, split window provides two views of the same file within a single file tab. The user can create a split window one of two ways:

- Via the *Split horizontally* and *Split vertically* commands in the *Window* tab (Ribbon mode) or the *Window* menu (Contemporary and Traditional menu modes)

- By dragging or double-clicking the horizontal splitter directly above the top scroll bar button (see Figure 5-2).

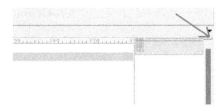

Figure 5-2. *Horizontal splitter above the top scroll bar*

To close a split window, simply double-click the splitter.

Any changes the user makes in one split window will be reflected in the other split as well. Each split window has its own independent editing, code folding, and bookmarks – however, everything else is shared.

In principle, windows can be split both vertically and horizontally. In fact, the user can split both orientations, creating a 2x2 view (4 different views) of the same file.

Switch Between Windows

There are four functions for switching between windows, and these functions can also be accessed via the *Window* tab (Ribbon mode) or the *Window* menu (Contemporary and Traditional menu modes):

- Last file: Moves the focus forward through the most-recently clicked file tab history (keyboard shortcut Ctrl+Shift+F6)

- Next file: Moves the focus backward through the most-recently clicked file tab history (keyboard shortcut Ctrl+F6)

- Previous tab: Activates the file tab immediately to the left of the active tab (keyboard shortcut Alt+Up Arrow)

- Next tab: Activates file tab immediately to the right of the active tab (keyboard shortcut Alt+Down Arrow)

Arrange

The Arrange category defines how several files are arranged. This applies mostly to tiling, cascading, and minimizing. Vertical scrolling of non-minimized windows can be synchronized via a special sync scrolling function:

- Enable tiling: Switches the editor window type from undockable to dockable. When this is enabled, the user can tile, cascade, rearrange, and minimize editor windows just as any other windows. Please note that enabling this will also enable dockable file tabs as a necessity of the windows framework.

- Sync scrolling: Synchronizes vertical scrolling for all non-minimized edit windows.

- Cascade & tile – Cascade: Arranges the edit windows (all open files) in an overlapped (cascading) fashion. This feature is only available if the first option *Enable tiling* is enabled.

- Cascade & tile – Tile horizontal: Arranges the edit windows (all open files) in non-overlapped horizontal tiles. This feature is only available if the first option *Enable tiling* is enabled

- Cascade & tile – Tile vertical: Arranges the edit windows (all open files) in non-overlapped vertical tiles. This feature is only available if the first option *Enable tiling* is enabled.

- Minimize all: Minimizes all edit windows (all open files). This feature is only available if the first option *Enable tiling* is enabled.

- Arrange minimized: Arranges and aligns all minimized edit windows. This feature is only available if the first option *Enable tiling* is enabled.

List

The List category contains only one function with the name *All windows*, which can be launched via the *Window* tab ➤ *All windows* (Ribbon mode), the *Window* menu ➤ *Windows* (Traditional menu mode), and the *Window* menu ➤ *All windows* (Contemporary menu mode).

The function opens the *Windows* dialog, which contains a list of all open windows including open files and any duplicate windows (see also Figure 5-3).

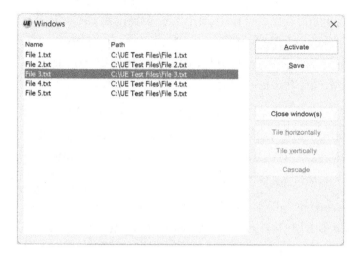

Figure 5-3. *Windows dialog with all open files*

In the dialog, the user will maybe immediately notice that the currently focused file is selected in the list. The list itself contains the file name and path in two columns.

Double-clicking an item in the list of open windows will activate that window in UltraEdit and immediately close the *Windows* dialog. The user can select one or more files in the list of open windows and then act upon them with the following right-side buttons and corresponding options:

- Activate: Makes the last selected item in the windows list active.

- Save: Saves all selected items.

- Close window(s): Closes all selected items.

- Tile horizontally/vertically/cascade: These buttons execute the tiling and cascading functionality in the Window tab (Ribbon mode) or Window menu (menu mode). These buttons are only enabled if the first option *Enable tiling* is enabled.

Application

This last category with the name *Application* launches a separate instance of UltraEdit/UEStudio. No file is open in this new instance, and the function is useful if the user wants to display certain content in a second process or present it on a second monitor.

Summary

In this rather compact chapter, we have learned about the various navigation options of UltraEdit with regard to open files, how these can be arranged, and how to obtain an overview of all open files using the *Windows* dialog. This display variety is particularly important when working with multiple files, and we will delve into actual file management and editing in the next part of this book.

3

CHAPTER 6

Basics of File Management

In this chapter, we will take a look at UltraEdit's file management possibilities and the many options that come with it, some of which have been developed over many years from user suggestions and customer requests. The basic functionality is always retained, and those who want to use it will continue to be able to do so. But if any user is willing to increase its efficiency, they will also find previously unknown functions and ways to handle files faster, easier, and more efficiently. This is what UltraEdit offers – not only in this sector – and this is what many users appreciate very quickly after using it.

In Ribbon mode, the quick start toolbar is located above the tabs, and below comes the *File* tab with the file functions, as well as the last opened and last closed files to the right of it (see Figure 6-1).

© Devid Espenschied 2025
D. Espenschied, *Mastering UltraEdit*, https://doi.org/10.1007/979-8-8688-1160-9_6

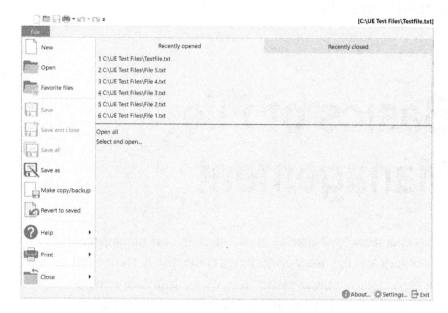

Figure 6-1. *File functions in the File tab on Ribbon mode*

Between the two menu modes, the Contemporary mode provides the most compact display, which is structure related comparable to the Ribbon mode (see Figure 6-2).

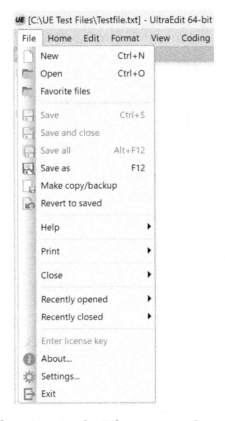

Figure 6-2. *File functions in the File menu on Contemporary menu mode*

If the user prefers really all available functions in the *File* menu, they will like the Traditional menu mode (see Figure 6-3).

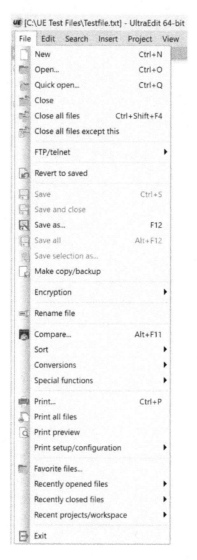

Figure 6-3. *File functions in the File menu on Traditional menu mode*

Most of the file functions are not only available via the menus and ribbons but also via the *File* tab context menu, which opens when the user right-clicks on the tab of the respective file. Therefore, we will not go through every option in detail below, especially since the naming and order change depending on the menu/ribbon modes. Instead, we will focus on the most important file functions that are relevant for the daily work with files and documents.

The original form of the *File* tab context menu is comparable to the Traditional menu mode, including the amount of details (see Figure 6-4).

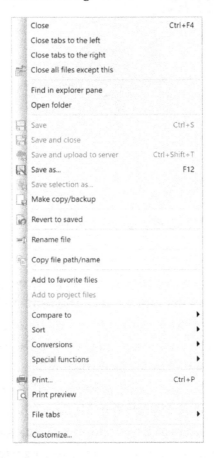

Figure 6-4. File tab context menu

The reference to the fact that this context menu is in its original form refers to the customization option that can be accessed via the *Customize* menu item at the bottom of the context menu, which opens the *Customize* dialog (see Figure 6-5).

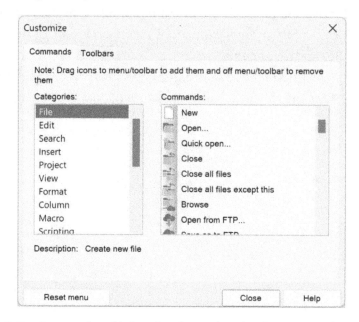

Figure 6-5. *Customize dialog for the individual change of the File tab context menu*

As soon as the *Customize* dialog is opened, the context menu switches to edit mode, which means that entries can be repositioned as required using drag and drop. Furthermore, existing entries can be deleted by opening a separate context menu with the right mouse button and selecting *Delete*.

The number of menu items can vary depending on which element has the focus – separator lines can also be focused in order to establish a more structured arrangement. As the *Customize* dialog is also used for editing the toolbar, this can also be conveniently adjusted. The following menu items exist in the separate context menu for customizing the File tab context menu:

- Copy Button Image: Copies the menu entry's image to the clipboard if an image is assigned

- Delete: Deletes the selected menu item from the File tab context menu

- Start Group: Inserts a group marker above the selected menu item that represents a separator line

As soon as the user right-clicks on a group marker (the previous mentioned separator line), another context menu opens with the following options:

- Reset to Default: Resets all options to default settings

- Copy Button Image: Copies the active button image to the clipboard

- Delete: Removes the selected separator line

- Image: Shows only the image for the active entry (if there is an existing icon)

- Text: Shows only text for the active entry

- Image and Text: Shows both image and text for the active entry

- Start Group: Inserts a group marker above the selected menu item that represents a separator line

The *Customize* dialog shows all the commands provided by UltraEdit, which are available in categories and listed in the command area on the right. If available, a short description is displayed below for each category and each command, and the user can drag and drop a command from the right-hand area into the context menu to the desired position and drop it there. This function allows the user to customize the context menu and adapt it to their own needs.

Create New File

The *New File* command can be used to create a new and empty file, which can be created simultaneously with the keyboard shortcut Ctrl+N.

The file name used is incremented numerically and is initially *Edit1*, then *Edit2* for the second file, and so on. Each newly created file must be saved to make the changes permanent.

There is another feature worth mentioning at this point: the Save State functionality. This function refers to the ability to close UltraEdit with unsaved changes and then have those unsaved changes reloaded the next time the application starts. For example, if the user is in the middle of making changes to several files as part of a larger project, and the operating system suddenly prompts to reboot to install an update, it can be stressful deciding whether or not to save one's own unsaved changes. With Save State, the user doesn't have to decide, because UltraEdit simply remembers the unsaved changes when it is closed down, and then restores them the next time it will be started. This behavior is controlled by various options in the settings category *File handling* ➤ *Session options.*

Open/Quick Open

UltraEdit offers a lot of different methods for opening any files. These include, for example, options via Quick Open Bar (on toolbars), Command Line, Drag-and-Drop, Windows File Explorer Context menu, File View (Explorer tab), Editor Context menu open (right-clicking on a valid file path in text), and the Command palette. We will discuss below the two classic methods: Quick Open, which is an option for fast opening files, and the regular Open function. The latter is within UltraEdit an advanced function with additional options, which we will discuss in a moment.

The Quick Open function can also be opened with the keyboard shortcut Ctrl+Q, and this opens the window with the same name, which looks relatively compact as shown in Figure 6-6.

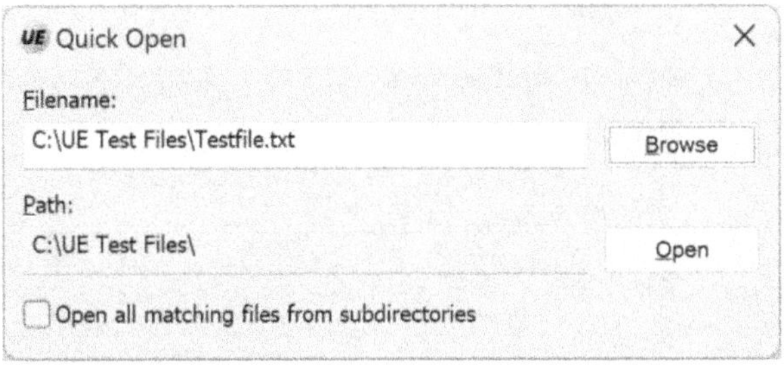

Figure 6-6. *Quick Open dialog*

In principle, this dialog "only" consists of two text fields, a check box, and two buttons. However, the flexibility is far greater than expected.

Any file name and extension can be entered relatively simply in the *Filename* input field. The relative path used for this and displayed in the *Path* input field is used based on the currently open file. Wildcards can also be used, such as *.txt or *.log. In this case, all files with the respective equivalent in the path would be opened by a single command.

The user can also enter a complete path with the file name in the *Filename* field, which can also be located on another accessible storage medium (e.g., j:\USBStick\UltraEdit\Testfile.log).

By using the option *Open all matching files from subdirectories*, UltraEdit allows the user to recursively search all subdirectories (of the specified path) and open all files that match the specified name/wildcard pattern.

The regular command for opening files/documents can also be launched with the shortcut Ctrl+O. UltraEdit then displays the *Open file dialog* (see Figure 6-7) and then displays every opened file in a new window.

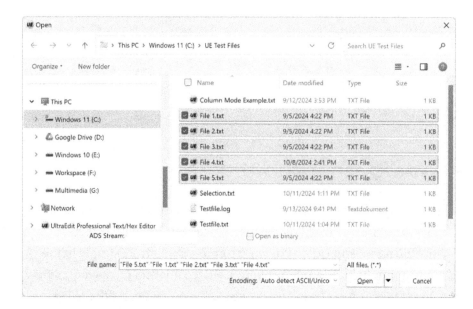

Figure 6-7. *Open file dialog with multiple selected files to open*

As can be seen in Figure 6-7, this dialog also works for multiple files that are selected, and those files can be opened at the same time with UltraEdit. If there are multiple files, these are listed one after the other in the edit field *File name*, enclosed in double quotation marks.

This dialog is basically the same as a standard Windows open dialog, but it has been extended to include several options. These include, for example, the ADS Stream, which means alternate data stream and allows files to be associated with more than one data stream (and is only supported if files are on an NTFS drive). For example, a file such as text.txt can have an ADS with the name of text.txt:secret.txt (of form filename:ads) that can only be accessed by knowing the ADS name or by specialized directory browsing programs.

With the option *Open as binary*, UltraEdit forces the file to be opened in binary format (hex mode). We will discuss this special mode in more detail later.

The encoding for the file to be opened can also be influenced by the combo box with the same name, although an auto-detection is performed by default. Alternatively, the user can select ASCII and various UTF types.

Another way of opening files can be done by dragging them from the *File Manager* into UltraEdit's window and dropping them (releasing the mouse button).

Renaming Files

This command allows the user to rename the active file and can be launched via *Home* ➤ *Rename* (Ribbon and Contemporary menu mode), *File* ➤ *Rename file* (Traditional menu mode), or the *Rename file* option in the File tab context menu.

The rename command shows a dialog allowing the user to specify the new file name. Only the name should be entered there, and the path will be the same as the existing path.

If the file cannot be renamed, or the new name is invalid, an error message will be displayed.

Saving Files

UltraEdit offers various options for saving opened and edited files/ documents.

The classic *Save* command can be executed via the ribbon icons and menu bar, as well as with the keyboard shortcut Ctrl+S. It saves the active document under its current name in the current directory. When a document is saved for the first time, UltraEdit first asks for the name and directory using the *Save As* dialog. This dialog is structured similarly to the *Open* dialog, with the additional option of selecting the file type in the *Save as type* combo box. When the file type is selected, UltraEdit automatically adds the file extension to the name. At the same time, the user can also add the extension manually by typing a dot and the extension directly after the file name.

The *Save and close* command saves the active file and then closes it immediately, which is very helpful if the user doesn't want the file to remain open in UltraEdit after saving.

If the name and/or directory of an existing document is to be changed before it is saved, the *Save As* command is used. This can also be launched using the F12 key, and UltraEdit opens the *Save As* dialog, in which the name, type, and directory can be selected. Within the program settings in the section *Directories*, there is the *Default save directory* edit field in which a default directory can be defined that is used each time the *Save As* dialog is opened. This option is helpful if files are to be saved to a certain directory by default, from which further sorting can take place – all depending on the user and its environment.

The *Save All* command can be used to save all modified documents with their respective names in their respective directories. The keyboard shortcut Alt+F12 can also be used to perform this function. If a file in the file list is to be saved for the first time, the *Save As* dialog appears, allowing the definition of a name, type, and directory.

There is another save option called *Save selection* that is only available when at least one character is selected in the document. This command can be launched via *Edit* ➤ *Save selection* (Ribbon and Contemporary menu mode), *File* ➤ *Save selection as* (Traditional menu mode), or the *Save selection* option in the File tab context menu. With this command, UltraEdit first opens the *Save As* dialog, in which the name, type, and directory are defined. Then only the selected area is saved in this file, which is often useful if the user wants to save and forward a section of a file separately.

The *Make copy/backup* option allows the user to create a backup copy of the active file (with all the current changes) without affecting the active file. The active file maintains the current file name and does not change name unlike the *Save As* command.

The last command in the *Save* category is called *Revert to saved*, which means that the active document is closed and then reloaded, discarding any changes made since it was last saved. Therefore, a saved or unsaved modification of the saved file is the requirement, which means that the command will consequently not work if the file is unnamed and unsaved. As an added safeguard measure, a prompt will appear asking whether the user wants to reload the file, with the simultaneous loss of the last changes.

Deleting Files

There are situations in which a file should actually be deleted, which in Windows is usually solved by a fail-safe system called the Recycle Bin.

UltraEdit offers a function for deleting files that does not take the Recycle Bin into account – the file is really deleted and is therefore hidden in a separate submenu to avoid accidental deletion. This command can be launched via *Home* ➤ *Delete* (Ribbon and Contemporary menu mode), *File* ➤ *Special functions* ➤ *Delete active file* (Traditional menu mode), or the *Special functions* ➤ *Delete active file* option in the File tab context menu.

As soon as the *Delete active file* command is executed, a security question appears asking whether the file should really be deleted. As soon as OK is clicked here, the deletion process begins without any further warning.

Closing Files

There are three different commands for closing files, which are named differently in the Traditional menu mode and in the Ribbon mode/ Contemporary menu mode.

The classic command is named *Close active file* or simply *Close* and can be launched with the keyboard shortcut Ctrl+F4, a double-click on the tab of the file name, or via the "X" in the file tab. When the user closes a file, all windows containing the active document are closed, and UltraEdit suggests on modified files to save them first. If the file has not yet been named and saved, UltraEdit displays the *Save As* dialog, in which the file name and directory for the document can be defined.

Note   Whether or not an opened and active file has been modified can be seen from the fact that a modified file will display a red diamond status icon in the left side of its file tab (by default). If the option *Display status icons* is disabled in the UltraEdit settings in the category *Application layout* ➤ *File tabs* ➤ *Miscellaneous*, then an asterisk is used instead.

The collection function for closing more than a single file is called *Close all* or *Close all files* and can also be accessed via the keyboard shortcut Ctrl+Shift+F4. This function is used to close all currently open files in UltraEdit. Each opened file is checked for unsaved modifications, and if so, the user will be asked if they want to save them before closing.

The third close function is called *Close all except* or *Close all files except this* and means that UltraEdit closes all open files except the active file. Again, if there are any unsaved modifications, the user will be asked if they should be saved before closing. This function is particularly useful if the user opens a lot of files to find something specific and then wants to close all previously opened files except the target file with the found information.

Using File Encryption/Decryption

The encryption and decryption function of UltraEdit is designed to protect the contents of files from foreign eyes, and an Advanced Encryption Standard (AES) algorithm is used for this purpose.

The command *Encrypt file(s)* opens the dialog with the same name, which contains the files to be encrypted in the upper edit field, along with the path and separated by a semicolon (see Figure 6-8).

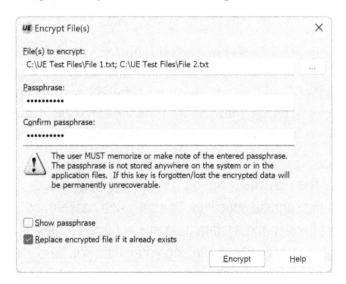

Figure 6-8. *Encrypt File(s) dialog with two files to encrypt*

The passphrase is the actual password and is therefore case-sensitive. It can be between 8 and 32 characters and must be confirmed in a second edit field to ensure correctness based on identical passphrases (the double confirmation is only necessary if the option *Show passphrase* is disabled).

The option *Show passphrase* displays the edit field with the passphrase in plain text, without representing the content by dots. The last option can be used to overwrite an existing encrypted file if it already exists, and this option is exactly named like this behavior.

The *Encrypt* button starts the process, and a log window lists the status for each individual file (see Figure 6-9).

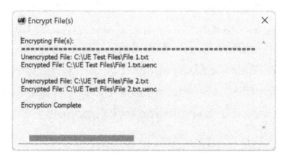

Figure 6-9. *Encrypt File(s) status window*

As we can see from the status window, UltraEdit has appended *.uenc* to the file name so that anyone can tell from the name that the file is encrypted when handling the file (e.g., via a file manager or via email).

Warning   The user **must** memorize or make note of the encryption passphrase specified. The specified passphrase is not stored anywhere on the system or in any application files. If this passphrase is forgotten/lost, the encrypted data will be permanently unrecoverable.

Let's now go the other way around, based on encrypted files that we want to decrypt using a known passphrase. The opposite dialog, *Decrypt File(s)*, is used for this purpose (see Figure 6-10). The files to be decrypted are specified in the upper edit field, and here again several files are separated by a semicolon. Below that, the passphrase is entered, which is used to attempt the decryption.

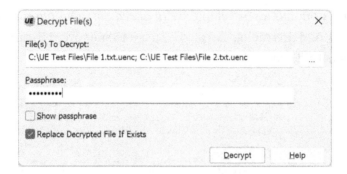

Figure 6-10. *Decrypt File(s) dialog with two files to decrypt*

Two further options are almost identical to the *Encrypt File(s)* dialog and allow a display of the passphrase in plain text and the replacement of decrypted files if they already exist.

The process is started with the *Decrypt* button, and just as with encryption, a status window shows whether the decryption of each individual file was successful.

Note   Within the UltraEdit settings in the category *File handling* ➤ *Encryption*, there are some useful options for encryption, including deleting the original file(s) or backup file(s) after encryption, or automatically re-encrypting a file when it is closed. We have described these options in more detail in Chapter 4.

Sorting Files

The *Sort file* command sorts each line of the active file according to predefined sort options. If only one section is selected, only this section will be sorted – the rest of the file will remain unchanged.

The sort options can be set in the *Advanced Sort/Options* dialog (see Figure 6-11), and this dialog can also be used to start a sort in addition to the separate menu command.

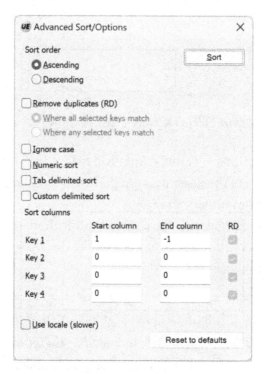

Figure 6-11. *Advanced Sort/Options dialog*

Note   The following sorting options are partially so advanced that they should not be categorized as basic file management functions. However, we do not want to split this function across two different chapters, so we will describe the sorting options in detail and in context below.

The options can be briefly summarized as follows:

- Sort order: Ascending ("a" to "z", 0–9) or Descending ("z" to "a", 9–0).

- Remove duplicates: If enabled, then the associated radio button options *Where all selected keys match* and *Where any selected keys match* become active and may be selected.

  - Where all selected keys match: If selected, duplicate strings/characters must exist in all active sort keys for a line to be considered a duplicate and be removed.

  - Where any selected keys match: If selected, a line is considered a duplicate if duplicate strings/characters exist in any of the active sort keys. Active keys are designated using the check boxes under the *RD* heading. This allows the user greater flexibility in determining which defined keys are used for the Remove duplicates sort operation.

- Ignore case: Lines are considered identical if the characters are the same with the only difference being the case of them. This option should be enabled if the user wants the search to be insensitive to case, i.e., "CAT" is considered the same as "cat". It should be disabled if the sort should consider "cAT" different from "cat".

- Numeric sort: The sort will perform a numeric sort on the selected columns. Typically, a sort is non-numeric, and the values 1,11,111 would be sorted before 2,22,222 as 1 comes before 2. If the numeric sort is enabled, the values would be sorted in numeric order (1,2,11,12,111,222). The numeric sort is not possible with a locale-specific sort or when using the alternate sort method. The numeric sort option should only be used with numeric characters.

- Tab delimited sort: Sorting is performed based on fields defined by tabs in the active document.

- Custom delimited sort: Sorting works as described above for tab delimited sort, but the user may specify a custom delimiter character to be used for sorting.

- Sort columns: Up to four sort keys may be selected to sort on, and each sort key contains a range of columns that will be sorted (normal value for the range is from column 1 to 9216). The start and end columns for unused keys should be set to 0, and the following rules apply:

  - If multiple keys are used, the sort order is based on the first key, followed by the second key, and so on.

  - To sort by complete line, the start column should be set to 1 and the end column to -1.

  - If any key has a value of -1 for the end column, the sort will be from the start column to the end of line.

  - If any key is set to sort the complete line, the rest of the sort keys will be ignored.

  - If the start column is 0 for any sort key (and not sorting by line), the start column will be the column of the cursor.

Sorting performance is better when less keys are used and when less columns are sorted on.

- Use locale (slower): This specifies that the sort should be locale specific. For some languages (e.g., German), this is required to change the default sort order. The locale to be used can be specified under *Advanced* ➤ *Code Page* (Ribbon mode and Contemporary menu mode) or via *View* ➤ *Set code page* (Traditional menu mode). When using this setting, the sort may be slower than if the option were not active.

- Reset to defaults: When this button is pressed, all sort options will be reset to default values.

Format Conversions

Format conversions are used in many areas, for example, to adapt formats or character sets between source and target environments. Therefore, UltraEdit offers various conversion options, which can be found in *Advanced* ➤ *Conversions* (Ribbon mode and Contemporary menu mode) or *File* ➤ *Conversions* (Traditional menu mode).

Depending on the format of the original file, UltraEdit allows customized conversion options (see Figure 6-12).

Unix/Mac to DOS

DOS to Mac

DOS to Unix

EBCDIC to ASCII

ASCII to EBCDIC

OEM to ANSI

ANSI to OEM

ASCII to Unicode

UTF-8 to Unicode

Unicode to ASCII

UTF-8 to ASCII

ASCII to UTF-8 (Unicode editing)

Unicode/UTF-8 to UTF-8 (Unicode editing)

Unicode/ASCII/UTF-8 to UTF-8 (ASCII editing)

Unicode To Unicode big-endian

Unicode big-endian to Unicode

Unicode to ASCII-escaped Unicode

ASCII-escaped Unicode to Unicode

Figure 6-12. *Possible conversions depending on the source file format*

- Unix/Mac to DOS: Corrects the end of line characters for the display in UltraEdit and other text editors. Some documents generated from Unix-based systems (and some other systems) do not terminate each line with a carriage return and line feed. UltraEdit requires all lines to be terminated with a carriage return and line feed character.

  This conversion searches the file for all carriage return and line feed characters:

  - If a carriage return character is found without an accompanying line feed character, a line feed character is added.

- If a line feed character is found without a preceding carriage return character, a carriage return character is inserted.

- If a line feed is found preceding a carriage return, the characters are reversed.

- DOS to Mac: Converts the file to a Mac (Classic) format. This will replace the carriage return and line feed combinations to a carriage return only.

- DOS to Unix: Converts the file to a Unix format. This will replace the carriage return and line feed combinations to a line feed only.

- EBCDIC to ASCII: Converts the complete file from EBCDIC format to ASCII. This is useful in dealing with files that are in the EBCDIC file format (usually on Mainframe computer systems).

  EBCDIC stands for Extended Binary Coded Decimal Interchange Code and is an 8-bit character encoding used mainly on IBM mainframe and IBM midrange computer operating systems.

- ASCII stands for American Standard Code for Information Interchange and is a 7-bit character code where each individual bit represents a unique character.

- ASCII to EBCDIC: Converts the complete file from ASCII to EBCDIC format. This conversion is the opposite of the previously described EBCDIC to ASCII conversion.

- OEM to ANSI: Converts a file that uses the OEM character set (usually DOS-generated text files) to the ANSI (Windows) character set.

  ANSI stands for American National Standards Institute and means in the Windows world that code pages refer to a collection of 8-bit character sets that are compatible with ASCII but incompatible with each other.

- ANSI to OEM: Converts a file that uses the ANSI (Windows) character set to the OEM (DOS) character set.

- ASCII to Unicode: Converts the complete file from ASCII to Unicode (16-bit wide characters). The conversion uses the active code page. The status bar will show a "U-" in front of the file type (DOS/Unix/Mac) to indicate the file is Unicode.

- UTF-8 to Unicode: Converts the complete file from UTF-8 to Unicode. When the file is saved, it will remain as Unicode unless specifically converted to another format by the user. The status bar will show a "U-" in front of the file type (DOS/Unix/Mac) to indicate the file is Unicode.

  UTF stands for Unicode Transformation Format and is a method of mapping Unicode characters onto sequences of bytes.

- Unicode to ASCII: Converts the complete file from Unicode to ASCII. The conversion uses the active code page. For Unicode files, the status bar will show a "U-"

in front of the file type (DOS/Unix/Mac) to indicate the file is Unicode. Following the conversion, this indicator would not be present.

- UTF-8 to ASCII: Converts the complete file from UTF-8 to ASCII. When the file is saved, it will remain as ASCII unless specifically converted to another format by the user. It will use the current code page for conversion, and it's possible that not all characters may be converted correctly – in this case, a default character (?) will be used.

- ASCII to UTF-8 (Unicode editing): Converts the complete file from ASCII to UTF-8. When the file is saved, it will remain as UTF-8 unless specifically converted to another format by the user. The status bar will show "UTF-8" in the field following the file type (DOS/Unix/Mac).

- Unicode/UTF-8 to UTF-8 (Unicode editing): Converts the complete file from Unicode or UTF-8 (ASCII representation) to UTF-8 (with the file internally as Unicode). When the file is saved, it will remain as UTF-8 unless specifically converted to another format by the user. The status bar will show "UTF-8" in the field following the file type (DOS/Unix/Mac).

  Internally the file will be in Unicode format and converted back when the file is saved to UTF-8 encoding. In hex mode, the file will be shown with its current internal representation.

- Unicode/ASCII/UTF-8 to UTF-8 (ASCII editing): Converts the complete file from Unicode, ASCII, or UTF-8 (Unicode representation internally) to UTF-8 encoding. The file will, however, not be internally stored as Unicode, and as such, the multi-byte UTF-8 characters will display as upper ASCII characters and not the UTF-8 character they represent. When the file is saved, it will remain as UTF-8 unless specifically converted to another format by the user. The status bar will not indicate this file format as it has no different structure from an ASCII file.

- Unicode to Unicode big-endian: Converts the complete file from Unicode encoding to Unicode (Big Endian) encoding. Endian refers to the order in which bytes are stored. On Windows platforms, which are mostly little endian, UTF-16LE is just called "Unicode", and UTF-16BE is just called "Unicode (Big Endian)". This is much less confusing for the majority of people who do not work cross-platform.

- Unicode big-endian to Unicode: Converts the complete file from Unicode (Big Endian) to Unicode encoding. This conversion is the opposite of the previously described Unicode to Unicode big-endian conversion.

- Unicode to ASCII-escaped Unicode: Converts the complete file from Unicode (UTF-16) to ASCII-escaped Unicode, which allows the file to maintain its Unicode bytes while in ASCII format.

- ASCII-escaped Unicode to Unicode: Converts the complete file from ASCII-escaped Unicode to Unicode (UTF-16).

What is already apparent from this list is that there are many flexible options for performing conversions from and to all possible formats. This also happens across platforms, because UltraEdit is available not only for the Windows platform but also for Mac and Linux.

Printing Files

Printing files/documents has been part of the standard features of text editors since their inception and is still available today in the age of digitalization. UltraEdit offers a variety of print options that cover almost all needs and requirements.

The classic function is called *Print* (in Traditional menu mode) or *Print file* (in Ribbon mode and Contemporary menu mode) and can also be started using the keyboard shortcut Ctrl+P. This opens the Windows Print dialog, where the user can define the number of pages or the current selection, the number of copies, the destination printer, and other printer options (see Figure 6-13).

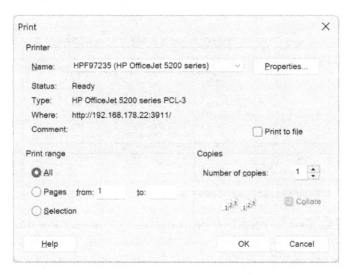

Figure 6-13. *Windows Print dialog with various selectable options*

With the OK button, the printing process is launched, taking into account the options from the Windows Print dialog.

If there are multiple documents to print, the user can use the *Print all* (in Ribbon mode and Contemporary menu mode) or *Print all files* (in Traditional menu mode) function, which prints all open documents using the current page setup and printer settings. The latter can be customized using the *Page Setup* and *Print Setup* options, which we will discuss in a moment.

The print preview allows the user to see what the printout of the current document would look like with the selected printer and settings. Once the *Print Preview* function has been started, UltraEdit replaces the main window with the *Print Preview* window, which displays one or two pages in their printed format (see Figure 6-14).

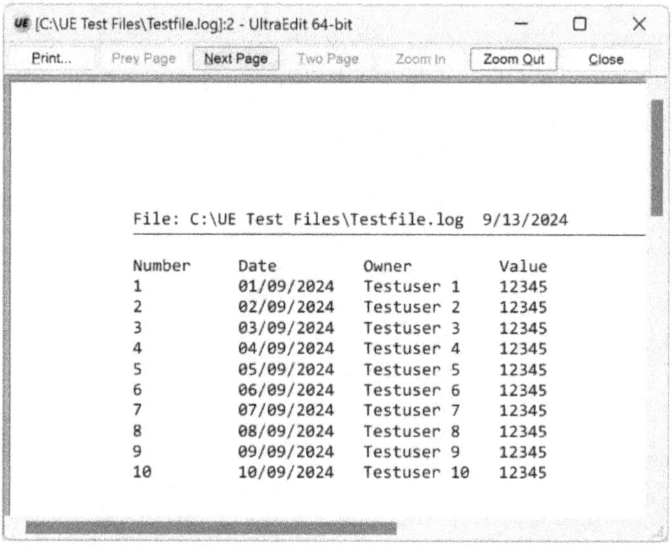

Figure 6-14. *Print Preview window with toolbar for the navigation*

The toolbar offers various buttons for either displaying one or two pages at a time, moving back and forth through the document, zooming in and out of pages, and initiating a print job:

- Print: Brings up the print dialog box to start a print job

- Prev Page: Previews the previous printed page

- Next Page: Previews the next printed page

- One Page/Two Page: Previews one or two printed pages at a time

- Zoom In: Takes a closer look at the printed page

- Zoom Out: Takes a larger look at the printed page

- Close: Returns from print preview to the editing window

We now come to the two dialog boxes that contain advanced printing options and should be familiar if documents need to be printed.

The *Print Setup* dialog is provided by Windows and has already been discussed above in Figure 6-13.

The *Page Setup* dialog, on the other hand, represents a dialog allowing the user to set up page headers, footers, and margins for printing (see Figure 6-15).

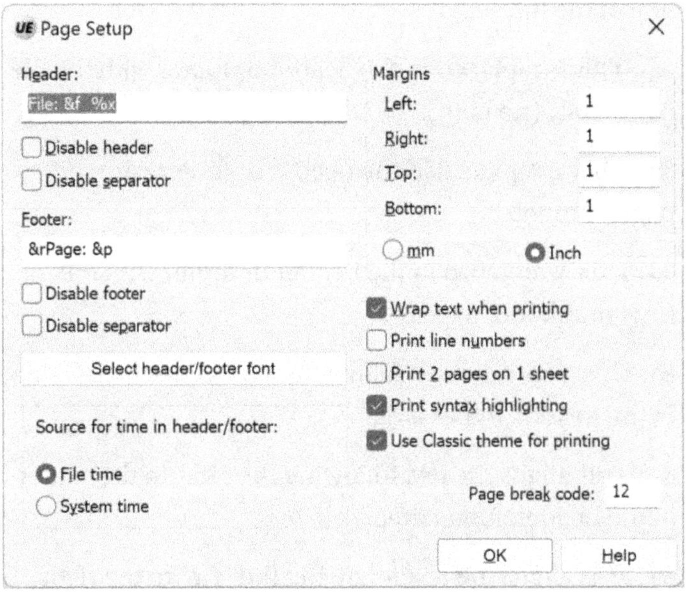

Figure 6-15. Page Setup dialog with extensive Print settings

If configured, the page header is printed at the top of every page and the page footer at the bottom of every page. While a page footer or header is configured, a single line is printed across the page between the header or footer and the text to be printed.

The header or footer may be disabled by selecting the appropriate check boxes, and if the header or footer is enabled, the separator line that is normally printed between the header/footer and the page text may optionally be disabled.

The page header and footer may include text defined by the user and additionally special characters to allow the file name and page numbers to be printed in the header or footer. The special characters are

- &f: This is replaced in the header or footer with the full file name including path.

- &fl: This is replaced in the header or footer with the first line of the file.

- &n: This is replaced in the header or footer with the file name only (no path).

- &p: This is replaced in the header or footer with the page number.

- &t: This is replaced in the header or footer with the total number of pages.

- &l: This aligns the text following the "&l" to the left side of the header/footer area.

- &c: This aligns the text following the "&c" to the center of the header/footer area.

- &r: This aligns the text following the "&r" to the right side of the header/footer area.

Note   Please consider that the colons contained in the previous bullet points and the following bullet points are not part of the special characters and are only used for the bullet points themselves.

Additionally, the header or footer may include the file date and time or system date and time. Two radio buttons allow the selection of either the file date or the system date to be included in the header or footer. The radio buttons select the source of the date and time, and additional special characters used in the header or footer specify if the date and time are to be printed and what format is used.

The characters used to specify the time and date format are shown below, where the absence of any of these characters results in the time and date not being printed:

- %a: Abbreviated weekday name

- %A: Full weekday name

- %b: Abbreviated month name

- %B: Full month name

- %c: Date and time representation appropriate for the locale

- %d: Day of the month as a decimal number (01–31)

- %H: Hour in 24-hour format (00–23)

- %I: Hour in 12-hour format (01–12)

- %j: Day of the year as a decimal number (001–366)

- %m: Month as a decimal number (01–12)

- %M: Minute as a decimal number (00–59)

- %p: Current locale's AM/PM indicator for a 12-hour clock

- %S: Second as a decimal number (00-59)

- %U: Week of the year as a decimal number, with Sunday as the first day of the week (00-51)

- %w: Weekday as a decimal number (0-6; Sunday is 0)

- %W: Week of the year as a decimal number, with Monday as the first day of the week (00-51)

- %x: Date representation for current locale

- %X: Time representation for current locale

- %y: Year without the century as a decimal number (00-99)

- %Y: Year with the century as a decimal number

- %Z: Time zone name or abbreviation; no characters if time zone is unknown

- %%: Percent sign

We would like to illustrate these characters and special characters with examples to make their implementation easier:

> The date is July, 4th 1994 and the time is 9:00pm:
>
> "%X, %x" prints 21:00, 07/04/94
>
> The date is July, 4th 1994 and the time is 9:00pm:
>
> "%c" prints 07/04/94 21:00
>
> The date is Jan, 10th 1991 and the time is 5:00am:
>
> "%A, %B %d, %Y %I:%M %p" prints Tuesday, January 10, 1991 05:00 AM

Using these characters and the examples just discussed, the user can put together their own customized headers and footers, depending on its own requirements and preferences.

Further options are available in the right-hand area of the dialog box:

- Margins: The page margins may be set up in either inches or millimeters (mm). Each margin, top, bottom, left, and right may be set independently. The margins are applied before the headers and footers are generated. If the printer is set up to have a minimum margin that is greater than the margin selected in UltraEdit, the printer margin will be in effect.

- Wrap text when printing: Causes automatically the printed output to wrap the text to additional lines of any line that exceeds the width of the printable area of the page.

- Print line numbers: Causes the line numbers to be printed for each line on the left-hand side of each page. If a line is wrapped, the line number is printed with the first line only. This setting is independent from UltraEdit's *Display Line Number* setting.

- Print 2 pages on 1 sheet: Allows two logical pages to be printed on a single sheet of paper. The logical page data is scaled to print two pages side by side. This scaling may mean that a little more or less data may fit side by side than when the pages are printed on a single sheet. This option is particularly useful for saving paper on printouts.

- Print syntax highlighting: Prints the file with the color used for syntax highlighting if a color printer is used. This will also show shades of gray on a Postscript monochrome printer.

- Use Classic theme for printing: The Classic theme will be used when printing, and if disabled, the active theme will be used. This was specifically added to save ink as attempting to print with a dark theme will use a heavy amount of ink.

- Page break code: The page break code may be set to any ASCII character and originally defaults to a form-feed character, 12 (0C hex). This may be changed if required but should not be set to any printable character, as a page break will be inserted on every occurrence of this character when printing occurs. It may be desirable to change this character if the font being used does not allow the page break character to be seen.

There are two additional print commands, which are called *Set printer font* and *Mirror display font* and which can be accessed via the print submenu of the Traditional menu mode.

The *Set printer font* command displays the *Font* dialog that allows the selection of different fonts and font sizes for the usage by the printer. The selection made will apply only to the printer fonts. Font selections may be reset to default values by selecting the *Reset fonts* command.

The second command is *Mirror display font* and means that the printout will be in the same font that is configured for UltraEdit and the editor window.

Favorite Files

The *Favorite files* function of UltraEdit allows the user to store the file names of frequently opened files or favorite files that the user wishes to quickly reference and open in the future. When the *Favorite files* menu item is selected, a dialog with the same name is displayed that allows the user to open one or more of the favorite files and modify the list of favorite files (see Figure 6-16).

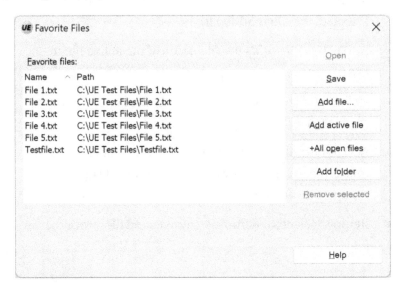

Figure 6-16. *Favorite Files dialog with a list and its editing options*

The following buttons can be used to manage the list:

- Open: Opens the selected files from the list and closes the dialog. This implies some notes about this behavior:

  - Multiple files may be selected from the list and opened at once.

  - Any changes to the list are saved.

  - A double click of any files in the file list will open the file in UltraEdit.

  - If one of the selections is a directory, a file open dialog is shown initialized to the specified directory.

- Save: Saves all changes to the favorite files list.

- Add file: Displays a file open dialog allowing the user to browse for a file to add to the list. If a valid file is selected, the file is added to the list.

- Add active file: Adds the file name of the active file to the file list.

- +All open files: Adds the file names of all open files to the file list.

- Add folder: Allows a user to browse for a folder and add this to the list. This allows the user to quickly open files from a favorite folder.

- Remove selected: Removes any selected files from the file list.

Recent Files

Depending on whether UltraEdit is in Ribbon or in one of the two menu modes, the most recently opened or closed files are displayed differently.

In Ribbon mode (see Figure 6-1), the lists are at the top right and can be switched between them using two tabs. In Contemporary menu mode (see Figure 6-2), the two menu items are named *Recently opened* and *Recently closed*. In Traditional menu mode (see Figure 6-3), there are even three menu items with the names *Recently opened files*, *Recently closed files*, and *Recent projects/workspace*.

Via command for recently opened files or recently closed files, the user can select the file they wish to edit from up to 32 files. A simple click or the Enter key opens the file for editing in UltraEdit. Files closed on application shutdown, via macro or script, or when closing a project are not added to the list of recently closed files.

In the program settings and the section *Toolbars/menus* ➤ *Miscellaneous*, the maximum list size for the *Recently opened* and *Recently closed* file lists can be defined. This is done via the option *Number of recent files on File menu*. The settings also include options for manually clearing the history or automatically doing so when the program ends.

When UltraEdit is in Ribbon mode, there are two options at the bottom of the *Recent opened* and *Recent closed* files:

- Open all: Opens all the files contained in the respective list, provided they are still existent at the last saved position.

- Select and open: Switches the display so that a check box appears in front of each file, allowing the files to be opened to be selected. At the same time, the buttons at the bottom change to *Open selected* and *Cancel*, where the first option opens the previously selected files if they are still existent at the last saved position.

When UltraEdit is in Traditional menu mode, there is a third function here called *Recent projects/workspace*. This allows the user to select a project from a list of recently edited projects and load it again. Please note that possible entries in this section require UltraEdit to have already worked with projects.

Summary

In this chapter, we have described the many basics of file management and the possibilities that UltraEdit offers. Beyond what is possible with a simple open-save-close scenario, the user will quickly be able to manage files after a short learning period and will also appreciate powerful functions such as encryption/decryption, sorting of file contents, as well as conversions to all possible formats and for multiple platforms.

Favorites can be used to access specific files in a targeted manner, while the Recent files lists allow quick access to recently opened and closed files, as well as entire projects.

In the next chapter, we will take a look at the core functionality, text editing. This is where UltraEdit once again demonstrates its strengths and shows what is possible today.

CHAPTER 7

Edit, Insert, and Columns

The core functionalities of UltraEdit include editing and inserting data as well as the so-called column mode. In the following sections, we will discuss the many ways to handle data in files, as well as how to use the spell checker and hex mode. The latter allows files to be edited in hexadecimal format.

We continue with the insertion of data, which includes not only the date and time but also files, literal characters, and templates. We have already mentioned the template concept in Chapter 3, and here we describe the creation and modification of templates with the help of many practical examples.

Column editing with the powerful column mode is a central topic in the last third of this chapter, as it has created a new way of editing data and performing CSV conversions at the same time.

Edit

Editing text does not only mean inserting text into a document but also handling text in all its facets.

In this aspect, text selecting also plays a role, as does hex mode, spell checking, encoding and decoding, and the entire topic of comments. We will describe all these aspects below.

© Devid Espenschied 2025
D. Espenschied, *Mastering UltraEdit*, https://doi.org/10.1007/979-8-8688-1160-9_7

Copy, Cut, and Paste

One of the oldest functions of text editing applications is copying text to the clipboard. This is done using the *Copy* command, which can be executed using the keyboard shortcut Ctrl+C and copies selected data to the clipboard.

In addition to this, there is the *Copy & append* command, which appends selected data to the data currently available in the clipboard. The keyboard shortcut Ctrl+Shift+C can also be used for this purpose. Normally, data in the clipboard is replaced by newly copied data, and *Copy & append* provides a useful way to enrich the clipboard with multiple data blocks before processing the entire clipboard content.

Furthermore, there are three additional copying options in the *Copy special* category:

- Copy as HTML document: Copies the selected data as a well-formatted HTML document including doctype declaration, <head> tags, and all styling in CSS classes added to the head of the document. This function should be used if the user wants to create a completely new HTML page to contain all selected data.

- Copy as HTML: Copies the selected data as an HTML fragment with inline CSS styles. This function should be used if the user wants to paste the selected data into an existing HTML page.

- Copy as RTF: Copies the selected data as an RTF fragment (Rich Text Format). If the user wants to quickly paste a snippet of data (i.e., source code) into an email or a Microsoft Word document with its syntax highlighting intact, this function sends it to the clipboard, and then the user can paste it into any application which supports the Rich Text Format such as Outlook, Word, Thunderbird, etc.

The *Cut* command, in contrast to the *Copy* command, removes the currently selected data from the document and stores it in the clipboard. The keyboard shortcut Ctrl+X can also be used for this.

Just as there is an extension called *Copy & append* for the *Copy* function, *Cut & append* can be used to append cut data to the existing contents of the clipboard. Alternatively, the keyboard shortcut Ctrl+Shift+X can be used for this.

The third command in this category describes how to paste data that has been copied or cut to the clipboard. The keyboard shortcut Ctrl+V can be used as an alternative. The *Paste* function is determined by the insertion point, which is defined by the caret.

UltraEdit also offers various additional functions for this, such as *Paste & Copy* with the additional keyboard shortcut Ctrl+Shift+V. This pastes the clipboard text into the selection (which replaces it) and then copies the selected text back to the clipboard.

Via *Paste column*, UltraEdit pastes the selected text at the cursor position as if in column mode without toggling column mode.

Two more special functions allow advanced paste modes:

- HTML source: This will paste the necessary HTML code to reproduce what was selected and copied from the browser.

- Raw RTF: This will paste the necessary raw RTF content to reproduce the same in an RTF file opened in Microsoft Word.

241

Undo and Redo

The Undo command is available via the Quick Access Toolbar or the two keyboard shortcuts Ctrl+Z and Alt+Backspace. In general, the user can use their command to reverse the last editing action, if possible. UltraEdit supports multiple levels of undo (the specific number varies based on the items being undone). Repeated Undo commands will attempt to step backward through the previous commands and undo one at a time.

There is also a so-called *Grouped undo* function, and if enabled, it will be executed on a word-by-word rather than character-by-character basis. If the corresponding option in the UltraEdit settings and the category *Editor* ➤ *Advanced* is enabled, Undo is toggled during the editing of a document (and the undo buffer is partially created with both settings). The Undo functionality will reflect the settings in place at the time the document was created. This could cause part of the text in a file to be undone as grouped characters and part to be undone character by character.

In contrast, there is the Redo command, which can also be performed via the Quick Access Toolbar or the keyboard shortcut Ctrl+Y. It allows commands that have previously been undone with the Undo command to be redone. If commands are undone and then a new command is performed, the Redo command will no longer allow previously undone actions to be redone.

Clipboard

UltraEdit provides up to nine user clipboards for use with the Cut, Copy, and Paste commands as well as the standard Windows Clipboard.

The active clipboard may be changed from either *Home* ➤ *Windows Clipboard* (Ribbon mode and Contemporary menu mode), *Edit* ➤ *Clipboards* (Traditional menu mode), or the right click context menu. Additionally, Ctrl+1-9 will switch to the user clipboards, and Ctrl+0 will switch to the Windows clipboard.

When changing the active clipboard, the contents of the clipboards are not modified. With the exception of the standard Windows Clipboard, the contents of the clipboards are destroyed when UltraEdit is closed.

The active clipboard is shown in the Status Bar following the Line and Column indicator separated with a comma.

Selecting Data

The selection of text and characters is implemented in UltraEdit using a variety of functions that can be found in the *Edit* tab (Ribbon mode), in the *Edit* menu (Contemporary and Traditional menu modes), and in the context menu.

The *Select All* command highlights the entire file and can also be accessed using the shortcut Ctrl+A. This allows an easy mechanism to select the complete file and cut it to the clipboard.

The *Select Line* command highlights the line in which the cursor is positioned. The end of line characters are also highlighted, and this allows an easy mechanism to select a line and cut it to the clipboard. A line may also be selected by triple-clicking the mouse, which will cause the complete line to be selected including the hard return at the end of line.

The *Select Word* command highlights the word in which the caret is positioned.

With the *Select next occurrence* command, UltraEdit adds a multi-selection of the next word matching the word under the caret or currently selected. This can also be invoked with the keyboard shortcut Ctrl+;.

Via the *Select range* command, UltraEdit opens a dialog allowing the user to select a range set by starting line/column number and ending line/column number. If UltraEdit works currently not in column mode, it will switch automatically to column mode if the start and end columns are specified with different values.

UltraEdit's last selection function, the *Persistent selection*, offers a way to keep a selection active and at the same time supports navigating in other parts of the file without affecting the active selection. This function also has a keyboard shortcut, which consists of the two keyboard shortcuts Ctrl+P and Ctrl+S in a quick sequence.

Note   Typically, the keyboard shortcut Ctrl+P is assigned to the print function, and Ctrl+S is assigned to the file save function. Pressing both keyboard shortcuts in quick succession enables the "Persistent selection" function.

Once the Persistent selection is active, the user defines the selected text (through keyboard commands or cursor movement), and then the menu option should be selected again or the keyboard shortcut should be invoked to terminate the definition of the selection.

It is not necessary to hold the Shift key while defining this selection. The anchor point for the active selection may be changed by holding down the Ctrl key and left-clicking with the mouse at the desired file position.

Once the *Persistent selection* has been defined and the user moves the caret to another position and types, the selection will be dismissed and text inserted at the current caret position. If the selection is defined and the caret is not moved, any key entered would replace the selected text (or in the case of Backspace or Delete would remove the selected text).

If desired, the user may extend the defined selection by selecting the menu option and clicking outside the current selection and then selecting the menu option again to terminate the definition of the selection.

Deleting Data

The deleting of text and characters is implemented in UltraEdit using a variety of functions that can be found in the *Edit* tab (Ribbon mode), in the *Edit* menu (Contemporary and Traditional menu modes), and in the context menu.

The basic function is called simply *Delete*, and this deletes the selected text or, if no text is selected, the character at the cursor position.

Via *Delete line*, UltraEdit deletes the line in which the cursor is positioned, and the end of line characters are also deleted. This command can also be performed with the keyboard shortcut Ctrl+E.

Both commands *Delete to start of line* (Ctrl+F11) and *Delete to end of line* (Ctrl+F12) delete all contents of the current line from the position of the caret to the beginning/end of the line containing the caret.

The *Delete all bookmarked lines* command deletes all bookmarked lines in the current file. Bookmarks are useful for marking certain positions so that they can be found again more quickly later.

The delete functions are concluded with the commands *Delete all hidden lines*, *Delete all empty lines*, and *Delete all empty and whitespace-only lines*. Via *Delete all hidden lines*, UltraEdit deletes all lines in the active document currently hidden by code folding operations, and *Delete all empty lines* causes UltraEdit to delete all lines in the active document that have nothing on them (including whitespace). The last command *Delete all empty/whitespace-only lines* means that UltraEdit deletes all lines in the active document that have nothing on them and lines that only have whitespace characters on them.

Active Line Actions

UltraEdit combines various functions for the active line in this category, which can be found in the *Edit* tab (Ribbon mode) or in the *Edit* menu (both Contemporary and Traditional menu modes).

By *Move up*, UltraEdit moves the active line (including all soft-wrapped portions of the line) up one line, and *Move down* does the same but down one line.

The *Duplicate line* command is quite helpful for everyday use and inserts a copy of the active line below the current caret position. The caret may be positioned anywhere on the active line when this feature is invoked. This command can also be performed using the keyboard shortcut Alt+Shift+D.

The last UltraEdit function for the active line is called *Join lines* and can also be accessed using the keyboard shortcut Ctrl+J. *Join lines* will join two or more contiguous lines, and this works differently depending on whether or not text is selected. With one or less lines selected (no line ends in selection), join lines will join the active line to the one immediately following it. With two or more lines selected (one or more line ends in selection), join lines will join all selected lines and the active line.

All trailing spaces from a line being joined with a line below it and all leading spaces from a line being joined with a line above it will be removed if the option *Preserve leading spaces when joining lines* is enabled. This option can be found in the UltraEdit settings in the category *Editor* ➤ *Advanced*. A single space will be inserted between two joined lines. The following example clarifies this explanation:

```
Join line example (· represents space, » represents tab)
```

```
»  ·····line·1
»  ·······line·2····
```

This is the output after join lines:

```
»  ·····line·1·line 2····
```

The caret will be positioned at the end of the joined lines after lines are combined.

During daily work, the usage of certain functions can be performed with predefined keyboard shortcuts, and in addition, the user can either use them normally or reassign them via the UltraEdit settings. The possibility of this reassignment once again underlines the flexibility of UltraEdit to customize everything to your own preferences.

Word Wrap

The word wrap function toggles the word wrap state of the active document. This function can be accessed either via the *Edit* tab (Ribbon mode), the *Edit* menu (both Contemporary and Traditional menu modes), or the keyboard shortcut Ctrl+W.

Within the UltraEdit settings in the category *Editor ➤ Word wrap/ tab settings*, there are many options for word wrap, which we have already discussed in detail in Chapter 4 (see Figure 7-1).

In certain scenarios, however, a maximum line length is necessary so that a wrap can be performed after a defined position. This position wrap can also be combined with a CR/LF. With the last option *Absolute wrap after column #*, the line is wrapped exactly at the defined position without a word wrap, even if the respective word is separated as a result.

Figure 7-1. *UltraEdit settings for the editor word wrap function*

Tip   Before performing the word wrap function, it is advisable to define the corresponding settings. The default setting already offers good results, but if a specific wrap position is required, this should be configured first and then activated with Ctrl+W.

Spellcheck

UltraEdit includes a spell checker based upon the Microsoft Windows native spell checker API available in Windows 8, 10, and 11. This spell checker can be accessed either via the *Edit* tab (Ribbon mode), the *Edit* menu (both Contemporary and Traditional menu modes), or the keyboard shortcut Ctrl+K.

In principle, only the selected text is checked if there is a selection. If there is no selection, the check is always applied to the entire file.

The text database is based on dictionaries, several of which can be selected in the UltraEdit settings in the category *Spell checker* ➤ *Dictionary* (see Figure 7-2).

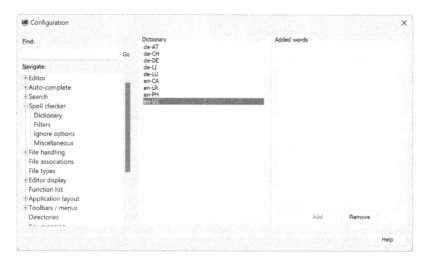

Figure 7-2. *UltraEdit Configuration and selection of the Spell checker dictionary*

The dictionary contains a language code for the main language (such as "en" for English and "de" for German) and, after a hyphen, a language code for the sublanguage (such as "LR" for Liberia and "CH" for Switzerland).

Note   At this point, it should be mentioned that there are many more options for the spell checker in the settings, which we have already discussed in Chapter 4, such as filters, ignore options, and a few other options. Therefore, please refer to Chapter 4 to customize this function in its subtleties.

If we take a closer look at the spelling check process, the *Check Spelling* dialog appears if a word requiring the user's attention is detected and will list words detected as misspelled in the field *Not in Dictionary*. The user can use the dialog to specify whether the word should be ignored or changed (see Figure 7-3).

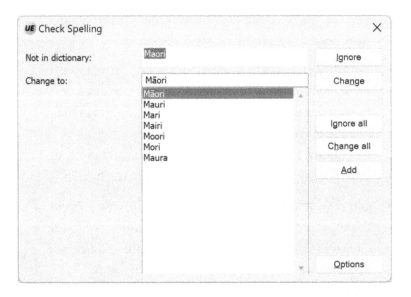

Figure 7-3. Checking Spell dialog if a word isn't found in the selected dictionary

This dialog consists of several buttons that allow further control of the spell checking process and the not found word in the selected dictionary:

- Not in dictionary: Contains the word which wasn't found in the currently selected dictionary.

- Change to: Contains a word which will replace a misspelled word when the user selects the *Change* or *Change all* buttons. The user can enter a word in the *Change to* field by typing, or they can select one of the suggested replacements from the suggestions list.

- Ignore: Causes this occurrence of a misspelled word to be skipped. If the same misspelled word appears later, it will be reported.

- Change: Causes the reported word to be replaced with the word in the *Change to* field. Only this occurrence of the reported word is replaced, and if the user wants this and all following occurrences of the word replaced, they need to select the *Change all* button.

- Ignore all: Causes this and all further occurrences of a misspelled word to be skipped. The user might use this button if the word reported as a misspelling is actually spelled correctly. If the word is one word they use frequently, they may wish to ignore it permanently or add it to the dictionary by selecting the *Add* button.

- Change all: Causes this and all following occurrences of the reported word to be replaced with the word in the *Change to* field. If the user wants only this occurrence of the word to be replaced, they need to use the *Change* button.

- Add: Causes the reported word to be added to the personal dictionary for the dictionary currently selected in the dictionary configuration dialog and displayed there in the list of *Added Words*. The user can use the *Add* button if a correctly spelled word they use often is reported as a misspelling (e.g., your family name). If the word is not used frequently, they may want to select the *Ignore* or *Ignore all* button instead.

- Options: Opens the configuration dialog to the *Miscellaneous* topic for *Spell checker* options.

Read-Only

The Read-only command can be accessed either via the *Edit* tab (Ribbon mode), the *Edit* menu (both Contemporary and Traditional menu modes), or the *R/W* respectively *R/O* field in the status bar. It toggles the state of the read-only status of the file. If the read-only status is set, the file cannot be modified, and if the file has already been modified, the modifications are maintained and the file may be saved.

The default behavior of the read-only status can be configured in the UltraEdit settings in the category *File Handling* ➤ *Miscellaneous*. This determines if the file is read-only when it is opened. As we have already discussed these settings in detail in Chapter 4, we would like to refer to this chapter at this point.

Word Count and Character Info

The Word count and Character info functions can be accessed either via the *Edit* tab (Ribbon mode) or the *Edit* menu (both Contemporary and Traditional menu modes). Word count is accessible in addition with the keyboard shortcut Alt + ^ and Character info with Alt+Enter.

The Word count function calculates statistical data for the current document and selection and determines the number of words, lines, and characters (with and without spaces) and displays the result. If a portion of the file is selected, the results are shown for that portion of the file and the complete file (see Figure 7-4).

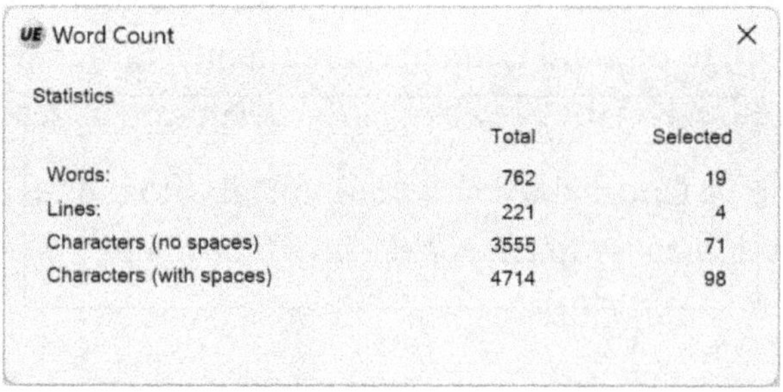

UE Word Count			✕
Statistics			
		Total	Selected
Words:		762	19
Lines:		221	4
Characters (no spaces)		3555	71
Characters (with spaces)		4714	98

Figure 7-4. *Word count function with total and selected statistics*

The number of lines determined is real lines terminated with the line terminator. If a line is wrapped in the display, this is not counted as multiple lines.

The Character info command shows a dialog containing the decimal and hexadecimal values of the active byte as well as how this will be displayed (this may vary based on font and script). Along with this, the offset of the active byte is displayed in both decimal and hexadecimal formats (see Figure 7-5).

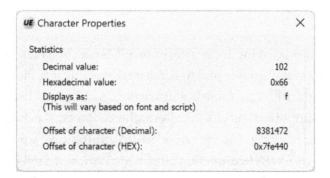

Figure 7-5. *Character Properties function with character statistics*

Hex Edit and Hex Mode

UltraEdit offers editing in hexadecimal format apart from the regular text editing in ASCII format. In the hexadecimal system, numbers are represented in a positional numeral system based on 16. While the decimal system represents the digits using 10 symbols, the hexadecimal system uses the values 0 to 9 and "A" to "F". This results in the values from 0 to 15, or 16 in total. The letters "A" to "F" can be written in either upper- or lowercase, which has no significance for the interpretation.

The so-called hex mode can be accessed via the keyboard shortcut Ctrl+H and switches between ASCII and hex mode. Alternatively, the mode can be accessed via *Edit* ➤ *Hex mode* (in Ribbon mode), via *Edit* ➤ *HEX functions* ➤ *Hex edit* (Traditional menu mode), or *Edit* ➤ *Hex mode* ➤ *Hex edit* (Contemporary menu mode).

Tip   It is also possible to create a new empty file with the *New File* command or the keyboard shortcut Ctrl+N and then directly switch to hex mode by pressing Ctrl+H.

Basics

Hex mode is intended for processing non-ASCII files in which certain characters are not printable and in cases not involving text files in the classic sense. In addition, there is a restriction in hex mode because Insert mode is not supported – this is the alternative to Overstrike mode, which is used for regular editing. For the non-existing Insert mode, we will discuss a separate *Hex Insert/Delete* function later, which works independently of it.

As soon as UltraEdit is in hex mode, the display is switched, and the file content is displayed in three sections (see Figure 7-6).

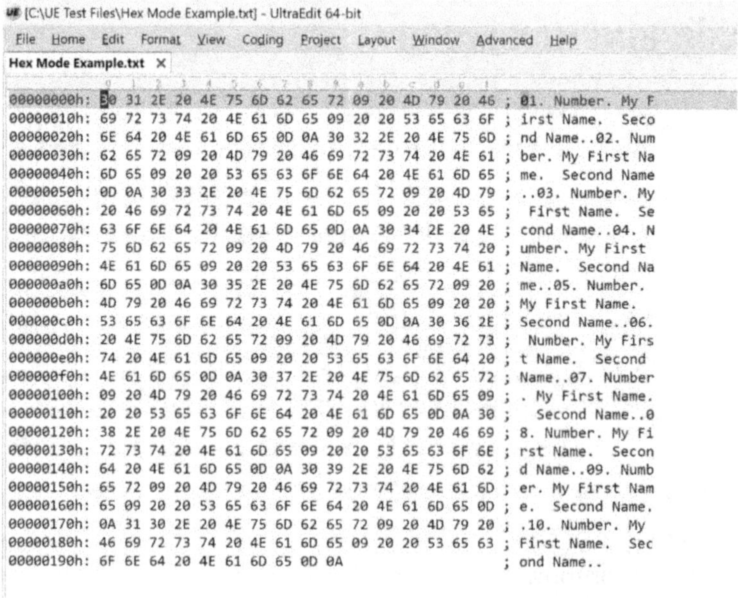

Figure 7-6. Hex mode representation

- File offset: Contains the byte numbering of the hex data. This data position is also hexadecimal and starts with 00000000h.

- Hexadecimal representation: Depending on how many hexadecimal characters are displayed per line, the hex values are displayed with two characters and separated by a space. If the hex value is a single digit (e.g., F), a zero is added to the front to achieve a two-digit display for all hex values (in this case, 0F).

- ASCII representation: Contains the ASCII representation of the values from the hexadecimal column, which corresponds exactly to the same quantity. Only printable ASCII characters are displayed, and nonprintable characters are replaced by a dot.

Data Editing

When data is changed in hex mode, whether in the hexadecimal representation or in the ASCII representation, this is always performed in Overstrike mode. That means that entering a new value overwrites the existing value. When a value is entered in one representation column, the other representation column is automatically adjusted.

Here follows an example (see Figure 7-7).

File Offset	Hexadecimal representation	ASCII representation
00000000h:	54 65 73 74 20 56 61 6C 75 65	; Test Value

Figure 7-7. *Unmodified sample output "Test Value"*

If in this example the value 56 (this is the 6th value from the left) is replaced by 76 in the hexadecimal representation, UltraEdit automatically updates the ASCII representation (see Figure 7-8).

File Offset	Hexadecimal representation	ASCII representation
00000000h:	54 65 73 74 20 76 61 6C 75 65	; Test value

Figure 7-8. *Modified sample output "Test value"*

Basically, the Windows Character Map is a good source for all ASCII characters and their hexadecimal position in the ASCII character set (see Figure 7-9).

Figure 7-9. *Windows Character Map with the selected "V" character and its hex value 56 at the bottom*

There are also scenarios in which hex values must not only be changed but inserted or deleted. For this purpose, UltraEdit offers the *Hex insert/delete* function, which can be accessed via the keyboard shortcut Ctrl+D. Alternatively, the function can be accessed via *Edit* ➤ *Insert/delete* (in Ribbon mode), via *Edit* ➤ *HEX functions* ➤ *Hex insert/ delete* (Traditional menu mode), or *Edit* ➤ *Insert/delete* (Contemporary menu mode).

The current caret position is always decisive for the *Hex Insert/Delete* dialog, and one or more bytes can be inserted via a selection. The default insert value is a hexadecimal value of 20 (ASCII space). If desired, users may specify a different decimal/hex value to be inserted and may also specify the number of bytes to be inserted.

The *Insert* button below adapts to the function selection and is always labeled the same as the selection above (see Figure 7-10).

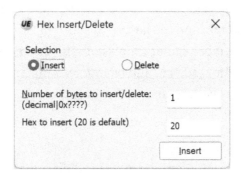

Figure 7-10. *Hex Insert/Delete dialog*

If *Delete* is selected, the specified number of characters will be removed from the file beginning at the cursor position. Likewise, the user can select a single hex value or range in the hexadecimal or ASCII representation and delete those selected values by pressing the Delete key.

EBCDIC Encoding

EBCDIC stands for Extended Binary Coded Decimal Interchange Code and is an 8-bit character encoding used mainly on IBM mainframe and IBM midrange computer operating systems.

The hex/EBCDIC mode works almost identically to the standard hex mode with the exception of converting the EBCDIC data for viewing purposes only and showing this as ASCII. The content of the file will not be modified; however, the right-hand side that shows the ASCII representation in hex mode will show the data converted to ASCII from EBCDIC.

While in this hex/EBCDIC mode, editing in the ASCII area will allow data to be entered as ASCII and it will be automatically converted to EBCDIC in the file. Editing in the hex area will allow data to be entered directly as hex, and the ASCII representation (converted from EBCDIC) will be shown in the ASCII area.

Find/Replace in this mode will allow ASCII strings to be used and correctly found/replaced according to the settings in the *HEX Find/Replace* dialog. The keyboard shortcut Ctrl+F opens the *HEX Find/Replace* dialog with the *Find* tab, and the keyboard shortcut Ctrl+R does the same but with the *Replace* tab. Regular expressions, however, cannot be used in this mode because the results would be indeterminate. Therefore, regular expressions are only available in ASCII mode.

Settings

The hex mode can be configured in the UltraEdit settings and is located in the category *Editor* ➤ *Hex mode* (see Figure 7-11).

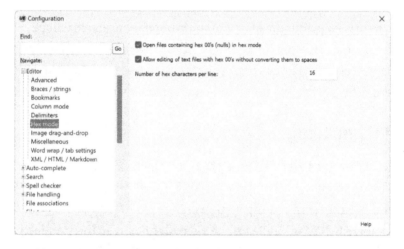

Figure 7-11. *UltraEdit's hex mode settings*

As we have already discussed these settings in detail in Chapter 4, we would like to refer to this chapter at this point.

Practical Use

There are many practical approaches to hex mode, all of which together would fill a book of their own. Every executable file (extension exe) and library (extension dll) in the Windows world is based on the so-called Portable Executable File Format (PE for short), whereby Portable Executable means that the format is not architecture dependent.

Microsoft has defined a structure for this that can be used to determine many file properties, such as the machine type, pages per file, checksums, symbol tables, and various characteristics – such as whether the application can process >2 GB addresses. Microsoft has listed the structures on its own home page: `https://learn.microsoft.com/en-us/windows/win32/debug/pe-format`.

Other scenarios for hex mode can be found in IT forensics, where images of disks and RAM are created and these images are examined or searched for evidence using a hex editor. Data can also be extracted from swap files and the Hiberfil.sys, as well as remnants of deleted files or other concealed information.

For computer games, hex editors can be used to falsify game saves, and there are instructions on the Internet that explain exactly which files need to be edited for which games – however, this requires the game saves to be saved on the local system. Games with an online link, such as Steam, synchronize their scores and achievements with online databases and can therefore only be modified to a limited extent.

The practical use of hex editors is always necessary when an interpretation of the data is to be prevented. When the user opens a picture in a hex editor, Microsoft Paint is not tasked with the interpretation, but the user does have access to the picture and metadata in hexadecimal raw form. This is a control level that is incredibly powerful but also requires precise knowledge of data interpretation.

In conclusion, UltraEdit's hex mode allows the complete editing of files from the first to the last byte, regardless of whether the characters they contain are printable or not. This makes the hex mode suitable for many areas of application, such as software development, administration, security experts, and forensic analysis, where raw data must be evaluated precisely for the collection of evidence.

The clear presentation in both ASCII and hex format combined with the ability to process extremely large files and data streams (such as disk and memory images) makes UltraEdit suitable for all conceivable application scenarios.

Insert

In this section, we discuss the insert functions of UltraEdit, which are provided in addition to regular data processing and can also be categorized as text editing functions. These functions can be found as a separate insert category in the *Edit* tab (Ribbon mode, see Figure 7-12), in the *Edit* menu (Contemporary menu mode), and in the *Insert* menu (Traditional menu mode).

Figure 7-12. *Insert functions from the Edit tab of the UltraEdit Ribbon mode*

Date and Time

The date/time command inserts the date and time at the cursor position and is also accessible via the F7 key. The date and time are formatted according to the control panel settings, and a single space is inserted between the date and time.

If the user wishes to customize the date/time, they can use the templates (which are discussed later in this chapter).

Line

The Line command can be used with the keyboard shortcut Ctrl+Enter and inserts a new blank line below the current cursor position. The cursor may be positioned anywhere on the active line when this feature is invoked.

The predefined keyboard shortcut can be customized as desired in the UltraEdit settings and the category *Key mapping*.

Color

With the Color command, the user can select a color value and insert it into a document. The dialog that opens for this is called *Select Color* and allows the user to view or choose a color and then have the value of the color inserted into the document (see Figure 7-13).

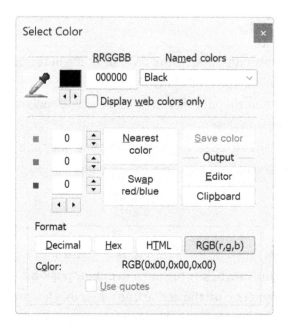

Figure 7-13. *Select Color dialog for the insertion into a document*

This dialog is a very flexible tool that may be used to insert numeric values for colors in four different formats: Decimal, Hex, HTML, and RGB (red, green, blue). When the dialog is first displayed, the color value will default to the selected color (if there is a value selected) in the active file. UltraEdit will try to determine the format of this, which is also based on the selection. The following options and buttons are available in this dialog:

- Eyedropper tool: The eyedropper in the upper left is a tool that may be used to import colors to the dialog. Clicking on the eyedropper and dragging it over any item will import its color values to the dialog.

- Color block: Clicking on this upper left-hand corner block presents the standard Windows Color dialog, where basic colors may be selected or custom colors may be defined. Whether a standard color is selected in the Color dialog or a custom color is created, whatever color is shown in the *Color/Solid* field will be the color shown if the user presses the OK button in the Color dialog.

- RRGGBB text field: If the user is familiar with the standard RGB color codes, they can directly specify a color by typing in this field. The specified color should be immediately reflected in the Color Block. If the user is defining a color in hexadecimal format, there should be six alphanumeric characters used to do so (e.g., F08FFF).

- Named colors: A list of 72 default colors used for web development is provided in the drop-down, and selecting one of these will automatically change the value reflected in the Hex/RRGGBB field. This can be very helpful in quickly selecting colors for development.

- Display web colors only: There are a limited number of colors that display the same regardless of what browser they are displayed in. If this option is enabled, only browser-safe colors will be displayed in the dialog.

- RGB text fields: Next to the red, green and blue color blocks there are text fields where values for these colors (from 0 through 255) may be directly entered. The up/down arrows by each text field may also be used to modify the color values. To increase/decrease all three color values simultaneously, the "-" and "+" buttons below the RGB text fields can be used.

Users may define custom colors using these controls and name them by entering the name in the *Named colors* combobox. Custom colors may be removed by selecting the color name in the *Named colors* combobox and pressing the Delete key on the keyboard and then pressing the *Save color* button. Any color saved with an empty name will be removed from the color list.

- Nearest color: Selects the closest color to the custom values currently defined from the default colors listed in the drop-down. The Color Block will change to reflect this color as will the Color field value in the Format section and the color name listed in the drop-down.

- Swap red/blue: Switches the values for red and blue for the currently specified color. This change is reflected throughout the Select Color dialog.

- Output: Users may select whether they want the color value to be inserted in either Decimal, Hex, HTML, or RGB format using the appropriate buttons. Pressing the *Editor* button will send the output to the active edit window, and pressing the *Clipboard* button will send the output to the active clipboard. If the *Use quotes* option is selected, the value will be inserted in the desired format and enclosed in double quotes. Please note that the RGB value is never inserted in double quotes as this is generally used for C macros, and this behavior would not be appropriate in this context.

The actual color value is shown in one of the specified formats:

- Decimal: The decimal value for the color value in RGB (Red, Green, Blue).

- Hexadecimal: The hexadecimal value for the color value in RGB (Red, Green, Blue).

- HTML: This is the format required for display in an HTML document. The # is added to the value.

- RGB(r,g,b): This format contains the identifier *RGB* followed by the three color values in hexadecimal notation.

File and Multiple Files

The *Insert File* command can be used to insert an existing document (file) into the active document. This command opens a dialog allowing the selection of the file to insert.

The *Encoding* drop-down is used to specify the encoding of the file which is being inserted into the active file. This will enable UltraEdit to convert the file to the format of the target file if necessary.

The complete contents of the selected file are inserted in the active document at the cursor position.

The same procedure for more than one file works with the *Insert Multiple files* command. This command opens the *Insert multiple files* dialog, in which the files can be specified for the insert process (see Figure 7-14).

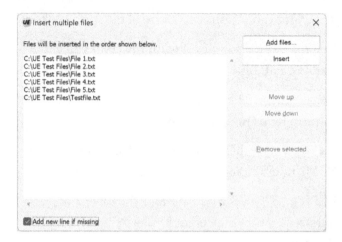

Figure 7-14. *Insert multiple files dialog with the definition of files and their order*

This dialog contains the following controls:

- Centrally aligned file list: Contains the files to be inserted along with their paths in exactly the order that will be followed during the insertion process.

- Add files: Displays an open dialog which may be used to select file(s) to populate the *Insert multiple files* dialog. Users may select multiple files from a single folder or may repeat the process to select files from different folders.

- Insert: This button inserts all files from the file list in the specified order into the active file.

- Move up/Move down: Used to reorganize the files in the list. It is important to note that files will be inserted into the active file in the order listed when the *Insert* button is pressed. Files may also be removed from the list by pressing the *Remove selected* button.

- Remove selected: Removes the selected file or files from the list.

- Add new line if missing: In some cases, a file may not have a line terminator on the last line of the file. If desired, users may select this option so that a line terminator is added when necessary.

The complete contents of the specified files are inserted in the active document at the cursor position.

Page Break

The Page Break command inserts a page break character at the current cursor position, and this page break character can be configured in the page setup dialog.

When the document is printed, the page break character is replaced with a page break. Printing continues on the next page following a page break character.

This *Page Setup* dialog has already been discussed in detail in Chapter 6 within the "Printing Files" section, so we would like to refer you to this chapter at this point.

Literal Character

This command allows a literal character (such as Control C) to be inserted into the file. Pressing the keyboard shortcut Ctrl+I tells UltraEdit that the next character is to be inserted directly into the file without any translation.

This is useful for inserting control codes that may be needed by printers or other devices. Let's talk about two samples that describe this command in more detail:

- Ctrl+I followed by Ctrl+C inserts a Control C character into the file.

- Ctrl+I followed by Escape inserts an escape character into the file.

String at Every Increment

The *String at every increment* command allows a user-specified string to be inserted at a constant user-specified increment in the file from some start point in the file to some end point in the file.

When handling large database type files, it is sometimes necessary to split the file into "records" or known line lengths as the file has been output without any delimiters/separators between records.

This command opens the *Insert String at Increment Specified* dialog, in which the string and positions can be specified for the insert process (see Figure 7-15).

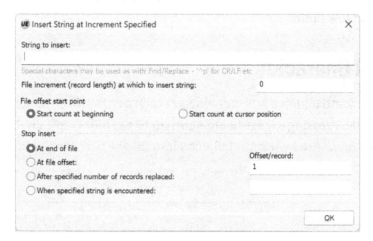

Figure 7-15. *Insert String at Increment Specified dialogwith string and position definitions*

- String to insert: Here the user can specify the exact string or character which needs to be inserted at every specified increment. Special characters can also be used in this field – for example, "^p" to insert a new line at every specified increment.

- File increment (record length) at which to insert string: This text field contains the length at which the string is to be entered. As an example, if the user does have database records that are not separated by a new line, and each record is exactly 40 characters long, they would enter "40" here to insert a line break and new line after each individual record.

- File offset start point: This option allows the user to set whether UltraEdit will begin counting the file increment (record length) from the start of the file or from the current cursor position. As an example, if the user selects *Start count at cursor position*, and the cursor is currently at column position 5, the string would be inserted at position 45 instead of 40.

- Stop insert: This option allows to specify where the string insertion should be terminated:

  - At end of file: The string insertion will continue to the end of the file.

  - At file offset: Requires to specify an absolute string position in the file where the string insertion will terminate. As an example, if the user set this offset to "80", UltraEdit will insert the string only two times: once at position 40 and once at position 80 in the file.

- After specified number of records replaced: Requires to specify a number of records in the corresponding dialog where the insertion will stop. This ending point will cause UltraEdit to terminate the string insertion at this number of records, based on the setting in the *File increment* field. As an example, if the user set this to "4" and the file increment is "40", UltraEdit will insert the string four times: once after the ending character of each 40-character record.

- When specified string is encountered: Requires to specify a string (any character(s)) where UltraEdit will terminate the insertion once the string is encountered. As an example, if the user set this to "**$**", UltraEdit will stop inserting the string as soon as it encounters the first "$" in the records.

Templates

Templates are a proven concept in UltraEdit and describe predefined text that can be inserted at the cursor position as required. In Chapter 3, we have already described this concept in detail because the *Template List* on the right program area of UltraEdit already offers integrated functionality.

To insert templates, the user can either use predefined templates or create a new one using the *Modify Template* dialog. Existing templates can be inserted at the current cursor position using the *Edit* tab ➤ *Insert template* (Ribbon mode), *Edit* ➤ *Insert template* (Contemporary menu mode), or *Insert* ➤ *Individual templates* (Traditional menu mode). At the same time, a predefined keyboard shortcut is assigned to each template that can be inserted. Starting with Alt+0 for the first template, it continues with Alt+1 for the second template and so on.

What we have not yet discussed is the *Modify template* dialog, which can be used to define new templates and modify existing ones (see Figure 7-16).

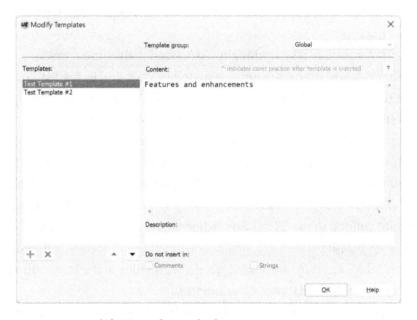

Figure 7-16. *Modify Templates dialog*

Templates are organized in four groups: *Global, Layouts, Languages,* and *Projects*:

- Global templates are always available.

- Layout templates are only available when the layout they're associated with is loaded.

- Language templates are associated with languages specified for syntax highlighting and are only available when editing files with extensions that match that language.

- Project templates are only available when the project they're associated with is loaded.

An unlimited number of templates can be defined. Each of the first 20 global templates can be recalled at a later time using the keyboard shortcuts Alt+0 through Alt+9, and Shift+Alt+0 through Shift+Alt+9, or any of the templates can be recalled with the *Insert Template* dialog or by user-defined hotkeys.

Each template can be optionally associated with a name that, if defined, will show up on the tooltips on the toolbar and in the list of templates when inserting a template. They will also appear in auto-complete, and the name is the trigger for the auto-suggest feature.

Global templates are always available no matter which layout, project, or coding language is used. They are stored in the *UETMPLTE.TPL* file in the default templates directory (which is typically *%APPDATA%\Roaming\ IDMComp\UltraEdit\templates* on Windows), or the *Template directory* manually defined in the UltraEdit settings in the category *Directories*.

Layout templates are only available when the layout they're associated with is loaded. They are stored in layout-related files in the environment's subfolder of the global template's directory.

Language templates are associated with coding languages specified for syntax highlighting and are only available when editing files with extensions that match that language as defined in the wordfile. They are stored in the default wordfiles directory which is defined in the UltraEdit settings in the category *Editor Display* ➤ *Syntax Highlighting*.

Project templates are only available when the project they're associated with is loaded. They are stored in the directory/file specified in the *Project settings* dialog.

Let's talk about adding and modifying templates, whereby each template must be named, and the name is then used in the ribbons, menus, toolbars, as well as in the *Template list*. The name is shown in the template list column in the left side of the *Modify templates* dialog. The following options and buttons are available in this dialog:

- Template group: Controls in which category the templates are displayed, whereby various subgroups exist in addition to the main groups *Global*, *Layout*, *Language*, and *Project*. In the case of languages, for example, specific programming languages can be selected, thus creating a meaningful grouping.

- Templates: Represents the list of templates available in the current group context with the associated name.

- Add (+)/remove (x) buttons: These buttons can be used to add and delete templates from the selected group.

- Up/down buttons: These buttons can be used to move the selected template up or down in the template list. The order of templates shown in the template list of this dialog is also the same order used to display templates in the *Template list*.

- Description: Every template can include an optional description of up to 79 characters. The description is shown in the tooltip displayed when hovering over the template in the *Template list*. If a description is not provided, the tooltip will show an extract of the template itself.

- Do not insert in Comments/Strings: These options are only available for language templates. If enabled, the template will not be automatically suggested when its name is typed in a comment or string of the associated syntax highlighting language.

- ? button: This button opens a dialog with a list of available template variables and formatting options.

- Content field: To create a template, simply type the text of the template into this field. The options and variables that can be used in this field are so diverse that we describe them separately in the following subchapter.

Template Content

This subchapter describes the template content in detail, and in general, the caret (^) can be used in the template to represent where the caret should be positioned after the template is inserted. For example, if the user does have a template consisting of *<mySampleTag></mySampleTag>*, and the caret needs to be positioned between the two tags, the template would be created as *<mySampleTag>^</mySampleTag>*. To include a literal caret (^) as part of the template, escape it with itself – for example, "^^" would insert a literal "^".

Placeholder Variables

By using the syntax *[+VariableName+]* within a template, the user can define so-called placeholder variables in templates. When the template is inserted, the value for a placeholder can be typed. All occurrences of the placeholder variable within the template are then updated. Pressing the Tab key will move the focus to the next placeholder variable.

For example, if we insert the following template:

```
// function [+function+]
[+scope+] function [+function+] () {
    ^

}
```

and type "myFunc" for the *[+function+]* variable and "private" for the *[+scope+]* variable, we get the following output:

```
// function myFunc
private function myFunc () {
  ^<-- caret blinking here
}
```

Selectable Value Variables

Selectable values allow inserting a variable with several different predefined choices which can be selected during the template insertion via the auto-complete drop-down. To add selectable values to a template variable, we use the following syntax:

```
[+defaultVal|selectableVal1|selectableVal2|selectableVal3+]
```

The pipe character (|) is used to delimit different selectable values. In the example above, when the template is inserted, the variable would have a default value of *defaultVal*, and the auto-complete dialog would open immediately to allow to choose one of the other three options. Once an item from the auto-complete drop-down is selected by pressing Enter, UltraEdit will shift its focus to the next variable (or if this is the only variable, insert the template).

In some cases, the user may prefer to use a completely different value for a template variable instead of one of the predefined values. In this case, he can simply press the tab key to navigate to the variable during the template insertion and begin typing a new value. The auto-complete dialog will disappear after the typing of new text begins. At any time, Ctrl+Spacebar can be pressed to make the auto-complete dialog with the selectable values visible again.

Special Template Variables

A template can contain special text strings that are translated at the time the template is recalled. These special strings are

- [DATE_DMY]: Is translated into the current date with the format day/month/year.

- [DATE_MDY]: Is translated into the current date with the format month/day/year.

- [DATE_TEXT]: Is translated into the current date with the date displayed as text.

- [TIME]: Is translated into the current time in 24-hour format.

- ^: This indicates the position at which to place the cursor after the template has been inserted.

- [FULL_FILE_NAME]: Is translated into the full path and file name of the active document.

- [FILE_PATH]: Is translated into the drive and path of the active document.

- [FILE_NAME]: Is translated into the root file name of the active document.

- [FILE_EXTENSION]: Is translated into the file extension of the active document with the point, i.e., ".txt", ".log", or ".csv".

- [FILE_EXTENSION_NP]: Is translated into the file extension of the active document without the point, i.e., "txt", "log", or "csv".

- [$REPLACE$]: Is replaced with selected text in the active document. The selection will be converted to uppercase text when inserted with the template.

- [$replace$]: Is replaced with selected text in the active document. The selection's current case will be maintained when it is inserted with the template.

Note   ^ refers to the character '^', not the Ctrl key.

Customizing Time/Date Format

For extended date and time formatting, UltraEdit supports special template strings.

To specify and customize the format of the local time, the following syntax can be used within a template:

`[TIME_USER]...format custom here...[TIME_USER_END]`

To specify and customize the format of the UTC (GMT, or Greenwich Mean Time) time, the following syntax can be used within a template:

`[TIME_USER_SYS]...format custom here...[TIME_USER_SYS_END]`

The following time format customizations are available:

- h: Hours with no leading zero for single-digit hours (12-hour clock)

- hh: Hours with leading zero for single-digit hours (12-hour clock)

- H: Hours with no leading zero for single-digit hours (24-hour clock)

- HH: Hours with leading zero for single-digit hours (24-hour clock)

- m: Minutes with no leading zero for single-digit minutes

- mm: Minutes with leading zero for single-digit minutes

- s: Seconds with no leading zero for single-digit seconds

- ss: Seconds with leading zero for single-digit seconds

- t: One character time marker string (such as A or P)

- tt: Multi-character time marker string (such as AM or PM).

If spaces are used to separate the elements in the format string, these spaces will appear in the same location in the template. The letters must be in uppercase or lowercase as shown in the list above (e.g., "ss", not "SS"). Characters in the format string that are enclosed in single quotation marks will appear in the same location and unchanged in the template. For example, to get the time string *11:29:40 PM*, the following format string between the time markers has to be used:

```
[TIME_USER]hh':'mm':'ss tt[TIME_USER_END]
```

To specify and customize the format of the local date, the following syntax can be used within a template:

```
[DATE_USER]...format custom here...[DATE_USER_END]
```

To specify and customize the format of the UTC date, the following syntax can be used within the template:

```
[DATE_USER_SYS]...format custom here...[DATE_USER_SYS_END]
```

The following date format customizations are available:

- d: Day of month as digits with no leading zero for single-digit days

- dd: Day of month as digits with leading zero for single-digit days

- ddd: Day of week as a three-letter abbreviation

- dddd: Day of week as its full name

- M: Month as digits with no leading zero for single-digit months

- MM: Month as digits with leading zero for single-digit months

- MMM: Month as a three-letter abbreviation

- MMMM: Month as its full name

- y: Year as last two digits, but with no leading zero for years less than 10

- yy: Year as last two digits, but with leading zero for years less than 10

- yyyy: Year represented by full four digits

If spaces to separate the elements in the format string are used, these spaces will appear in the same location in the template. The letters must be in uppercase or lowercase as shown in the list above (e.g., "MM", not "mm"). Characters in the format string that are enclosed in single quotation marks will appear in the same location and unchanged in the template. For example, to get the date string Wed, Aug 31 94, the following format string between the date markers has to be used:

```
[DATE_USER]ddd',' MMM dd yy[DATE_USER_END]
```

Columns and Column Mode

UltraEdit provides extensive support for columns and their editing, including the Column mode. We would like to discuss this power feature and other column-based insert functions in more detail in the following subchapters.

Column mode is one of the most popular features of UltraEdit for many users, and experience has shown that those who have become familiar with it no longer want to go without it.

This powerful feature changes the way in which UltraEdit selects and edits text. Normally this is done horizontally from character to character, and Column mode changes this mechanism to vertical processing.

This mode is activated program-wide via the keyboard shortcut Alt+C and can be activated simultaneously via *Edit* ➤ *Column/block* (Ribbon mode), *Edit* ➤ *Column mode* (Contemporary menu mode), or *Column* ➤ *Column mode* (Traditional menu mode). The default appearance of this ribbon section can be seen in Figure 7-17.

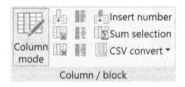

Figure 7-17. *Column and block functions in the Ribbon section*

For further understanding, we will use a simple example with a text file consisting of three columns and ten lines. Once activated, UltraEdit will highlight the text based on the column position of the first character the user selects to the column of the last character they select. Text selected in Column mode does not automatically include all text between the start and end position but does include all text in the *columns* between the first and last character which is selected.

Assuming we would like to insert text before the second column, the position in the column and for the desired rows is marked so that we find the marker seen in Figure 7-18. This simple marker does not select a character or word, but a simple vertical position. By entering new text, for example, the word "My", this is now done across all selected lines (see Figure 7-19).

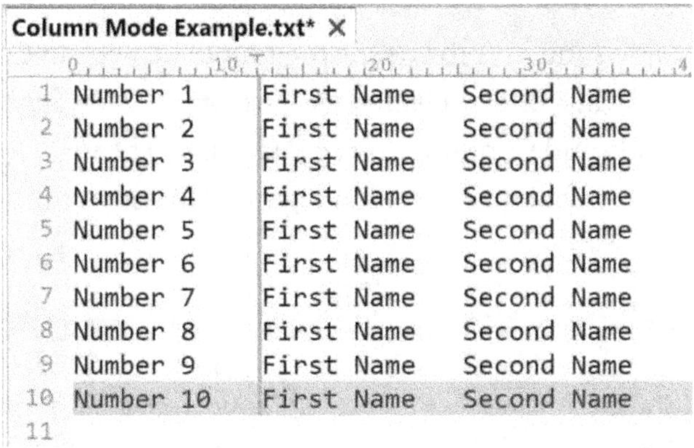

Figure 7-18. *Vertical marker selection before changing content*

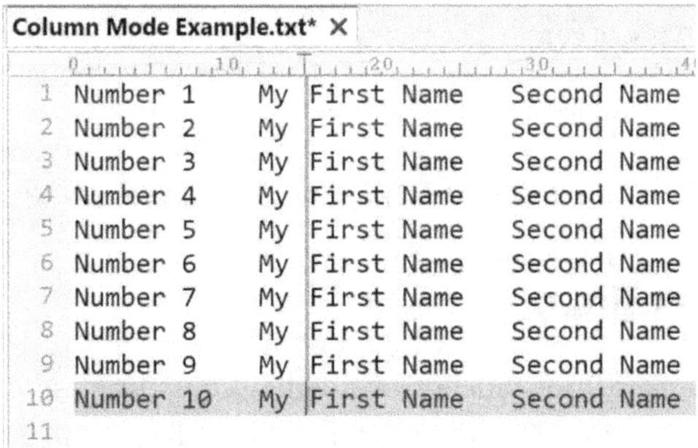

Figure 7-19. *Vertical marker selection after changing content*

Tip   If fast editing without prior separate activation of the Column mode is important, the Quick Column mode is a good option. The same column selection can also be used via Alt + Click and drag, which automatically activates Column mode. Column mode is then deactivated as soon as the caret is repositioned.

UltraEdit allows the user to specify the font to be used in Column mode separately. This font is selected via *View* ➤ *Fonts* ➤ *Set hex/column font* (Ribbon mode and Contemporary menu mode) or *View* ➤ *Set hex/column font* (Traditional menu mode). Figure 7-20 shows the access to this setting in Ribbon mode.

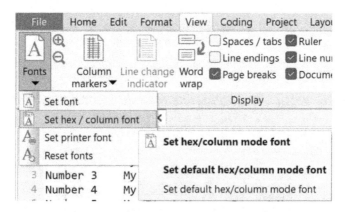

Figure 7-20. *Font setting especially for the Column mode*

Basic Functions

Basically, there are three functions for editing columns, described in more detail below. The *Insert/fill columns* function can be used to enter text that is inserted into a special column. If several rows are selected, the text is entered in these selected rows. If no lines are selected, text is entered for all lines in the file. The dialog *Insert/Fill Columns* appears for this, in which the text is entered (see Figure 7-21). The lower option is called *Do not insert/fill on empty last line* and prevents this text from being inserted in the last line of the file if this line is empty.

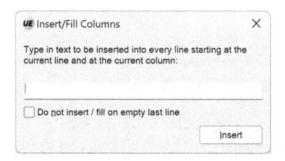

Figure 7-21. *Insert/Fill Columns dialog*

The further options *Cut columns* and *Delete columns* open a separate dialog in which the number of columns to cut/delete from every line starting at the current line and the current column can be specified (0 means to cut/delete columns based on highlighted text). Please see Figures 7-22 and 7-23 for this.

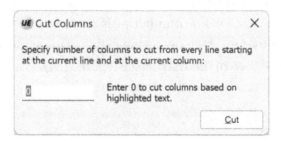

Figure 7-22. *Cut Columns dialog*

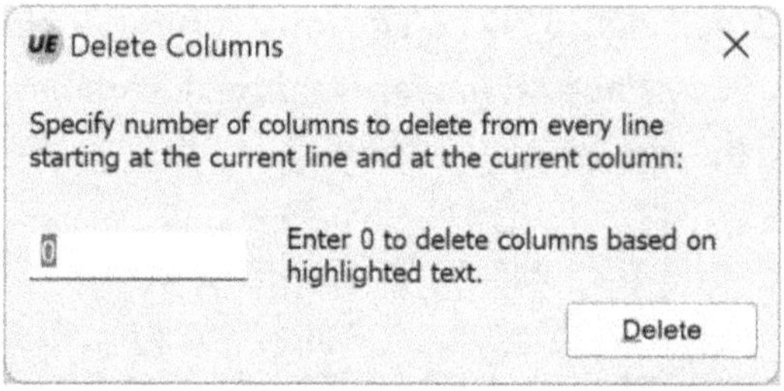

Figure 7-23. *Delete Columns dialog*

By using the justify options for left, center, and right, the user can justify a selected column of data, with the boundaries of the selection acting as the margins. Left-justifying a column of data will justify the data against the left of the selection, while right-justifying will do the opposite. Center-justifying the column of data will center the data within the selection.

The Column justify commands can be accessed via *Edit* ➤ *Column Left/Center/Right justify* (Ribbon mode), *Edit* ➤ *Left/Center/Right justify column* (Contemporary menu mode), or *Column* ➤ *Left/Center/Right justify* (Traditional menu mode).

As soon as any kind of line numbering is required, the *Insert Number* function is quite useful, which opens the dialog of the same name. Various options can be defined in this dialog (see Figure 7-24).

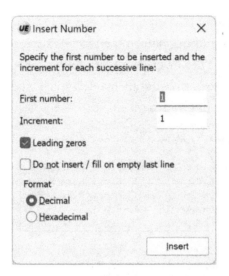

Figure 7-24. *Insert Number dialog with various insert options*

The following options are available here:

- First number: Describes the first starting number for the counting

- Increment: Defines the steps in which the number is to be increased

- Leading zeros: Determines whether shorter numbers are padded with leading zeros to match the longest number (such as 001 to 100)

- Do not insert/fill on empty last line: Prevents the numbering in the last line if it is empty

- Format: Allows a distinction between decimal and hexadecimal notation

If we use our original Column mode example from the beginning and want to insert a number before each row, we select rows 1 to 10 in the first column, open the *Insert Numbers* dialog, and press *Insert* at the bottom. We could also subsequently insert a space after the rows or a dot, depending on the requirements (see Figure 7-25).

Column Mode Example.txt* ✕

1	01. Number 1	My First Name	Second Name
2	02. Number 2	My First Name	Second Name
3	03. Number 3	My First Name	Second Name
4	04. Number 4	My First Name	Second Name
5	05. Number 5	My First Name	Second Name
6	06. Number 6	My First Name	Second Name
7	07. Number 7	My First Name	Second Name
8	08. Number 8	My First Name	Second Name
9	09. Number 9	My First Name	Second Name
10	10. Number 10	My First Name	Second Name
11			

Figure 7-25. *Column mode example withadded numbering at the beginning of the lines*

Tip   In our Column mode example, we indeed have an 11th empty line, so it would make sense to enable the option *Do not insert/fill on empty last line* inside the *Insert Numbers* dialog.

The *Sum* function can be used to convert selected text numbers into digits and add them up to a total. The condition must be that the text is already displayed as numeric characters. For example, if the user does have a text "one hundred thirty-two" selected, UltraEdit is not going to internally convert that text into an integer equaling 132.

To launch the *Sum* function, the user can select the area in Column mode and then select the *Sum selection* function, and the *Sum Selected Text* dialog appears (see Figure 7-26).

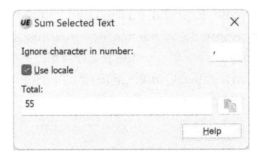

Figure 7-26. *Sum Selected Text dialog*

The following dialog components are available in this dialog for the summation:

- Ignore character in number: Because some number formats contain non-digit characters, such as commas, dots, or dashes, these characters can be ignored – leaving only the pure digits for the sum.

- Use locale: Uses the Windows locale for the thousand separators, for example, "," or "."

- Total: Contains the final result of the sum function.

- Copy to Clipboard: Copies the sum to the clipboard.

- Help: Opens the UltraEdit help system.

In our example above, we have selected the numbers added via the *Insert Number* function at the beginning of the line, and these are the line numbers 01 to 10. The sum of these line numbers is then 55, as calculated correctly by UltraEdit.

Another great strength of the Column mode is the handling of CSV files. These text files, known as **C**haracter-**S**eparated **V**alues, are often used for lists, whereby several columns are separated from each other by a separator character (often a comma). Many spreadsheet programs allow tables to be saved and exported in this format. However, editing these files where column manipulation is required can be difficult because the column widths vary and do not have a fixed size. UltraEdit therefore has two functions that convert a CSV file to a file with a fixed column width and the reverse process via a conversion to a CSV file.

The first function is called *Convert to fixed-width* and opens the dialog *Convert to Fixed Columns* (see Figure 7-27).

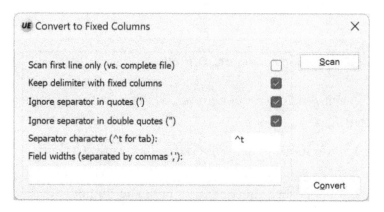

Figure 7-27. *Convert to Fixed Columns dialog*

In this dialog, the user can define the properties before UltraEdit analyzes the file content with the *Scan* button and finally converts it with the *Convert* button:

- Scan first line only (vs. complete file): Instructs UltraEdit to search just the first line for the field widths.

- Keep delimiter with fixed columns: Means that when converting to fixed width columns, the delimiter character for the fields will not be removed. If this option is disabled, the conversion process will remove the delimiter between fields.

- Ignore separator in quotes ('): If enabled, separator characters which are enclosed in single quotes will not be taken into account when scanning to determine column spacing for alignment.

- Ignore separator in double quotes ("): This option is identical to the previous option, except that double quotes are taken into account instead of single quotes.

- Separator character (^t for tab): Defines the delimiter character between fields (for the Tab character, "^t" should be used). In all other cases, a single character should be entered, and UltraEdit uses this character to determine the field boundaries.

- Field widths (separated by commas ","): Represents a list of comma-separated field widths used for the conversion process. If there are more fields than entries, the last entry will be used as the field width for the remaining fields, which allows the user to set a single entry, if all fields are required to be the same width. Please note that this field must not be left empty when the conversion to fixed columns is executed. It may be populated automatically by pressing the *Scan* button after specifying the conversion options, or the user may manually specify field widths if desired.

- Scan: UltraEdit scans the file (or first line) and determines the maximum field widths for each field. This will determine the maximum width required for each field and place the results (comma separated) in the *Field widths* edit field.

- Convert: Performs the conversion from character delimited text to fixed column according to the defined settings – the complete file will be converted.

The opposite can be performed with the *Convert fixed-width to CSV* function, which opens the *Convert to "Characters Delimited" text* dialog (see Figure 7-28).

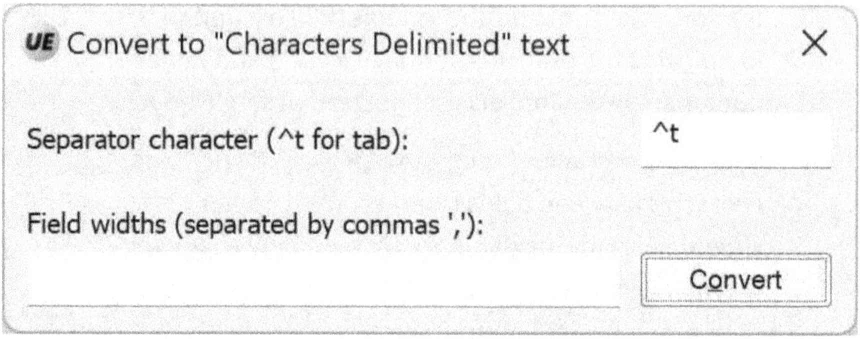

Figure 7-28. *Convert to "Characters Delimited" text dialog*

The following dialog components are available in this dialog:

- Separator character (^t for tab): Defines the delimiter character between fields (for the tab character, "^t" should be used). In all other cases, a single character should be entered, and UltraEdit uses this character to determine the field boundaries.

- Field widths (separated by commas ','): Represents a list of comma-separated field widths used for the conversion process. If there are more fields than entries, the last entry will be used as the field width for the remaining fields, which allows the user to set a single entry, if all fields are required to be the same width.

- Convert: Performs the conversion from fixed column to character delimited text according to the defined settings – the complete file will be converted.

Settings

The performance of a function essentially depends on its flexibility and configurability, and here UltraEdit offers fine-grained settings. These can be opened either via *Advanced* ➤ *Settings* (Ribbon mode), *Advanced* ➤ *Configuration* (Traditional menu mode), or *Advanced* ➤ *Settings* (Contemporary menu mode). All three options open the *Configuration* dialog, in which all settings are contained in a central location. Within this dialog, the user needs to navigate to the category *Editor* ➤ *Column mode* to open the options for Column mode (see Figure 7-29).

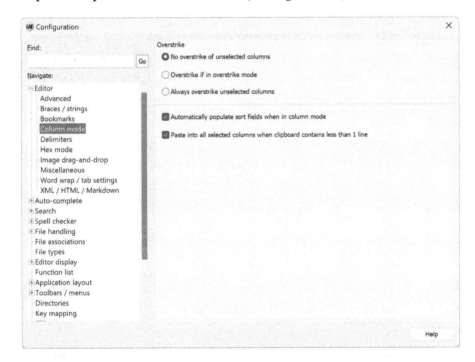

Figure 7-29. *UltraEdit settings for the Column mode*

As we have already discussed these settings in detail in Chapter 4, we would like to refer to this chapter at this point.

Practical Examples

Finally, we would like to describe two practical scenarios that can be used to understand the performance of the Column mode. Even if the following two scenarios appear relatively compact, these options should always be considered on a larger scale. A realistic question would be: *How much time and effort would I save if I had to edit not just a 10-line log file, but a 1,000,000-line log file?*

Scenario 1

For this first scenario, we have Delphi source code, and as can be seen in Figure 7-30, the procedure *Button1Click* is shown, which describes certain activities as soon as the button with the name *Button1* is pressed. We now extend the source code with a so-called if-then query, which describes a coherent code action with a subsequent *begin*, which is terminated again with *end;* (see Figure 7-31). This begin-end block is usually indented two positions to the right, which favors a more structured syntax. We therefore activate the UltraEdit Column mode and first mark the lines to be indented at the respective position (see Figure 7-32). If we now insert a space twice with this positioning, the entire selected block is indented to the right and we have achieved our result (see Figure 7-33).

```
109   procedure TForm1.Button1Click(Sender: TObject);
110   begin
111       Action1.Visible := cb1Visible.Checked;
112       Action2.Visible := cb2Visible.Checked;
113       Action3.Visible := cb3Visible.Checked;
114       Taskbar1.ApplyButtonsChanges;
115   end;
```

Figure 7-30. *Delphi source code with the procedure Button1Click*

```
109   procedure TForm1.Button1Click(Sender: TObject);
110   begin
111      if ComboBox1.Enabled then
112      begin
113         Action1.Visible = cb1Visible.Checked;
114         Action2.Visible = cb2Visible.Checked;
115         Action3.Visible = cb3Visible.Checked;
116      Taskbar1.ApplyButtonsChanges;
117      end;
118   end;
```

Figure 7-31. Delphi source code with an if-then query added

```
109   procedure TForm1.Button1Click(Sender: TObject);
110   begin
111      if ComboBox1.Enabled then
112      begin
113      Action1.Visible := cb1Visible.Checked;
114      Action2.Visible := cb2Visible.Checked;
115      Action3.Visible := cb3Visible.Checked;
116      Taskbar1.ApplyButtonsChanges;
117      end;
118   end;
```

Figure 7-32. Delphi source code with the marked lines to be indented

```
109   procedure TForm1.Button1Click(Sender: TObject);
110   begin
111      if ComboBox1.Enabled then
112      begin
113         Action1.Visible := cb1Visible.Checked;
114         Action2.Visible := cb2Visible.Checked;
115         Action3.Visible := cb3Visible.Checked;
116         Taskbar1.ApplyButtonsChanges;
117      end;
118   end;
```

Figure 7-33. Delphi source code with the already-indented code block between begin and end;

Tip   The same method can also be used to comment out a code block of any size by entering the two characters // instead of two spaces. In Object Pascal and C++, this means that the respective line is commented out, which is then applied to the entire selected block in Column mode.

Scenario 2

In this second scenario, we use a log file, as they exist in many IT sectors; UltraEdit is known for processing extremely large files. Our log file consists of 4 columns and 11 lines, of which the first line is the header. The columns are named Number, Date, Owner, and Value (see Figure 7-34).

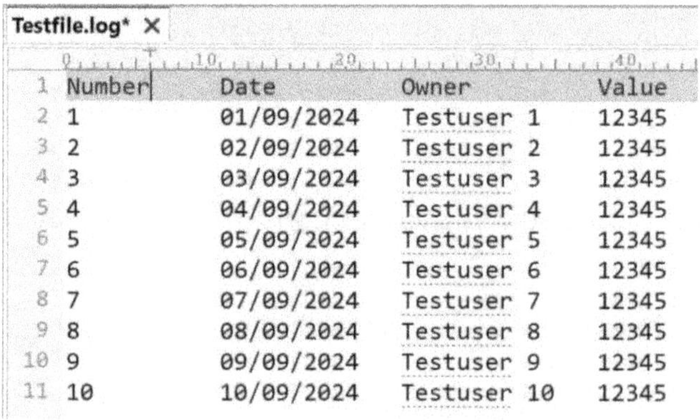

```
Testfile.log*  ×
     0.........10.........20.........30.........40.....
  1  Number|       Date         Owner          Value
  2  1            01/09/2024     Testuser 1     12345
  3  2            02/09/2024     Testuser 2     12345
  4  3            03/09/2024     Testuser 3     12345
  5  4            04/09/2024     Testuser 4     12345
  6  5            05/09/2024     Testuser 5     12345
  7  6            06/09/2024     Testuser 6     12345
  8  7            07/09/2024     Testuser 7     12345
  9  8            08/09/2024     Testuser 8     12345
 10  9            09/09/2024     Testuser 9     12345
 11  10           10/09/2024     Testuser 10    12345
```

Figure 7-34.   Our log file with four columns

First, we want to use the *Sum selection* function and therefore activate the Column mode, select the *Value* column in lines 2–11 (without the header row), and select *Sum selection* (e.g., from the *Edit* ➤ *Column/block* tab in Ribbon mode). The *Sum Selected Text* dialog box then opens, and the sum is displayed correctly in the Total field with 123450 (see Figure 7-35).

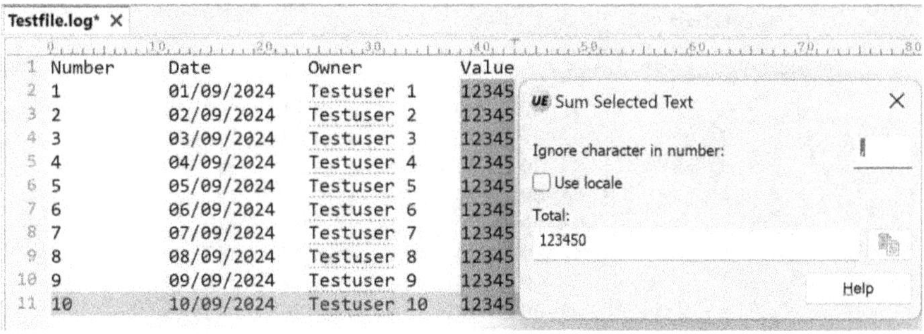

Figure 7-35. *Log file with the fourth column selected and the Sum Selected Text dialog*

In the next step, we would like to replace the slashes in the date column with hyphens. A "01/09/2024" should therefore become a "01-09-2024". To do this, we select the first slash column in column 2 within rows 2–11 (without the header row) as seen in Figure 7-36 and activate Overstrike mode by entering a hyphen. This means that the slash in all selected rows is overwritten by a hyphen. We repeat the same process in the second position of the slash so that we achieve a result as shown in Figure 7-37.

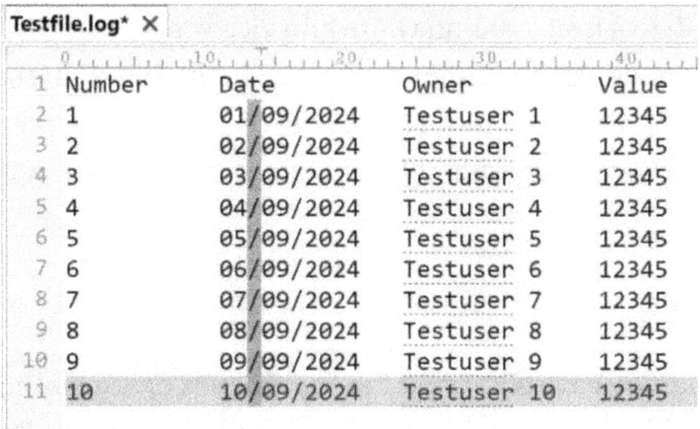

Figure 7-36. *Log file with selected column in which a slash is to be replaced by a hyphen*

```
Testfile.log*  X
   0         10        20        30        40
 1  Number       Date         Owner        Value
 2  1            01-09-2024   Testuser 1    12345
 3  2            02-09-2024   Testuser 2    12345
 4  3            03-09-2024   Testuser 3    12345
 5  4            04-09-2024   Testuser 4    12345
 6  5            05-09-2024   Testuser 5    12345
 7  6            06-09-2024   Testuser 6    12345
 8  7            07-09-2024   Testuser 7    12345
 9  8            08-09-2024   Testuser 8    12345
10  9            09-09-2024   Testuser 9    12345
11  10           10-09-2024   Testuser 10   12345
```

Figure 7-37. *Log file with selected column, where the replacement was finalized*

UltraEdit's Column mode is a powerful feature for editing text and source code in a new way than was previously possible. Combined with the flexibility and processing of extremely large files, even gigabyte-sized log files can be edited vertically.

Additional functions allow the handling of new/existing columns, the change of alignment (left/center/right), the flexible insertion of numbers, a sum function, as well as the conversion to and from CSV files with variable column width to a fixed column width and vice versa.

Column mode can be further configured in the UltraEdit settings, and the experience with customers has shown that anyone who has got to know this function appreciates it and no longer wants to work without it.

Summary

In this chapter, we have described the possibilities of text editing with all the associated functions, including several clipboards, active line actions, the spell checker, statistical word and line details, and the powerful hex mode.

For insertion options, we have discussed date and time, color values, literal characters, strings, and templates, with the latter concept being discussed in more detail with placeholder variables, selectable value variables, and special template variables.

Finally, we described the Column mode with its possibilities and how powerful this editing function actually is using two practical examples.

CHAPTER 8

View, Format, and Find

In this chapter, we will look at the fundamental elements of text editing, including the many view functionalities of UltraEdit. How data is displayed is of enormous importance for the practicable navigation and editing of this data.

We will also talk about formatting options, such as indentation, various conversion functions, the *Trim* command, and paragraph editing including setup and alignment.

In the third major topic area, we will look at the search and replace functions, which are very comprehensive and enable an effective search in individual files as well as entire directory structures and drives.

View

The *View* section in UltraEdit contains all the functions that affect the screen display. This noteworthy aspect of text editing defines how the edited data and the various UltraEdit tools are displayed.

This view area can be categorized into different sub-areas, including display, highlight, hide/show lines, and mode.

© Devid Espenschied 2025
D. Espenschied, *Mastering UltraEdit*, https://doi.org/10.1007/979-8-8688-1160-9_8

Display

The *Display* section is the main group within the view category and contains functions for font selections, column markers, line change indicators, word wrap, and the display of various text editing tools.

Set Font

The *Set font* function opens the *Font* dialog where the user can choose the font that UltraEdit will use for normal plain-text editing, as well as the style and size (see Figure 8-1).

Figure 8-1. *Font dialog*

This dialog includes a list of all installed fonts on the system as well as the available styles for each font. It is highly recommended that for plain-text editing, a fixed-width, monospace font (such as Consolas or

Courier New) is selected. Using proportional fonts like Arial or Lucida with a plain-text position-based text editor like UltraEdit will likely cause caret positioning and ruler issues.

The *Script* combobox allows the user to choose a different code page script for the font, based upon the scripts that the font supports. In general, it should not be necessary to change this setting since UltraEdit will automatically detect a file's encoding/code page on open and automatically select the correct script for the font as required.

The *Set hex/column font* command presents the same *Font* dialog that was discussed above, and it allows the selection of different fonts and font sizes. For this special function, the selection will apply when editing in hex mode or in Column mode. UltraEdit will automatically switch to this font when hex or Column mode is selected.

The *Set printer font* command presents also the same *Font* dialog that was discussed above, and for this special function, the selection affects different fonts and font sizes for use by the printer. The here performed selection will apply only to the printer fonts.

The last font command is called *Reset fonts* and instructs UltraEdit to reset user selections of the screen and printer fonts to the default settings. Any user selections of the screen fonts made with the *Set font* command or *Set printer font* command will be lost.

Increase/Decrease Font Size

These two options allow the user to increase or decrease the font size by one unit. If the initial value of the font size is set to 10, this function increases this value to 11 and decreases it to 9.

Additionally, there is a faster way for changing the font size. The user can quickly increase and decrease the size of the active font for a zoom effect by holding the Ctrl key and spinning the mouse's scroll wheel. This will globally change the font size for all open files.

Column Markers

This is a marker for columns that are relevant for visual purposes. The *Show column markers* command is used to switch the visibility of the active column markers.

At the same time, the *Set column markers* command provides a dialog of the same name in which column marker settings can be defined (see Figure 8-2).

Figure 8-2. *Set Column Markers dialog*

In principle, the user can define groups in this dialog and then assign any column markers to each individual group. The upper list represents the column marker groups, and the lower list represents the column markers based on the selection of the upper group list:

- Column groups: This list allows the selection of a group name by clicking on it and editing it by clicking on it again. It allows column groups to be assigned unique names. The Column groups list has four associated buttons:

    - Set active: Sets the selected group active and displays associated column markers in the edit window

    - New: Inserts a new column group item into the list

    - Modify: Toggles the selected column group name to edit mode so it may be renamed

    - Delete: Removes the selected column group from the list

- Column markers: This list consists of two separate columns: *Enabled* and *Column number*. When a column group is selected in the first list, the column markers associated with that group may be defined within the lower list.

    When a column marker is created, a check box appears in the *Enabled* column. The user can enter a column number at which the marker should be displayed in the *Column number* column. The column marker is only displayed if the *Enabled* option is checked. In the column markers list, the user can select a column number by clicking on it and edit it by clicking on it again. The Column markers list has three associated buttons:

- New: Inserts a new column marker item and its associated check box into the list

- Modify: Toggles the selected column marker number to edit mode so it may be modified

- Delete: Removes the selected column marker from the list

The last function for the Column markers is called *No scroll left of marker 1*, and if this is enabled, the columns to the left of the 1st column marker are fixed and do not scroll horizontally, while the columns to the right of the column marker will scroll as normal when the horizontal scroll bar is used or when the caret is positioned to the right-hand side of the window forcing a horizontal scroll.

If this feature is enabled, columns to the right of the marker will scroll horizontally, while columns to the left will not. While the horizontal scroll is in effect, any mouse selection or clicking of the primary mouse button within the fixed portion of the display will cause the horizontal scroll position to be reset, allowing viewing and editing of the continuous columns.

If the 1st column marker is disabled or set to 0, this function will have no effect.

By using the settings in Figure 8-2 and setting the Delphi column group as active, the Delphi source code results in the marker output shown in Figure 8-3.

```
DelphiAIDev.DB.Utils.pas  ×
  1  ⊟unit DelphiAIDev.DB.Utils;
  2
  3    interface
  4
  5    uses
  6      System.SysUtils,
  7      Vcl.StdCtrls;
  8
  9  ⊟type
 10      TDelphiAIDevDBUtils = class
 11      private
 12      public
 13        class procedure ClearComboBox(const AComboBox: TComb
 14        class procedure FillComboBoxDatabases(const AComboBo
 15      end;
 16
 17    implementation
 18
 19    uses
 20      DelphiAIDev.DB.Registers.Fields,
 21      DelphiAIDev.DB.Registers.Model;
 22
 23    class procedure TDelphiAIDevDBUtils.ClearComboBox(const
 24    var
 25      i: Integer;
 26      LObj: TObject;
 27  ⊟begin
 28      for i := 0 to Pred(AComboBox.Items.Count) do
 29  ⊟    begin
 30        if not Assigned(AComboBox.Items.Objects[i]) then
 31          Continue;
 32
 33        LObj := AComboBox.Items.Objects[i];
 34
 35        if LObj is TDelphiAIDevDBRegistersFields then
 36          TDelphiAIDevDBRegistersFields(LObj).Free;
 37      end;
 38
 39      AComboBox.Items.Clear;
 40    end;
```

Figure 8-3. *Column markers for the Delphi column group with marker positions at offset 2, 4, and 6*

Line Change Indicator

If the line change indicator function is enabled, modified lines will be indicated with a special-colored shading between the line numbers and the first character on the line. The colors used to indicate saved and unsaved changes to a file within an editing session are configured in the *Manage Themes* dialog. This dialog can be accessed via *Layout* ➤ *Themes* ➤ *Manage Themes* (Ribbon mode and Contemporary menu mode) and *View* ➤ *Themes* ➤ *Manage Themes* (Traditional menu mode). Figure 8-4 shows this dialog with the Line change indicator options for saved and unsaved files (color preset green and red).

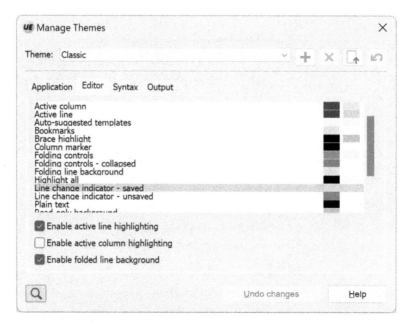

Figure 8-4. *Manage Themes dialog with the Line change indicator options*

If the undo buffer is cleared during an editing session, the line change indicators would be reset as well.

If the Line change indicator option is toggled on/off via the *View* tab (Ribbon mode) or the *View* menu (both Contemporary and Traditional menu modes), this will only affect the active document – global changes for this feature are set under the UltraEdit settings in the category *Editor Display* ➤ *Line Change Indicator*.

Word Wrap

The Word Wrap function can be toggled simultaneously with the keyboard shortcut Ctrl+W and configured in the UltraEdit settings in the category *Editor* ➤ *Word wrap/tab settings* (see Figure 8-5).

Figure 8-5. *Word wrap option in the UltraEdit settings*

We have already described this function in detail in Chapter 7 and therefore refer to this chapter here.

Display of Various Text Editing Tools

This section allows the display of various text editing tools that are visual in nature and facilitate the editing and navigation of files depending on the scenario. In Ribbon mode, these are individual check boxes that can be activated/deactivated in the *View* tab, while in the Contemporary and Traditional menu modes, there are separate menu items in the *View* menu that can be toggled. We would like to discuss these text editing tools in more detail below:

- Spaces/tabs: Allows the displaying of spaces, tabs, and new line characters as visible characters on the screen. It does not change the document but allows the user to clearly distinguish between the different characters.

- Spaces are shown as '·'

- Tabs are shown as '»'

- New lines are shown as '¶'

If there is not enough room to show the '»' with the tab, the tab will appear as normal and nonvisible. The color used to display these characters may be modified by using the already-described *Manage Themes* dialog.

- Line endings: This will display line endings (carriage returns and line feeds) as visible characters on the screen. It does not actually alter the contents of the file but allows the user to visibly see the line endings. With this option enabled:

  - DOS/Windows style line endings (carriage return, line feed – hex 0D 0A) are shown as '¶'

  - Unix style line endings (line feed – hex 0A) are shown as '¬'

  - Mac (legacy) style line endings (carriage return – hex 0D) are shown as '±'

- Page breaks: This will display the page break character as defined in the UltraEdit Page setup as a line drawn across the screen. Any text following the page break character will start on the line following the page break line. This will not modify the line numbering of the file, as line numbers are based on line terminators only. If this setting is disabled, the page break character will be printed as with any other character, and text will be displayed immediately prior to and following the character according to what is present.

- Ruler: This toggles the column ruler that displays the column numbers at the top of each window. The ruler indicates the column number in even increments. For fixed pitch fonts, this will show the correct column indication, and for variable pitch fonts, this will show the column numbers based on the average character width for the active font. All ruler colors can be configured within the already-described *Manage Themes* dialog.

- Line numbers: This toggles the line number display on the left-hand side of the window. The line numbers are shown in a fixed area on the left-hand side of the window for each file if this option is enabled. The font used is automatically selected based on the current font and is slightly smaller than the selected font for display. The color of the line numbers can be configured within the already-described *Manage Themes* dialog. If a file with line numbers is to be printed, a corresponding selection must be made in the *Page Setup* dialog, because the line numbers function just discussed is only relevant during text editing.

- Document map: This toggles the document map visibility. The document map is an element that allows users to quickly navigate in documents by pointing and clicking to reposition the active view. It shows an outline of the active document, like a filmstrip. A viewport or frame will indicate the portion of the active file currently visible in the edit window. Users may click at a different position in the document map to reposition the viewport or may click on the viewport and drag it to another location.

We have already discussed the document map and the associated context menu in detail in Chapter 3.

- Active line highlight: This toggles active line highlighting. The active line will be colored with the background and foreground colors set for this in the already-described *Manage themes* dialog.

- Active col. highlight: This toggles active column highlighting. The active column (to the immediate right of the caret) will be colored with the background and foreground colors set for this in the already-described *Manage themes* dialog.

- Line spacing: These three items change the usage of Single, 1 ½, and Double spacing. This allows a document to be viewed and printed with additional spacing between each line of text:

  - Single spacing: Each line is displayed and printed with the normal character height and line spacing.

  - 1 ½ spacing: Each line is displayed and printed with the 1 ½ the normal character height for the line. The actual characters are the normal height, but spacing allocated for the line is increased, giving additional room for notes to be handwritten between lines.

  - Double spacing: Each line is displayed and printed with the two times the normal character height for the line. The actual characters are the normal height, but spacing allocated for the line is increased, giving additional room for notes to be handwritten between lines.

Highlight

The *Highlight* section contains two useful functions for selecting text.

Highlight All Selected

The *Highlight all selected* option turns on or off the selection of strings matched by a Find with *Highlight All Items Found* selected when the option *Use persistent highlight all* is selected in the UltraEdit settings and the category *Search* ➤ *Advanced* or when all occurrences of the word under the cursor are highlighted. This command can also be invoked with the keyboard shortcut Ctrl + . (this means a dot in combination with the Ctrl key).

Make Selections

The *Make selections* option converts all highlighted strings to editable selections. This command can also be invoked with the keyboard shortcut Ctrl + , (this means a comma in combination with the Ctrl key).

Hide/Show Lines

The *Hide/show lines* section contains various functions for hiding and showing lines, which also includes the collapsing and expanding of text. The latter is a fundamental feature of code folding.

Hide/Show Selection

This function allows the user to select some number of lines and to hide these. In this case, they will not be visible on the screen, or if lines are hidden, they will be shown.

To hide a set of lines, the user needs to select the lines they wish to be hidden and invoke the *Hide/show selection* command from the *View* tab (Ribbon mode) and the *View* menu (both Contemporary and Traditional

311

menu modes) or by using the shortcut (Ctrl + "-" numeric keypad, the subtract key). If the lines are hidden, a "+" will be displayed in the folding gutter to the left of the edit window. When editing a file that does not have syntax highlighting, the following configuration options must be enabled in the UltraEdit settings in the category *Editor Display* ➤ *Code Folding* (see Figure 8-6):

- Enable show/hide lines and code folding

- Enable show/hide lines in nonsyntax highlighted files

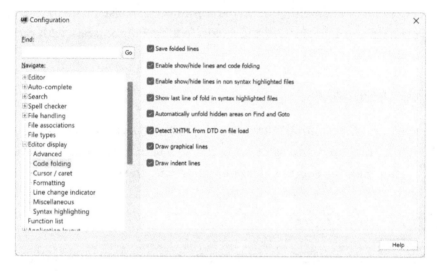

Figure 8-6. *UltraEdit settings with enabled show/hide line options*

Multiple sections can be hidden at one time. Changes made to the file will update the hidden regions in most cases, which means that the hidden lines are maintained. In a few instances (e.g., file sort), this may not be possible, and the hidden lines may be offset, requiring them to be hidden again.

Clicking the "+" in the folding gutter beside hidden lines will cause the section no longer to be hidden. This may be re-hidden by using this *Hide Lines* feature without a selection – in this case, the last set of lines that was hidden and then shown will be hidden again.

This command can be used from within macros.

To show already-hidden lines, the user can click the "+" in the folding gutter beside the hidden lines, or position to it via some other means and select the *Hide/show selection* command.

To save the hidden lines, the option *Save folding lines* in the UltraEdit settings in the category *Editor display* ➤ *Code folding* needs to be enabled. This means that the hidden line information will also be saved and reloaded when the file is next loaded.

Two additional commands exist for unchanged lines. The command *Hide unchanged lines* hides all lines with no unsaved changes in the current editing session. *Unhide unchanged lines* makes unchanged lines visible again after the command *Hide unchanged lines* has been used.

Collapse and Expand All

Text elements and structures can be collapsed to improve the overview in certain scenarios. These are key topics in code folding, in which certain source code passages are hidden. This often occurs in sections that must be fully contained in the source code but are not necessarily conducive to good readability.

The *Collapse all* command collapses all blocks in the active file bounded by the *Open/Close Fold Strings* defined in the active wordfile. If text is selected, this will affect only the selected region, and if no text is selected, this command will operate on the whole of the active file. This command can also be accessed via the keyboard shortcut Ctrl+Add.

In contrast to this, the *Expand all* command expands all blocks in the active file bounded by *Open/Close Fold Strings* defined in the active wordfile. The same behavior applies here, which means that if text is selected, this will affect only the selected region and if no text is selected, this command will operate on the whole of the active file. This command can also be accessed via the keyboard shortcut Ctrl+Multiply.

Note   When this command is invoked, strings hidden using the *Hide Lines* command will be expanded as well as folded sections of code.

Fold Lines

The *Fold lines* command toggles the visibility of guide lines based on code folding strings in the current wordfile.

Mode

The *Mode* section contains functions for file change polling and additional UltraEdit window display functions.

File Change Polling

File change polling defines a functionality to monitor file changes in a certain defined interval. When files are opened in UltraEdit and are being modified by external applications, this allows the user to control how quickly and precisely UltraEdit should reflect these file changes.

Toggle File Change Polling

The *Toggle file change polling* command toggles the file change polling for the active file. This can be very useful for log files or any other files that might be dynamically updated. When this command is enabled, UltraEdit checks the active file periodically based on a specified interval and is updated with any changes that have been made to the file.

The *File change polling* command will be grayed out in the *View* tab (Ribbon mode) and the *View* menu (both Contemporary and Traditional menu modes) unless the associated configuration item has been selected and a polling interval has been set. This item is called *Poll for file changes at force interval in seconds* and can be accessed through the UltraEdit settings in the category *File handling* ➤ *File change detection* (see Figure 8-7). A value of 0 means that this function is disabled.

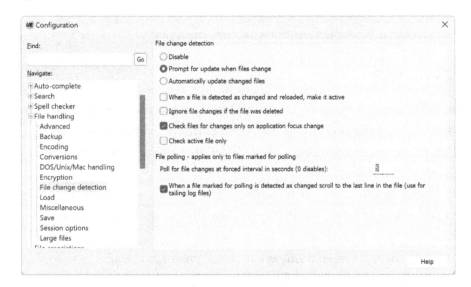

Figure 8-7. *UltraEdit settings with a five-second file polling interval*

Auto-scroll Polled Files

The *Auto-scroll polled files* command toggles the auto-scroll state of all files for which polling has been activated using the *File Change Polling* command. If this is selected, all polled files will automatically be scrolled to display the last line each time the files are polled.

In the case of dynamically updated files, such as log files, this ensures that the latest additions to the file are always visible when the polled file is active. This functionality is similar to the Unix tail command.

Always on Top

The *Always on top* command toggles the setting to display UltraEdit on top of all other applications.

This means that as soon as this function is active, no other application or its windows are allowed to come to the foreground. This function is quite useful if UltraEdit is to remain in the foreground at all times, for example, for demonstration purposes and to suppress all potentially disruptive overlaying applications or their windows.

Full Screen

The *Full screen* function allows the active file to be edited using the whole screen. The toolbar, status bar, and other UltraEdit windows that would normally be displayed as part of the UltraEdit application will be hidden while in this mode.

A small window with an icon on it will be shown to allow the user to switch back to normal editing. In addition, the Escape key can be used to cancel the full screen mode.

When the full screen mode is canceled, the main UltraEdit window and editing window will be returned to their previous state.

In the next two figures, we have compared the normal view mode (with the Contemporary menu mode) in Figure 8-8 and the full screen mode in Figure 8-9. As can be seen in full screen mode, there is a small symbol to the right of the text which actually represents a movable mini window and which exits full screen mode when the mouse is clicked (alternatively the Escape key).

Figure 8-8. *UltraEdit with its standard view (here with our previous Column mode example file)*

Figure 8-9. *UltraEdit in full screen mode (with the movable close window to the right)*

317

Format

The *Format* section in UltraEdit contains all the functions that allow the formatting of text in all its aspects.

This includes functions for the indent, case formatting, handling tabs and spaces, trim commands for leading and trailing spaces, and reformatting.

Indent

The topic of indentation is an important aspect in many IT areas, such as software development or editing websites using HTML. Certain lines or blocks of lines are indented a certain number of positions to the right to make the structure easier to understand and to highlight subsections. UltraEdit offers some functions for this structural improvement, which we will discuss in more detail below.

Reindent Selection

The *Reindent selection* command allows the user to reformat the selected text within the active file. This is typically used by developers to reformat existing text according to the indentation settings in configuration and the automatic indent settings for syntax highlighting.

When the reindenting is performed, UltraEdit will reindent the file line by line, starting with the indentation of the first selected line.

If the indentation of the first selected line is less than the indent setting, or falls between multiples of the indent setting, then the indentation will be rounded down to match the value or multiple of the indent setting.

For example, if the indent value is 4, and the first selected line is indented to 2, then the line will be assumed not to be indented as it will be rounded down to 0. If the line was indented to 6, then the line will be adjusted to be indented to 4 as it falls between the indent values of 4 and 8.

UltraEdit does try and determine if the statement causing a change in the indentation is commented out or part of a string and ignores it in this case. However, if the file contains preprocessor conditional statements (#ifdef, #ifndef, and so on), UltraEdit does not attempt to determine which text is valid and which is not. This may cause lines to be adjusted incorrectly.

To avoid problems with conditional statements, it is suggested that all conditional sections include the same number of open and close conditional statements. If an "*if (test) {*" statement is in the conditional text, the user should make sure the closing brace "}" is also in the conditional text and there should not be a problem.

In some cases, it may be desirable not to indent lines such as compiler directives or comments. UltraEdit provides for this capability by allowing strings to be ignored to be defined in the active wordfile.

Add Indents

The *Add indent* command presents a dialog that allows the user to specify the number of spaces to add at the beginning of each of the selected (highlighted) lines (see Figure 8-10).

Figure 8-10. *Add Indents dialog with the number of spaces to indent each line*

UltraEdit starts adding the specified number of spaces to each line beginning with the first highlighted line and ending with the last line that has at least one character selected (highlighted).

The Indents will be added to all lines stated above, irrespective to indentations that may already exist.

Remove Indents

The *Remove indents* command is the opposite of the *Add indent* command and opens a dialog that allows the user to specify the number of spaces or tabs to remove from the beginning of each of the selected (highlighted) lines (see Figure 8-11).

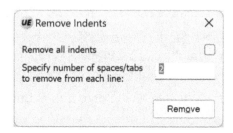

Figure 8-11. *Remove Indents dialog with the number of spaces/tabs to remove from each line*

If the check box *Remove all indents* is enabled, UltraEdit will remove all indentation at the beginning of the selected lines. UltraEdit starts removing the indents beginning with the first highlighted line and ending with the last line that has at least one character selected (highlighted).

If no indentation is found at the beginning of a selected line, no changes are made to that line.

Convert

This section describes various conversions, such as upper- and lowercase, spaces to tabs and vice versa, and word wrap to line ends and vice versa.

To Uppercase

The *To uppercase* command changes all selected text to uppercase and can also be invoked with the keyboard shortcut Alt+F5. There is no limit on the amount of text that may be selected.

If Column mode is selected, the selected columns only are converted.

To Lowercase

The *To lowercase* command changes all selected text to lowercase and can also be invoked with the keyboard shortcut Ctrl+F5. There is no limit on the amount of text that may be selected.

If Column mode is selected, the selected columns only are converted.

Capitalize

The *Capitalize* command can also be invoked with the F5 key and changes the first letter of all words in the selected text to uppercase and the remaining letters to lowercase. There is no limit on the amount of text that may be selected.

If Column mode is selected, the selected columns only are converted.

Invert Case

The *Invert case* command inverts the case of all selected text and can also be invoked with the keyboard shortcut Shift+F5. There is no limit on the amount of text that may be selected.

If Column mode is selected, the selected columns only are converted.

Tabs to Spaces

The *Tabs to spaces* command converts all of the tab characters within a file to spaces. This function uses the tab options within the UltraEdit settings to determine how the tab character/tab stop is to be interpreted. The conversion is performed, and at the same time, the formatting will remain the same.

If a portion of the file is selected/highlighted, only the selected portion is converted; otherwise, the complete file is converted.

Spaces to Tabs (All)

The *Spaces to tabs (all)* command converts all of the spaces in a file to tabs. This uses the tab options within the UltraEdit settings to determine how the tab character/tab stop is to be interpreted.

The conversion is performed, and at the same time, the formatting will remain the same. This will mean that where there are insufficient spaces to replace with a tab character and retain the same formatting, the spaces will be left in place.

If a portion of the file is selected/highlighted, only the selected portion is converted; otherwise, the complete file is converted.

Spaces to Tabs (Leading)

The *Spaces to tabs (leading)* command converts all of the (leading) spaces in a file to tabs. This uses the tab options within the UltraEdit settings to determine how the tab character/tab stop is to be interpreted.

The leading spaces refer to the space at the beginning of a line. Any spaces after the first non-space character in a line will not be converted. To convert all spaces in a line, the *Spaces to tabs (all)* command should be used.

The conversion is performed, and at the same time the formatting will remain the same. This will mean that where there are insufficient spaces to replace with a tab character and retain the same formatting, the spaces will be left in place.

If a portion of the file is selected/highlighted, only the selected portion is converted; otherwise, the complete file is converted.

Wrap to Line Ends

The *Wrap to line ends* command does a word wrap to the text based on either the width of the display window or a specified column number and writes CR/LF (carriage return/line feed) characters to the file. Please note that this concerns Windows files, and any files opened from a Unix system with Unix line terminators will appropriately use Unix line terminators (LF) for this function. The same applies for Mac Classic (CR), although these hardly exist anymore.

If a space is found at the position of the wrap, a single space is removed. This allows the document to be saved as viewed in the word wrap state with CR/LF characters inserted at the end of each word wrapped line.

When this command is selected, a dialog box is displayed, allowing selection of the wrap parameters (see Figure 8-12).

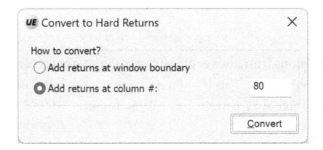

Figure 8-12. *Convert to Hard Returns dialog*

By default, the text will be wrapped based on the current view. This means that the text will be wrapped at the window boundary as shown on the screen. The dialog *Convert to Hard Returns* allows the selection of a column number at which the text should be wrapped. In this case, the text will be wrapped at the specified column or at the preceding word boundary on the line.

This command works on the complete file if no text is selected. If a selection is made, the feature only converts the selected area.

Line Ends to Wrap

The *Line ends to wrap* command removes the CR/LF (carriage return/ line feed) characters from the file, allowing the text to be word wrapped by UltraEdit. This feature removes all CR/LF characters from the text that is selected. If no text is selected, this function has no effect.

To remove all CR/LF characters from the file, the complete file needs to be selected. By positioning the cursor at the beginning of the file and pressing the keyboard shortcut Ctrl+Shift+End at the same time, this can be achieved.

Trim

The *Trim* functions trim lines at either the beginning or the end if there are spaces at either end. This is often useful when lines are padded with spaces (e.g., to achieve a certain vertical alignment).

Leading Spaces

The *Trim Leading spaces* command trims all leading whitespace (tabs and spaces) from each line.

Trailing Spaces

The *Trim Trailing spaces* command removes the trailing white space (tabs and spaces) from the ends of each line. This function removes the trailing white spaces from the end of every line in the file and positions back to the original cursor position when it is complete.

The UltraEdit settings in the category *File Handling* ➤ *Save* contain the option *Trim trailing spaces on file save*. This function causes UltraEdit to automatically remove the trailing white space (spaces/tabs) from the end of every line in the file and positions back to the original cursor position when it is complete each time a file is saved.

Paragraph

UltraEdit comes with a few paragraph commands that include a complete reformat with extensive setup. At the same time, there are text alignment commands to left-align, right-align, center, or justify text.

Reformat

The *Reformat* command (which can also be invoked via the keyboard shortcut Ctrl+T) can be used to format the current paragraph (or selected text) to the specified column number boundary. The column number and settings are specified in the *Reformatting Options* dialog (which we will describe in the next sections). A paragraph is determined as having two hard returns in succession (i.e., a blank line).

All hard returns are removed for the paragraph, and new hard returns are automatically inserted at the appropriate position based upon the settings in the *Reformatting Options* dialog. Please note that the reformat process will remove all bookmarks from bookmarked lines within the area selected for reformatting. An Undo executed after the completion of the reformat process will not restore removed bookmarks.

The whole file may be reformatted using the *Select All* command to first select the complete file (alternatively with the keyboard shortcut Ctrl+A), and then reformat it.

If the *Auto Indent* feature is enabled, the paragraphs will be automatically indented based on the first line of the paragraph.

Setup

The *Reformatting Options* dialog specifies the parameters used for reformatting. These parameters are used when one of the paragraph formatting commands is used (see Figure 8-13).

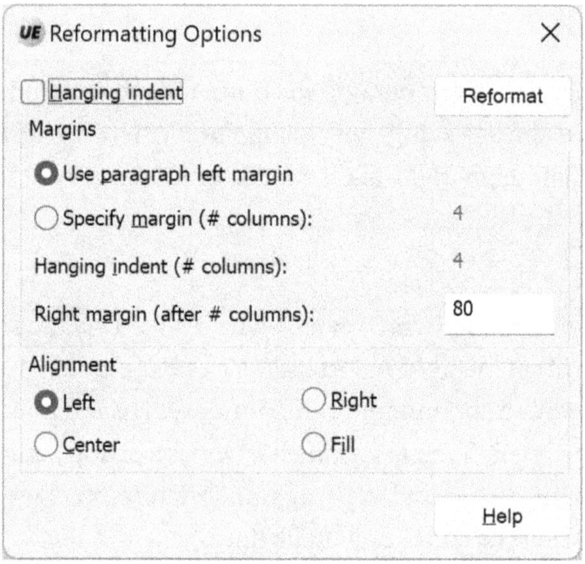

Figure 8-13. *Reformatting Options dialog*

- Hanging indent: This applies to the left alignment only. If enabled, the alignment will allow a second margin to be specified that is used for the second and successive lines of a paragraph. This causes the first line of a paragraph to be indented with one setting and the rest of the paragraph to have a different setting. If this is set, the hanging indent value may be entered in the dialog.

- Margins – Use paragraph left margin: This instructs UltraEdit to use the existing left margin of the paragraph that is being reformatted rather than specifying a new margin value.

- Margins – Specify margin (# columns): This setting instructs UltraEdit to use the left margin value entered in the dialog as the indentation for the left margin when reformatting the paragraph.

- Hanging indent (# columns): The value here specified controls the indentation of the first line of the paragraph or text to be reformatted. This option is only available if the *Hanging indent* option is enabled.

- Margins – Right margin (after # columns): This setting specifies the right margin to be used when reformatting the paragraph. This is the last column number (starting at 1) at which text may be placed.

The dialog allows the user to align the paragraph using the methods *Left Align*, *Center Align*, *Right Align*, and *Fill*. These alignment functions can also be accessed separately via icons (Ribbon mode) or menu items (both Contemporary and Traditional menu modes).

Align Paragraphs

The alignment commands, which can be accessed separately via icons or menu items, are described below:

- Left Align: Text will be left aligned against the left margin and will not extend past the right margin.

- Center Align: Text will be centered between the left and right margins.

- Right Align: Text will be right aligned against the right margin and will not extend past the left margin.

- Fill: Text will be aligned between the right and left margins with spaces added between words to ensure alignment to both margins. The last line of the paragraph will be aligned only to the left margin.

Find

UltraEdit includes very flexible and powerful search functions that go far beyond the normal functionality of a text editor. At the same time, there is the *Goto* command and the bookmarks concept to round off this chapter.

Every editor has a more or less good search function to search for text, numbers, and characters. UltraEdit has integrated so many flexible options for this functionality that it will warrant an extensive explanation; but it is a worthwhile investment as it provides the user with extremely powerful tools for their daily usage. We would like to describe the functionality in the following text and use various practical examples to show why the search functions of UltraEdit are considered so outstanding by many users.

Quick Find

Quick Find is the function that is intended for quick lookups and can be opened using the key combination Ctrl+F. This opens a small box in the top right-hand corner, which is helpful if the user wants to search quickly without using the large/normal search function (see Figure 8-14).

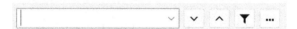

Figure 8-14. *Quick Find fly-out box*

The user can close Quick Find by either pressing the Escape key or by activating the normal Find dialog (if the Find dialog is in a floating state). Escape will always close Quick Find, even if focus is elsewhere in the application. Quick Find takes precedence over the Output Window (which is also closed with Escape).

It is particularly practical that UltraEdit enters the word at the position of the cursor in the search field by default. The Quick Find dialog contains the following elements:

- Search edit field: With focus on the Quick Find input, the user can begin typing a string, and UltraEdit will perform an incremental search as each character is typed. This is a basic character-to-character search; advanced functions such as regular expressions, case matching, and whole word matching are not available via Quick Find. Special characters via "^" are supported, however (^t, ^n, ^p, etc.).

- Find next: The user can move to the next occurrence of the search string by either pressing Enter while the Quick Find still has focus or by clicking the "Next" button next to the input field. If the user presses Enter to go to the next occurrence, focus will remain in the Quick Find so that the user can repeatedly press Enter to step through each match.

- Find previous: The user can move to the previous occurrence of the search string by either pressing Ctrl+Enter while the Quick Find still has focus, or by clicking the "Prev" button.

- Filter: The filter command reduces the display to only those lines that contain the search term.

- Expand to Find dialog: The user can expand to the Find dialog either by pressing the hotkey for it or by pressing the "Expand" button. If the user expands to the Find dialog while focus is in the Quick Find dialog, then the Find dialog will inherit the search string the user provided in the Quick Find dialog, overriding any existing behavior in regard to selected text/word under caret. Once the normal Find dialog is opened, the Quick Find will close, regardless of whether or not it has focus.

There are a few more tips and tricks for maximizing efficiency when using Quick Find:

- Match highlighting: As the user types the search string, the first/active match is selected (as with Find Next from a Find dialog). All other matches are highlighted with the "Highlight all items" color specified within the active theme. All match highlighting is cleared when the user closes the Quick Find dialog. The active match selection is not cleared when the user closes the Quick Find dialog, but remains selected.

- Returning focus back to Quick Find: If the Quick Find dialog has been left open and focus is elsewhere in the application, pressing the keyboard shortcut for Quick Find will not close it but instead move focus back to it.

- Interaction with existing Find Next/Previous: Any search strings entered via Quick Find are not added to UltraEdit's Find Next/Prev (F3/Ctrl + F3) histories.

- Status bar feedback: The leftmost portion of the status bar indicates how many matches are found as each incremental search via Quick Find is executed in the following format:

Find "searched text" – 123 matches

Note   The key combination Ctrl+F can be changed in the UltraEdit settings. To do this, the user needs to go to the *Key mapping* category in the UltraEdit settings and select *Quick find* in the list. The existing key combinations are displayed in the right area, and a new combination can be defined directly below (see Figure 8-15).

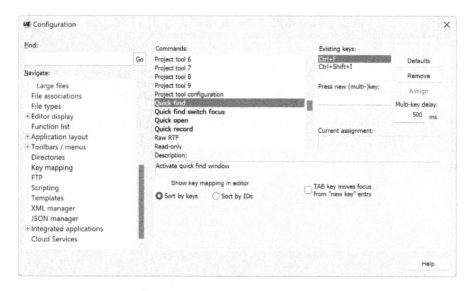

Figure 8-15. *UltraEdit settings with the key mapping of the Quick find function*

Find

The actual search is handled in UltraEdit via the *Find and Replace* dialog, which is displayed with four tabs at the top: *Find, Replace, Find in Files*, and *Replace in Files*.

This dialog can be launched via the menu, the ribbon icons, and various keyboard shortcuts, whereby the desired tab is preselected depending on the key combination:

- Find – keyboard shortcut Alt+F3: Comprehensive search for strings

- Replace – keyboard shortcut Ctrl+R: Replaces search results in Find

- Find in Files – keyboard shortcut Ctrl+Shift+F: Finds functionality in chosen files or directory

- Replace in Files – keyboard shortcut Ctrl+Shift+R: Replaces functionality in chosen files or directory

Figure 8-16 shows the *Find and Replace* dialog in its standard display, whereby the word located at the cursor is automatically transferred to the search field.

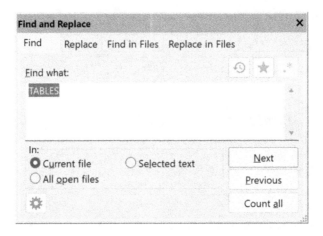

Figure 8-16. *Find and Replace dialog*

The search parameters are as extensive as the user wants them to be. In the default setting, the dialog shows basic functions. By using the gear symbol at the bottom, the advanced search options can be opened (see Figure 8-17).

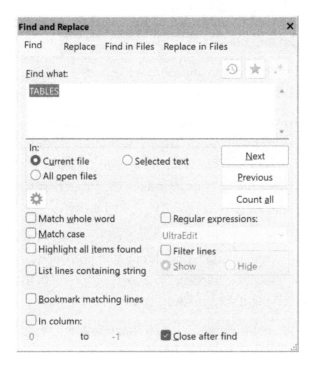

Figure 8-17. *Find and Replace dialog with its advanced options*

Three further keyboard shortcuts are additionally quite helpful to navigate through the search results (these functions are also available via buttons):

- F3: Find the next result.

- Ctrl+F3: Find the previous result.

- Shift+F3: Select all text from the current cursor position to the next matching search string.

What seems very obvious here is the *Find what* section. The search term is entered in this field.

There are three additional symbol buttons at the top right, which conceal powerful functions:

- Circle with clock inside: Shows a history of all previous search terms for possible reuse.

- Yellow star: Allows to define favorites that can be loaded for quick reuse. The context menu contains the menu items *Add to favorites*, *Edit favorites*, and *Favorites* – the last item contains the saved favorites in a selectable list.

- Green star and dot: Can be selected as soon as the option *Regular expressions* is enabled and opens a list of regular expression options appropriate to the selected regular expression engine.

The *In* section defines the used search parameters, which includes current/all open files or the selected text.

By default, the search will not be restricted to matching whole words only. The *Match whole word* option allows the search to be restricted to whole words only. This is useful for searching for "a" or "A" without finding all words including "a". If a search has already occurred in a document, the default selection will match the previous search.

With the *Match case* option and by default, the search will not be case sensitive. If a search has already occurred in the document, the default selection for case sensitivity is that of the previous search. This option also affects regular expressions. If this is disabled, [A-Za-z] and [A-Z] are equal to [a-z].

One feature that is often used is the highlighting of all matches found. When source code is written, as in the following screenshot in Object Pascal/Delphi, and the option *Highlight all items found* is enabled, all hits found are highlighted in color, which gives a better overview of where further adjustments may be necessary (see Figure 8-18).

Figure 8-18. *Find option for highlighting all items found*

The option *List lines containing string* is also extremely useful, whereby a new result dialog with the string matches is displayed after the search. By double-clicking on a line, UltraEdit jumps directly to the respective line. This option is very similar to the Microsoft Word search function, for example, whose results navigation is often appreciated, and many users are pleased that UltraEdit also makes this possible.

Regular expressions and the same-called option are also an important major topic in all kinds of searches and can be enabled here. UltraEdit also supports them extensively, and they will be described in more detail later in this chapter.

If the *Filter lines* option is enabled, the *Show* and *Hide* radio buttons become active and control what text is displayed in the file after the search is completed. By selecting the *Show* radio button, only lines matching the specified search string will be displayed in the active file. All non-matching lines will be hidden using code folding. By using the *Hide* radio button, all lines matching the specified search string will be hidden in the active file using code folding.

The option *Bookmark matching lines* allows the user to bookmark lines containing a particular string, then copy, cut, or delete them from the file. If the user wishes to remove bookmarks added by a search but still keep the other bookmarks, he can do this with the *Clear Find bookmarks* command. This command can be used via the *Home* tab ➤ *Bookmarks* ➤ *Clear Find bookmarks* (Ribbon mode), *Home* ➤ *Bookmarks* ➤ *Clear Find bookmarks* (Contemporary menu mode), or *Search* ➤ *Bookmarks* ➤ *Clear Find bookmarks* (Traditional menu mode).

By using the *In column* option, the search will be restricted to the specified start and end columns. The number specified for the end column must be greater than the number specified for the start column (except when searching an entire line). To search an entire line, "0" and "-1" should be used. It is important to note that column numbering begins with "0" so the initial column value would have to be set to "0" to search from the beginning of a line.

The last Find option is called *Close after find*, and if enabled, and a matching string is found when Next is pressed, the Find dialog is closed.

Replace

If we move from the classic *Find* function of text/code to the *Replace* function, the basic functionality is retained and in a simple sense is supplemented by a second string that replaces the search string. UltraEdit offers in the *Replace* tab the same basic functionality and extends it with the function buttons (see Figure 8-19).

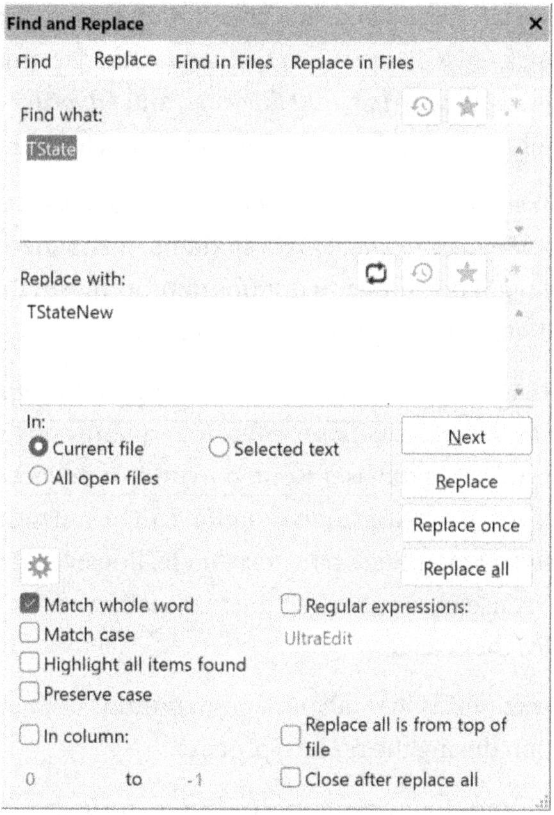

Figure 8-19. *Find and Replace dialog with the Replace function opened*

What is also very obvious here are the input fields *Find what* and *Replace with*. The search term is entered in the first input field and the term to be replaced in the second.

There are three additional symbol buttons for the *Find what* input field and four additional symbol buttons for the *Replace with* input field – all of them conceal powerful functions:

- Circle with clock inside: Shows a history of all previous search terms for possible reuse.

- Yellow star: Allows to define favorites that can be loaded for quick reuse. The context menu contains the menu items *Add to favorites*, *Edit favorites*, and *Favorites* – the last item contains the saved favorites in a selectable list.

- Green star and dot: Can be selected as soon as the option *Regular expressions* is enabled and opens a list of regular expression options appropriate to the selected regular expression engine.

- Two black arrows: Swaps the two strings of the *Find what* and *Replace with* sections. A frequently observed scenario is that the user wanted to undo a replaced string, for which the undo function can of course also be used. Depending on the text/code, however, it may make sense to simply swap the two sections and then replace them again.

The window contains in total four action buttons on the right-hand side for navigation during the replace process:

- Next: Jumps to the next occurrence of the text entered in the "Find what" section

- Replace: Replaces the string from the *Find what* section with the string from the *Replace with* section (keeps the *Find and Replace* dialog permanently open)

- Replace once: Replaces the searched string from the *Find what* section with the string from the *Replace with* section once (closes the *Find and Replace* dialog afterward)

- Replace all: Replaces all occurrences of the searched string from the *Find what* section with the string from the *Replace with* section (keeps the *Find and Replace* dialog permanently open)

The *In* section defines the used search parameters, which includes current/all open files or the selected text.

By default, the search will not be restricted to matching whole words only. The *Match whole word* option allows the search to be restricted to whole words only. This is useful for searching for "a" or "A" without finding all words including "a". If a search has already occurred in a document, the default selection will match the previous search.

With the *Match case* option and by default, the search will not be case sensitive. If a search has already occurred in the document, the default selection for case sensitivity is that of the previous search. This option also affects regular expressions. If this is disabled, [A-Za-z] and [A-Z] are equal to [a-z].

One feature that is often used is the highlighting of all matches found. When text or source code is written and the option *Highlight all items found* is enabled, all hits found are highlighted in color, which gives a better overview of where further adjustments may be necessary.

Also relevant for the *Replace* function and always very helpful is the option *Preserve case*. This power function causes UltraEdit to match the case of the replace string with the case of the found string with the condition of multiple rules:

- If the word found is all lowercase, the replacement word will be all lowercase.

- If the word found is all UPPERCASE, the replacement word will be all UPPERCASE.

- If the word found is MixedCase, the replacement word will match the casing of the replacement word.

Let's illustrate this function with an example from the Embarcadero Delphi world. A corresponding click event is created for a button on a form, and the procedure *Button1Click* is called as soon as the button is clicked. If we now enter "Button1Click" in the *Find* section and "ButtonActionClick" in the *Replace* section, the following for all occurrences happens:

- "button1click" will be replaced with "buttonactionclick".

- "BUTTON1CLICK" will be replaced with "BUTTONACTIONCLICK".

- "Button1Click" will be replaced with "ButtonActionClick".

Regular expressions and the same-called option are also an important major topic in all kinds of searches and can be enabled here. UltraEdit also supports them extensively, and they will be described in more detail later in this chapter.

By using the *In column* option, the search will be restricted to the specified start and end columns. The number specified for the end column must be greater than the number specified for the start column (except when searching an entire line). To search an entire line, "0" and "-1" should be used. It is important to note that column numbering begins with "0" so the initial column value would have to be set to "0" to search from the beginning of a line.

When the option *Replace all is from top of file* is enabled, the specified search will be executed from the top of the active file rather than the current cursor position.

The last replace option is called *Close after replace all*, and if enabled, the *Replace* dialog will automatically be closed after a *Replace all* is executed.

Find in Files

Now that we have talked in detail about finding and replacing in the currently open file/document, we come to the supreme discipline, namely, finding and replacing in complete files and directories.

This functionality is already known from various IDEs (Integrated Development Environments), such as Microsoft Visual Studio and Embarcadero RAD Studio, where it is used to search projects or entire project groups across multiple files, folders, and even drives.

UltraEdit's professionalism is now emphasized by providing this powerful feature of IDEs in a text editor, and we will take a closer look at it in Figure 8-20.

Figure 8-20. *Find and Replace dialog with the Find in Files function opened*

What seems very obvious here is the *Find what* section. The search term is entered in this field.

There are three additional symbol buttons at the top right, which conceal powerful functions:

- Circle with clock inside: Shows a history of all previous search terms for possible reuse.

- Yellow star: Allows to define favorites that can be loaded for quick reuse. The context menu contains the menu items *Add to favorites*, *Edit favorites*, and *Favorites* – the last item contains the saved favorites in a selectable list.

- Green star and dot: Can be selected as soon as the option *Regular expressions* is enabled and opens a list of regular expression options appropriate to the selected regular expression engine.

What is immediately noticeable here is the adjusted search focus in the *In* section, where the default setting is the *Files listed* option – this searches the files located in the two edit fields below: *In files/types* and *Directory*. While the *Directory* field can accept a directory either in text form, via the *Use active file path* button, or via the *Browse* button next to it, the upper field *In files/types* can be used to specify either individual files or wildcards. Multiple entries are separated by a semicolon, and three typical examples might look like this:

- *.pas;*.cpp
- Testfile.txt;*.cpp;*.h
- *.pas;TestForm.frm;*.dfm

In these examples, wildcards and named file names are mixed, which UltraEdit can easily handle when the semicolon is used as a separator.

Further *In* section options are available for open files, favorite files (*Application Menu ➤ Favorite Files*), and project files – the latter searches all files within a currently open project. These three options ignore the edit fields *In files/types* and *Directory*, as these are only used with the *Files listed* option.

Before we get to the actual search with the *Find* button, we would like to discuss the options below.

By default, the search will not be restricted to matching whole words only. The *Match whole word* option allows the search to be restricted to whole words only. This is useful for searching for "a" or "A" without finding all words including "a". If a search has already occurred in a document, the default selection will match the previous search.

With the *Match case* option and by default, the search will not be case sensitive. If a search has already occurred in the document, the default selection for case sensitivity is that of the previous search. This option also affects regular expressions. If this is disabled, [A-Za-z] and [A-Z] are equal to [a-z].

Via the option *Results to edit window*, UltraEdit will create an edit window (new file) for the results of the find. This allows editing of the results, saving, or printing the results. The default action is to capture the output in a list box window (Output Window) that allows the user to double-click on the result and have the file opened automatically.

When the *Interactive results* option is enabled, the *Find in Files* search will open a new *Interactive results* document. In this window, all the *Find in Files* results are returned, but these results are immediately editable and the user doesn't have to take intermediate steps to open matched files to edit the string that was searched for. This is effectively a window into the relevant portions of each matched file, and the users may edit results individually as desired (see Figure 8-21).

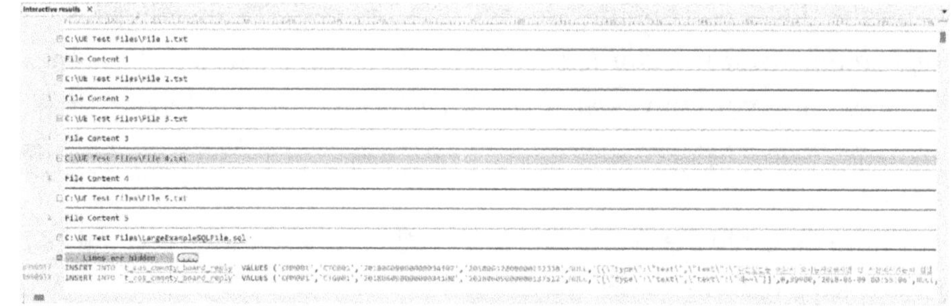

Figure 8-21. *Interactive results window from the Find in Files function*

If preferred and once the *Interactive results* document is opened, the user may switch to the *Replace* tab in the *Find and Replace* dialog. When focus is on the *Interactive results* document, the *All open files* option in the *Replace* dialog is dynamically changed to *All results*. If this option is selected, the user can use the replace operation interactively by pressing the *Replace* button or use *Replace all* to replace all matched strings in all files listed in the *Interactive results* document. When *All results* is selected in the *Replace* dialog, no other open files will be affected by the *Replace all* operation.

When direct editing of the results (either by typing or replace operations) is done, the user may close the *Interactive results* document. When the document is closed, a prompt appears asking whether the changes should be saved – changes would then be saved for all modified documents listed in the *Interactive results* document. This additional intermediate layer provides a clear way of keeping track of things, especially if there are many files that need to be changed.

The feature *For each match, show __ lines before __ lines after* allows the user to see the *Find in Files* results with any given number of lines before and after to provide context. By default, each of these values is set to "2", and when a matching line is found, two lines before and after the matching line are returned as well. To disable this, the values for "lines before" and "lines after" both need to be set to 0.

Regular expressions and the same-called option are also an important major topic in all kinds of searches and can be enabled here. UltraEdit also supports them extensively, and they will be described in more detail later in this chapter.

By using the *Match files/lines if string is not found* option, this will instruct UltraEdit to list only files that do not include the specified search string. The *lines* radio button instructs UltraEdit to list each individual line that does not match the search parameters. Whereas the files option only lists files that do not include the specified search string, this option returns data on a line-by-line basis.

Search subdirectories is also an important Find option, because by default, only files specified in the specified directory are searched. This option instructs UltraEdit to search all subdirectories of the specified directory. If the *Ignore hidden subdirectories* option is selected, then subdirectories which are hidden (as defined in Microsoft Explorer) will not be included in the search – multiple names should be separated by a semicolon. The user may also specify subdirectories, file names, or extensions which should be ignored in the edit fields *Subdirectories to ignore in search* and *File names/extensions to ignore in search*. For example, the text "*.cpp;index.*;" would instruct the search not to match files with a "*.cpp" extension or files that are named "index" (regardless of extension).

By using the *Open matching files* option, any files matching the specified parameters will be opened when the search completes.

The last option is called *Use encoding* and is disabled by default. When enabled, the drop-down may be used to specify the encoding to be used when searching for the specified string.

After all these options, the *Find* button closes the *Find and Replace* dialog, the search is then performed, and all results are displayed in the *Output Window* below. The respective files can be opened in the *Output Window* by double-clicking on the line with the file name. Anyone who is familiar with the *Output Window* will know that there are many more options available in a context menu via the right mouse button. These include collapsing/expanding the entire window content and copying the content to the clipboard. Figure 8-22 shows a possible display of this window.

Figure 8-22. *Output Window with the results of the Find in Files search function*

Replace in Files

The fourth major search function is *Replace in Files*, and here the *Replace* function is used in connection with listed files (names and wildcards as well as directories), favorite files, or project files. Please see at Figure 8-23 for this function.

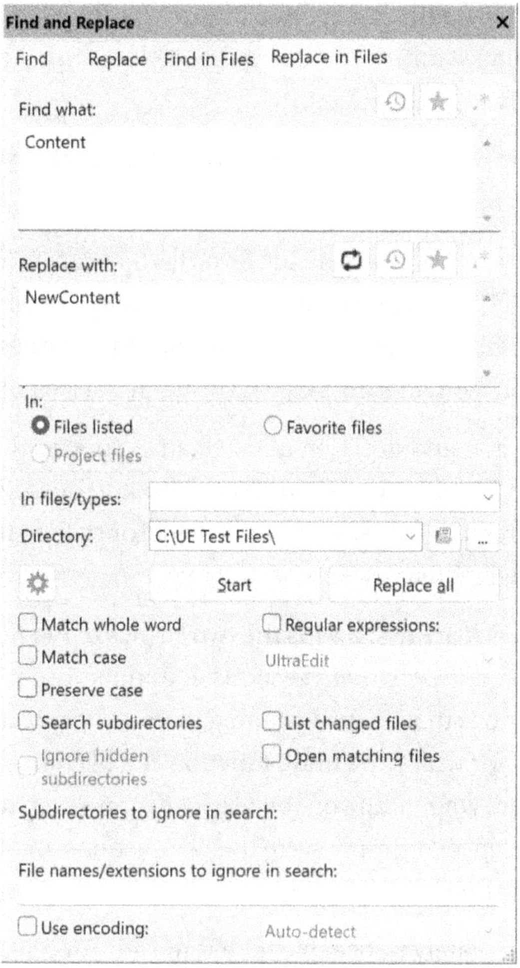

Figure 8-23. *Find and Replace dialog with the Replace in Files function opened*

What is also very obvious here are the input fields *Find what* and *Replace with*. The search term is entered in the first input field and the term to be replaced in the second.

There are three additional symbol buttons for the *Find what* input field and four additional symbol buttons for the *Replace with* input field – all of them conceal powerful functions:

- Circle with clock inside: Shows a history of all previous search terms for possible reuse.

- Yellow star: Allows to define favorites that can be loaded for quick reuse. The context menu contains the menu items *Add to favorites*, *Edit favorites*, and *Favorites* – the last item contains the saved favorites in a selectable list.

- Green star and dot: Can be selected as soon as the option *Regular expressions* is enabled and opens a list of regular expression options appropriate to the selected regular expression engine.

- Two black arrows: Swaps the two strings of the *Find what* and *Replace with* sections. A frequently observed scenario is that the user wanted to undo a replaced string, for which the undo function can of course also be used. Depending on the text/code, however, it may make sense to simply swap the two sections and then replace them again.

What is immediately noticeable here is the adjusted search focus in the *In* section, where the default setting is the *Files listed* option – this searches the files located in the two edit fields below: *In files/types* and *Directory*. While the *Directory* field can accept a directory either in text form, via the *Use active file path* button, or via the *Browse* button next to it, the upper field *In files/types* can be used to specify either individual files or wildcards. Multiple entries are separated by a semicolon, and we have already described three typical examples in the "Find in Files" section above. Further *In* section options are available for favorite files (*Application Menu* ➤ *Favorite Files*) and project files – the latter searches all files within a currently open project. These two options ignore the edit fields *In files/ types* and *Directory*, as these are only used with the *Files listed* option.

Before we get to the actual find and replace process with the *Start* and *Replace all* buttons, we would like to discuss the options below.

By default, the search will not be restricted to matching whole words only. The *Match whole word* option allows the search to be restricted to whole words only. This is useful for searching for "a" or "A" without finding all words including "a". If a search has already occurred in a document, the default selection will match the previous search.

With the *Match case* option and by default, the search will not be case sensitive. If a search has already occurred in the document, the default selection for case sensitivity is that of the previous search. This option also affects regular expressions. If this is disabled, [A-Za-z] and [A-Z] are equal to [a-z].

Also relevant for the *Replace in Files* function and always very helpful is the option *Preserve case*. This power function causes UltraEdit to match the case of the replaced string with the case of the found string with the condition of multiple rules:

- If the word found is all lowercase, the replacement word will be all lowercase.

- If the word found is all UPPERCASE, the replacement word will be all UPPERCASE.

- If the word found is MixedCase, the replacement word will match the casing of the replacement word.

Search subdirectories is also an important Replace option, because by default, only files in the specified directory are searched. This option instructs UltraEdit to search all subdirectories of the specified directory. If the *Ignore hidden subdirectories* option is selected, then subdirectories which are hidden (as defined in Microsoft Explorer) will not be included in the search – multiple names should be separated by a semicolon. The user may also specify subdirectories, file names, or extensions which should be ignored in the edit fields *Subdirectories to ignore in search* and *File names/ extensions to ignore in search*. For example, the text "*.cpp;index.*;" would instruct the search not to match files with a "*.cpp" extension or files that are named "index" (regardless of extension).

Regular expressions and the same-called option are also an important major topic in all kinds of searches and can be enabled here. UltraEdit also supports them extensively, and they will be described in more detail later in this chapter.

With the option *List changed files*, UltraEdit is going to list all the files that were modified in the *Output Window*. If enabled, each file change will be listed in the *Output Window* followed by the number of occurrences found and changed.

By using the *Open matching files* option, any files matching the specified parameters will be opened when the search completes.

The last option is called *Use encoding* and is disabled by default. When enabled, the drop-down may be used to specify the encoding to be used when searching for the specified string.

The window contains two action buttons at the bottom (when the dialog is collapsed ➤ gear symbol) or in the middle (when the dialog is expanded ➤ gear symbol) for the control of the replace process:

- Start: Starts the *Replace* process with the first found occurrence and prompts the user before modifying a file where the string is found. It does not open the file and allows the user to review it, but it does give the user the ability to skip the replacement on a file-by-file basis. This provides more granular control over the second button, which is described next.

- Replace all: Replaces all occurrences of the searched string from the *Find what* section with the string from the *Replace with* section without any prompts for user interaction after the standard warning prompt is displayed.

Regular Expressions

Regular expressions have been widely used for many years, and once the user has understood the principle, they will never want to miss them again. In UltraEdit, the option to activate regular expressions is available in all four tabs of the *Find and Replace* dialog. Once activated, it can be chosen between three different expression types:

- Perl: UltraEdit uses Perl style regular expressions based on the Boost C++ libraries.

- UltraEdit: UltraEdit uses its own style regular expressions.

- Unix: UltraEdit uses Unix style regular expressions.

Regular expressions are search strings where certain characters (symbols) have a special meaning. The following symbols and associated functions exist in the original UltraEdit syntax (please note that the colon after each symbol is not part of the symbol itself but only serves as a technical separation):

- %: Matches the start of line – this indicates the search string must be at the beginning of a line but does not include any line terminator characters in the resulting string selected.

- $: Matches the end of line – this indicates the search string must be at the end of line but does not include any line terminator characters in the resulting string selected.

- ?: Matches any single character except newline.

- *: Matches any number of occurrences of any character except newline.

- +: Matches one or more of the preceding single character/character set, where at least one occurrence of the character must be found.

- ++: Matches the preceding single character/character set zero or more times.

- ^b: Matches a page break.

- ^p: Matches a newline (CR/LF) (paragraph) (DOS files).

- ^r: Matches a newline (CR Only) (paragraph) (Mac files).

- ^n: Matches a newline (LF Only) (paragraph) (Unix files).

- ^t: Matches a tab character.

- [xyz]: Matches any characters between brackets (a character set).

- [~xyz]: Matches any characters not between brackets including newline characters (a negative character set).

- ^{A^}^{B^}: Matches expression A or B.

- ^: Overrides the following regular expression character.

- ^(...^): Brackets or tags an expression to use in the replace command. A regular expression may have up to nine tagged expressions, numbered according to their order in the regular expression.

  The corresponding replacement expression is ^x, for x in the range 1-9.

  Example:

  If ^(h*o^) ^(f*s^) matches "hello folks", ^2 ^1 would replace it with "folks hello".

These symbols and associated functions result in many examples, some of which are described below to give an idea of how they are used:

- m?n matches "man", "men", and "min" but not "moon".

- t*t matches "test", "tonight", and "tea time" (the "tea t" portion) but not 'tea

  time' (newline between "tea " and "time").

- Te+st matches "test", "teest", "teeeest", etc., but does not match "tst".

- [aeiou] matches every lowercase vowel with enabled match case option.

- [,.?] matches a literal ",", ".", or "?".

- [0-9a-z] matches any digit, or lowercase letter with enabled match case option.

- [~0-9] matches any character except a digit (~ means not the following).

The user can search for an expression A or B as follows:

"^{John^}^{Tom^}"

This will search for an occurrence of John or Tom – there should be nothing between the two expressions.

The user can combine A or B and C or D in the same search as follows:

"^{John^}^{Tom^} ^{Smith^}^{Jones^}"

This will search for John or Tom followed by Smith or Jones.

Tip   There are many helpful websites on the Internet for regular expressions, but we would like to recommend the website www. regex101.com at this point. Here the user can actively learn and fill the page with regular expressions and a test string. This is the basis for the explanation, which is supplemented by various match information and a quick reference.

The recommendation here is to actively use this page as a learning aid and to familiarize yourself with the handling once. The result is much more practical than just imparting theoretical knowledge, as the user can actively carry out exercises and receive extensive explanations of the regular expressions.

Goto

The *Goto* command has been used in text editors and development environments for over 30 years and is implemented to varying degrees depending on the manufacturer. UltraEdit follows a relatively straightforward intuitive approach and opens the *Go To* dialog either from the *Home* tab – *Goto* (Ribbon mode), *Home* ➤ *Goto* (Contemporary menu mode), and *Search* ➤ *Goto* (Traditional menu mode) – or via the keyboard shortcut Ctrl+G (see Figure 8-24).

Figure 8-24. *UltraEdit's Go To dialog*

This dialog allows the user to specify the line/column number, page break, or bookmark at which the cursor should be positioned. Users may also specify relative positions if desired. For example, "+6" would cause the caret to be positioned 6 lines below its current position, and "-8" would cause the caret to be positioned 8 lines prior to its current position.

- Page break: The cursor is positioned at the line with the specified page break character.

- Line/column: The cursor is positioned at the line/column specified, and the line is scrolled into view. Two additional conditions apply here:

  - If the line number is greater than the number of lines in the file, the cursor is positioned at the end of the file.

  - If the column number is greater than the number of columns in the file, the cursor is positioned at the end of the specified line.

- Bookmark: The cursor is positioned at the line with the specified bookmark.

When the Shift key is pressed at the same time as performing the *Goto* command, the current selection (if present) or a new selection will be extended to select text up to the cursor position following the command.

If UltraEdit is in hex mode, the *Go To* dialog allows the user to select the offset into the file at which the cursor should be positioned (see Figure 8-25). Should the offset be greater than the file size, the cursor is positioned at the end of the file.

Figure 8-25. *Goto dialog in UltraEdit's hex mode*

Bookmarks

Bookmarks are a common concept in many editors, development environments, and also Internet browsers, because they make it possible to find marked positions quickly. UltraEdit allows setting bookmarks to mark a position in a file. Once a bookmark has been set at a line, it may use menu or keyboard commands to move to that line.

By default, the column position is bookmarked with the line so that when jumping to the bookmarked line, the caret is positioned at the bookmarked column as well. This behavior can be changed in the UltraEdit settings in the category *Editor* ➤ *Bookmarks*.

Bookmarked lines are visually represented by a highlighted line number background, or the entire line depending upon the bookmark settings.

The UltraEdit bookmark commands are accessible via the *Home* tab – *Bookmarks* (Ribbon mode), *Home* ➤ *Bookmarks* (Contemporary menu mode), *Search* ➤ *Bookmarks* (Traditional menu mode), and the context menu of the *Bookmark Viewer*.

Bookmark Gutter and Bookmark Viewer

The bookmark gutter is displayed to the right of line numbers and to the left of the folding gutter. When this function is enabled, it toggles the gutter.

The bookmark gutter can be enabled via the *Layout* tab – *Bookmark gutter* (Ribbon mode), *Layout* ➤ *Bookmark gutter* (Contemporary menu mode), and *View* ➤ *Display bookmark gutter* (Traditional menu mode). A separate context menu includes the following options, which we will discuss in more detail later:

- Toggle bookmark: Toggles the bookmark at the current line

- Edit bookmark name: Shows the *Edit bookmark* dialog where bookmark names may be added or removed

- Hide bookmark gutter: Hides the bookmark gutter

- Clear all bookmarks: Removes all bookmarks from the active document

- Edit bookmarks...: Opens the *Edit bookmark* dialog

- Copy all bookmarked lines: Copies all bookmarked lines in the active file to the clipboard

- Cut all bookmarked lines: Cuts all bookmarked lines in the active file to the clipboard

- Delete all bookmarked lines: Removes all bookmarked lines from the active file

- Open bookmark viewer: Opens the *Bookmark Viewer* dockable window

The *Bookmark Viewer* displays all bookmarks currently specified for the active document. If no bookmarks are defined, the list will display "No Bookmarks".

The display can be toggled via the *Layout tab* – *Bookmarks* (Ribbon mode), *Layout* ➤ *Bookmarks* (Contemporary menu mode), and *View* ➤ *Views/lists* ➤ *Lists* ➤ *Bookmark viewer* (Traditional menu mode). An example of this can be seen in Figure 8-26.

Line ^	Col	Name	Text from file		
3	0	Test 3	03. Number	First Name	Second Name
6	0	Test 6	06. Number	First Name	Second Name
9	0	Test 9	09. Number	First Name	Second Name

Bookmark Viewer

Figure 8-26. *Bookmark Viewer with three bookmarks*

Double-clicking on a line jumps directly to the corresponding bookmark. Right-clicking on the column headers will present a pop-up menu where the user can select the column headers they wish to be visible in the *Bookmark Viewer*. If the option *Column Order* is enabled at the bottom of this context menu, a dialog is displayed where the user can specify the order in which columns should be displayed in the *Bookmark Viewer* (see Figure 8-27).

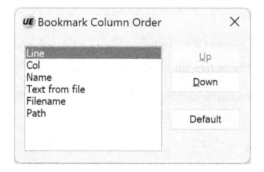

Figure 8-27. *Bookmark Column Order dialog*

Right-clicking in the *Bookmark Viewer* opens the context menu which includes the following options – we will discuss them in more detail later:

- List bookmarks for all files: Displays list of bookmarks in all open files. If this option is selected, the name of the file the bookmark exists in will also be displayed.

- Delete bookmarks: Deletes currently selected bookmark(s).

- Copy all bookmarked lines: Copies all bookmarked lines in the active file to the clipboard.

- Cut all bookmarked lines: Cuts all bookmarked lines in the active file to the clipboard.

- Delete all bookmarked lines: Deletes all bookmarked lines in the active file.

- Edit bookmark: Opens the *Edit Bookmark* dialog where the name of the bookmark can be edited.

Toggle Bookmark

This command and the commands from the following sections are accessible via the *Home* tab – *Bookmarks* (Ribbon mode), *Home* ➤ *Bookmark* (Contemporary menu mode), and *Search* ➤ *Bookmarks* (Traditional menu mode).

The *Toggle bookmark* command sets a bookmark to mark a position in a file. Once a bookmark has been set at a line, the user can use menu or keyboard commands to move to that line. Please note that the user can also toggle a bookmark gutter, precisely, whereupon the cursor will change to reflect a bookmark.

The cursor must be positioned in the line in which the bookmark is to be placed. Then the *Toggle bookmark* command is invoked. This command can alternatively be used with the keyboard shortcut Ctrl+F2.

In Figure 8-28, from our previous Column mode example, we have set bookmarks in lines 3, 6, and 9, which is reflected by the colored marking in the line number.

Column Mode Example.txt ✕			
1	01. Number	First Name	Second Name
2	02. Number	First Name	Second Name
3	03. Number	First Name	Second Name
4	04. Number	First Name	Second Name
5	05. Number	First Name	Second Name
6	06. Number	First Name	Second Name
7	07. Number	First Name	Second Name
8	08. Number	First Name	Second Name
9	09. Number	First Name	Second Name
10	10. Number	First Name	Second Name
11			

Figure 8-28. Bookmarks in lines 3, 6, and 9

Clear All Bookmarks

The *Clear all bookmarks* command removes all the bookmarks from the active file. This happens without any further confirmation and has an immediate effect on the bookmarks.

Clear Find Bookmarks

Find bookmarks can be added by using the *Bookmark matching lines* option within the *Find* dialog. This allows the user to bookmark lines containing a particular string, then copy, cut, or delete them from the file.

The *Clear Find bookmarks* command removes bookmarks added by a previous search but still keeps all other bookmarks intact and undamaged.

Edit Bookmarks

The *Edit bookmarks* command opens the *Edit Bookmark* dialog, where a bookmark in the selected row can be assigned a name, or that name can be renamed or deleted (see Figure 8-29).

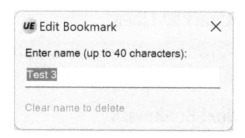

Figure 8-29. *Edit Bookmark dialog*

The purpose of these bookmark names is to use them in the *Bookmark Viewer* and the *Go To* dialog, where the user can also jump to bookmarks, and we will discuss this functionality in a moment. The bookmark name allows a clearer assignment of the line, which is particularly helpful when there are many lines.

At the same time, the name can be changed in the *Edit Bookmark* dialog or deleted using the *Clear name to delete* button at the bottom.

Copy All Bookmarked Lines

The *Copy all bookmarked lines* command copies all bookmarked lines in the active file to the clipboard.

This function is quite helpful if the user wants to copy certain lines from a file to the clipboard and then goes through the file line by line and activates the bookmarks using Ctrl+F2 in order to copy them collectively to the clipboard. From there, these lines can be re-inserted into UltraEdit or other applications for further processing.

Cut All Bookmarked Lines

The *Cut all bookmarked lines* command does almost the same as the *Copy all bookmarked lines* command, which means that it copies the bookmarked lines into the clipboard. The difference here is the cut command does not keep the copied lines at the original position but removes them and transfers them to the clipboard.

Delete All Bookmarked Lines

The *Delete all bookmarked lines* command removes all bookmarked lines from the active file.

Previous and Next Bookmark

Navigation through bookmarks can also be done using the *Previous Bookmark* and *Next Bookmark* commands. This automatically moves the line focus to the first position of the line with the previous or next bookmark.

The F2 key for the next bookmark and the keyboard shortcut Alt+F2 for the previous bookmark are particularly advantageous here. In conjunction with creating bookmarks using Ctrl+F2, the complete bookmark navigation can be achieved using the keyboard.

Also worth mentioning here in this context is the *Go To* dialog, in which bookmarks can be selected as jump marks (see Figure 8-30). In this case, the display in the middle of the dialog changes, with the active bookmarks appearing in the selection list and a name, if one has been set via the *Edit bookmarks* command. The listed bookmarks in this dialog start with a potential bookmark name, then *Ln* for line, and then the actual line number. This function also allows the user to jump to a specific bookmark very quickly and do everything with the keyboard if wished.

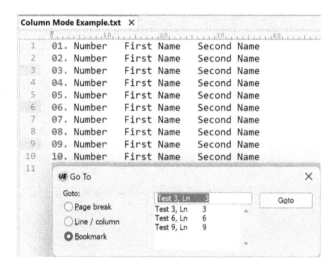

Figure 8-30. *Go To dialog with bookmarks selected and the display of bookmark names and lines*

Summary

We have discussed the various view functionalities, which include fonts, column markers, line change indicators, word wrap, highlight and selections, line folding, and various other text editing tools. Here the wide range of options can already be seen with something useful for every user type.

We have also described the format category, which provides a Reindent function, various conversions (such as upper- and lowercase as well as spaces to tabs and vice versa), two trim commands, and extensive paragraph reformatting functionality including setup and align options.

We have dealt with UltraEdit's search and replace functions that work either for individual files/documents or complete directory structures. Countless options allow the user to fine-tune the parameters and leave almost nothing to be desired. UltraEdit thus takes the step forward of providing much more powerful functions than many users are used to from a text editor. As a result of these options, productivity is increased and search and replace is as powerful as the user works with this functionality.

CHAPTER 9

More Powerful Functions

In this chapter, we would like to talk about some of the outstanding and advanced features of UltraEdit that every user should know about and that will significantly improve productivity.

We describe syntax highlighting for a visually improved view of source codes and web files, multi-caret editing for simultaneous editing at multiple caret positions, the Command palette as a complete overview of UltraEdit functions, FTP integration for editing remote files, the PowerShell terminal for automation, as well as the processing of very large files. The latter function is an enormous strength of UltraEdit with simultaneous flexibility and stability.

Syntax Highlighting

Syntax highlighting describes the color highlighting of certain words to increase readability, especially in source code during software development. This relatively widespread feature in text editors is also supported by UltraEdit, and we will look at the exact implementation below.

© Devid Espenschied 2025
D. Espenschied, *Mastering UltraEdit*, https://doi.org/10.1007/979-8-8688-1160-9_9

UltraEdit basically tries to recognize the programming language based on the file and then automatically selects the template for the syntax highlighting. An example of a C++ source code file can be found in Figure 9-1.

```
RelativePanel.cpp  ×
12   #include <vcl.h>
13   #pragma hdrstop
14   #include <tchar.h>
15   //--------------------------------------------------------------
16   USEFORM("uRelativePanel.cpp", RelativePanelForm);
17   //--------------------------------------------------------------
18   int WINAPI _tWinMain(HINSTANCE, HINSTANCE, LPTSTR, int)
19   {
20       try
21       {
22           Application->Initialize();
23           Application->MainFormOnTaskBar = true;
24           Application->Title = "TRelativePanel Demo";
25               Application->CreateForm(__classid(TRelativePanelForm), &RelativePanelForm);
26           Application->Run();
27       }
28       catch (Exception &exception)
29       {
30           Application->ShowException(&exception);
31       }
32       catch (...)
33       {
34           try
35           {
36               throw Exception("");
37           }
38           catch (Exception &exception)
39           {
40               Application->ShowException(&exception);
41           }
42       }
43       return 0;
44   }
45   //--------------------------------------------------------------
46
```

Figure 9-1. *Syntax highlighting for a C++ source code file*

The *Coding* tab (Ribbon mode), *Coding* menu (Contemporary menu mode), or *View* ➤ *View as (highlighting file type)* (Traditional menu mode) can be used to manually set the language type or install new ones. The language type can also be selected in the status bar.

The *Add another language* function opens the *Add and remove languages* dialog, which lists the languages that have already been installed and all optional additional languages (see Figure 9-2).

Figure 9-2. *Add and remove languages dialog*

The list of languages and associated file types shows that there are several hundred entries. This also shows how much effort and energy UltraEdit has invested in supporting as many programming languages and file types as possible. It is generally advisable to use the filter edit field at the top and type the language to be added. The appropriate entry with the link to the language file extension(s) will then appear. The language support is downloaded directly by activating this line with the check box at the beginning so that the programming language then appears in the active language list after the filter has been cleared with the *Clear* button.

Immediately after closing this window, syntax highlighting is already activated in UltraEdit for the newly added languages, if those files were already open or if new files are opened from now on.

Note   Behind every language within UltraEdit are so-called wordfiles, which are pure text configuration files. In addition to syntax highlighting, these files also contain definitions for other features such as code folding, brace matching, function listing, and more.

Multi-caret Editing

Multi-caret editing allows the user to activate two or more noncontiguous insertion points (identified by the blinking caret) within the active file. Each caret acts and operates independently of any other caret, and any edit operations the user executes are performed in all caret locations simultaneously.

This is an optional feature and may be disabled completely in the UltraEdit settings and the category *Editor Display* ➤ *Cursor/Caret*. The option is called *Enable multi-caret editing*. Please see Figure 9-3 to check if this function is already enabled.

Figure 9-3. *UltraEdit settings with the multi-caret editing option at the bottom*

Note   Multi-caret editing is not supported when Column mode or hex mode is active.

If we use our own Column mode example and use multi-caret editing to place the carets in the third column and the rows 2, 4, 6, 8, and 10, our output looks like Figure 9-4.

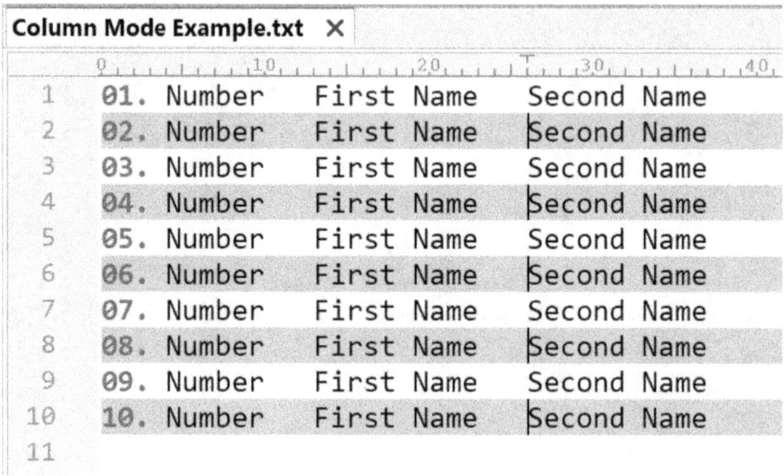

Figure 9-4. *Multi-caret editing in the third row of lines 2, 4, 6, 8, and 10*

The cursor blinks in these five selected lines as if it were a single cursor. If we now insert additional text (such as the word "My"), this word is inserted in all carets (see Figure 9-5).

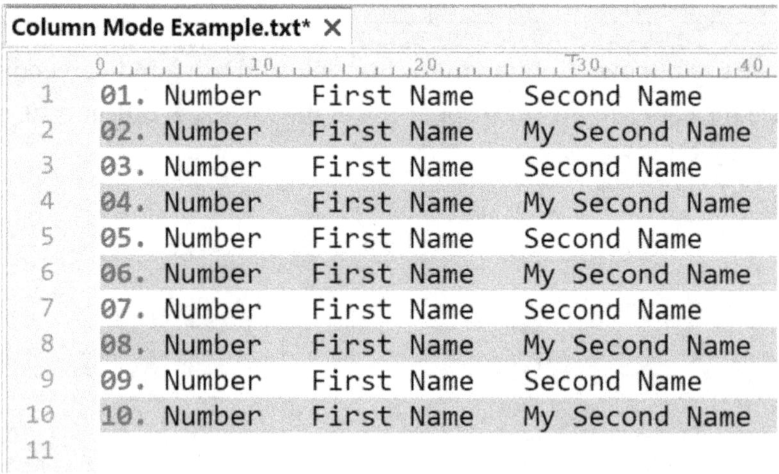

Figure 9-5. *Multi-caret editing after the insertion of the word "My" in lines 2, 4, 6, 8, and 10*

Tip   If the user wants to add text to different long lines at the same time, they need to select these lines and then press the Ctrl key and the mouse button in the free areas behind the selected lines, whereupon the caret is positioned at the end of each selected line and blinks. Now additional text can be entered, which affects each caret position and the selected lines.

Multi-caret via Mouse

Creating Multiple Carets via Mouse

Regardless of how many carets are active, the user can add a new caret by holding the Ctrl key and left mouse button clicking at any location within the file where they can normally click to reposition the caret, including beyond a line end if the editor is configured for it.

Adding a New Caret to an Existing Set via Mouse

If the user has created a caret set and released the Ctrl key and wishes to add a new caret to the active set, then, prior to clicking anywhere else in the file, they can press Ctrl again and click in a new position to add a new caret to the existing set.

Removing a Caret via Mouse

The user can remove a caret from the active set by holding the Ctrl key and clicking on the caret they wish to remove. No other carets are affected. The user can undo the last-created caret by pressing the keyboard shortcut Shift+Alt+Z.

Clearing All Multiple Carets via Mouse

To remove multiple carets, the user can release the Ctrl key and then click elsewhere in the file (not on an active selection). All carets will be removed, and the clicked position will become the only active caret. Alternatively, users can press the keyboard shortcut Ctrl+Shift+/ to remove all but the primary caret.

Multi-select via Mouse

Multi-select is a component of multi-caret that allows the user to select multiple noncontiguous sections of data.

Creating Multiple Selections via Mouse

Regardless of how many selections are active, the user can add a new selection by holding the Ctrl key and selecting any text within the file where they can normally do so. The selection can be created via

- Click-and-drag (standard selection)

- Double-/triple-click

- Click on line number

Adding a New Selection to an Existing Set via Mouse

If the user has created a selection set and released the Ctrl key and wishes to add a new caret to the active set, then, prior to clicking anywhere else in the file, they can press the Ctrl key again and select new text to add to the existing set.

Removing a Selection via Mouse

The user can remove a selection from the active set by holding the Ctrl key and clicking anywhere on the selection they wish to remove. No other selections are affected, and no caret is left where the user clicked.

Clearing All Multiple Selections via Mouse

To remove multiple selections, the user must release the Ctrl key and then click elsewhere in the file (not on an active caret/selection). All carets will be removed, and the clicked position will become the only active caret.

Multi-select Strings

Tip The user can see how many carets/selections exist in the file by looking at the status bar.

Select All Occurrences of String

The user can use multi-caret editing to quickly select all occurrences of a word regardless of its position in the file. To do this, a selection needs to be done, and the keyboard shortcut Ctrl + , (comma) needs to be pressed. If no selection exists, UltraEdit will select all occurrences of the word under the active caret.

Select Next Occurrence of String

To select the next occurrence of the selected string, the keyboard shortcut Ctrl + ; (semicolon) needs to be pressed. If no selection exists, UltraEdit will first select the word under the caret, and subsequent keypresses will select subsequent occurrences.

Select All Find Matches

The user can also load all matches from a search into multiple selections. To do this, first, a *Quick find* or *Find* with the enabled option *Highlight all items found* needs to be done. After the matched items are highlighted, the keyboard shortcut Ctrl + , (comma) needs to be pressed to load them into selections. When combined with Perl regular expressions, this provides a very powerful way of selecting multiple different strings all at once.

Movement of Multi-carets

With a caret/selection set active, the user can reposition them as they normally would by using basic movement keys on the keyboard. Some examples:

- Left Arrow will move all carets to the left one position.

- Down Arrow will move all carets down one line.

- Home will move all carets to the beginning of each line.

- Page Up will move all carets up one page.

Any movement which would cause the carets to converge into a unified location will result in a single caret. Examples include Ctrl+Home, Ctrl+End, Ctrl+Shift+Home, Ctrl+Shift+End, etc.

General Editing with Multi-caret

Once a user has a set of multi-carets and/or selections, they can perform any number of general editing operations.

Copy/Cut

All selections are copied or cut into the clipboard. Noncontiguous selections are separated on the clipboard by a line terminator. If the user has an option enabled which is called *Enable copy/cut of current line with no selection active*, then all lines where a nonselection caret is active are copied/cut.

Paste

All selections are overwritten with whatever data is on the clipboard.

Select

Using Shift, the user can select from each caret at once just as they would with a single caret.

Backspace/Delete

All backspace/delete functionality is available and operates independently upon each caret.

End of Line Carets

Special handling is provided for multiple contiguous end of line (EOL) carets. When this is enabled, the user can hold the Ctrl key and click and drag beyond the EOL for multiple contiguous lines and have a caret automatically activated at the end of each line. This way, the user does not have to manually Ctrl+Click at the end of each line. If the user continues to drag to a point that is not beyond EOL for a line, then the multi-carets will switch over to a regular selection (normal behavior when clicking and dragging).

Command Palette

The Command palette provides a method by which any user can quickly gain information regarding available features/settings in UltraEdit. It also allows the user to directly invoke the commands found after completing the search.

The Command palette can be opened via the list icon at the top right (Ribbon mode), via *Help ➤ Open command palette* (both Contemporary and Traditional menu modes), and via the keyboard shortcut Ctrl+Shift+P (see Figure 9-6).

Figure 9-6. *UltraEdit's Command palette*

The user begins by entering a search string in the text field at the top of the Command palette. The list of available commands and settings will then be filtered to show relevant matches. For example, searching for "hex" would return the output of Figure 9-7.

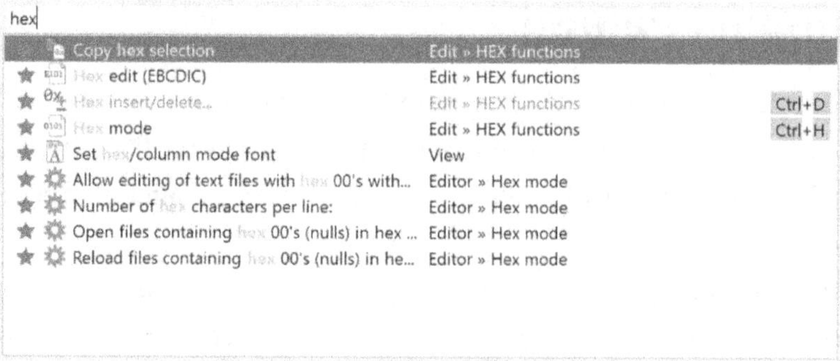

Figure 9-7. *Command palette with the search word "hex"*

Command names are sorted alphabetically and listed at the top of the results. The location of the command is shown in the second column, and keyboard shortcuts for the command (if they exist) are shown in the third column. Settings matching the filter are listed alphabetically below the commands. Once the user has selected a command they wish to use, they can press the Enter key to invoke that command. If a setting is selected, pressing the Enter key would open the relevant page in the Configuration dialog – so that setting can be modified as desired.

If the user clicks on the star to the left of a command name, it will be added to the Favorites list, with Recently used commands listed below the Favorites. To clear the Recently used list, a click on the X to the right of the Recently used heading is sufficient.

Launch Custom Macros, Tools, Scripts, and Templates

The user can launch custom macros, tools, scripts, and templates directly from the Command palette. They just need to type all or part of the item's name, or if not sure, they can type "play" or "insert" or "tool" to see a list of available items.

Pressing the Enter key means to insert or play the selected item.

Favorites/Recently Used

The user can click on the star to the left of a command or setting to add it to the favorites list which appears at the top of the Command palette. Clicking the star again removes a command or setting from the favorites list.

It is possible to access the last five recently used commands directly below the favorites. If the command history needs to be cleared, a click on the X to the right of the *Recently used* heading is sufficient.

Quick Open from History

The Command palette maintains a history of all files previously opened, similar to a web browser's browsing history. This allows the user to quickly re-open a file without having to remember the time or exact location from where it was opened. To open a file from the history, with the opened Command palette, the character "\" enters the history mode (without the double quotation marks at the beginning and end, that means a backslash). After that, the user can begin typing all or parts of the path/name of the file which needs to be opened. The user sees results filtered into the Command palette. Once the file to open is seen, it can be selected and opened immediately with the Enter key. This feature supports local, network, and (S)FTP files.

The history can be cleared by clicking the X to the right of the *Search recently opened files* heading.

Open Files

The Command palette also functions as a quick open for local files. To open files, with the Command palette open, the user can start typing the path beginning with the drive letter. Automatically auto-suggestions appear in the Command palette filtered based upon the path which was typed. By pressing the Tab key, the path with the selected item will be auto-completed. If a full file path is entered, the Enter key can be used to open it. The arrow keys can be used to move through the list of filtered results; then a press on the Enter key on the selected result opens it.

The user can use the asterisk (*) as a wildcard in the Command palette to open multiple files.

Relative paths can also be used (relative to the active file) and traverse parent directories with "..".

FTP Integration

UltraEdit includes the functionality of an FTP client that can be used to access, modify, and save files on an FTP server. This works in UltraEdit and supports the standard FTP and SFTP protocols as well as FTPS (FTP over SSL).

The FTP functionality is accessible via the *Home* tab ➤ *FTP* (Ribbon mode), *Home* ➤ *FTP* (Contemporary menu mode), and *File* ➤ *FTP/telnet* (Traditional menu mode).

The first step is to create an FTP account in UltraEdit, which is done via *the Account Manager* and the dialog of the same name (see Figure 9-8).

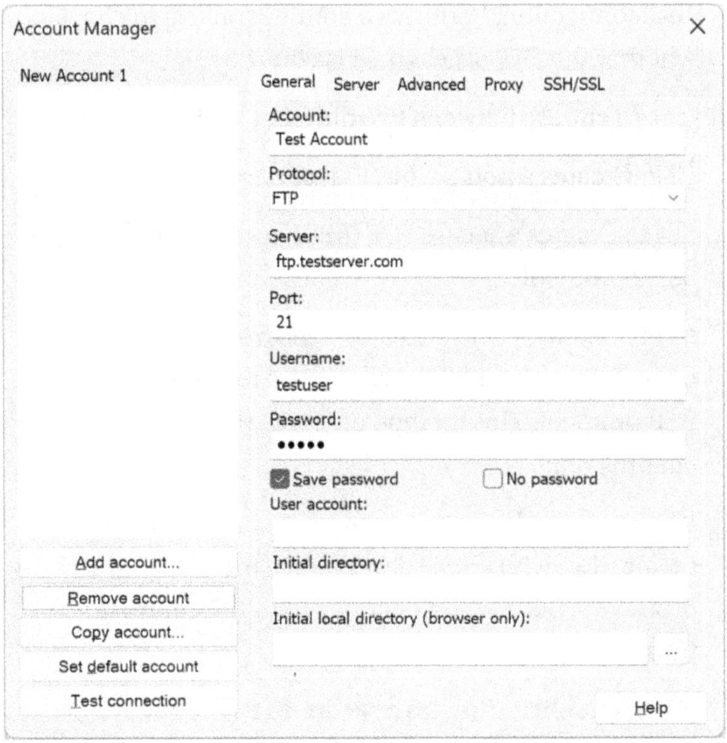

Figure 9-8. *Account Manager for FTP accounts within UltraEdit*

This dialog contains some buttons at the bottom:

- Add account: Allows to specify a new account name. Each account must have a unique name.

- Remove account: This button immediately removes the active/selected account from the accounts list.

- Copy account: Creates a copy of the selected account and adds the text "Copy of" to the front.

- Set default account: Sets the active/selected account as the default account specified by an asterisk "*" following the account name in the list.

- Test connection: Performs a connection test to check whether the FTP access data is correct.

The user can choose between five different FTP protocols:

- FTP: Creates a non-secure FTP connection.

- SFTP: Creates a secure FTP (SFTP) connection with the SSH2 protocol.

- FTPS – Control Only: Creates a secure FTP (FTPS) connection with an SSL layer below the standard FTP protocol. This method encrypts the control channel only.

- FTPS – Control + Data: Creates a secure FTP (FTPS) connection with an SSL layer below the standard FTP protocol. This method encrypts both the control and the data channels.

- FTPS – Implicit: Creates a secure FTP (FTPS) connection with an SSL layer below the standard FTP protocol. This is an older FTPS method and is not generally preferred, but is still supported on some servers.

The Account Manager has several options organized under five different tabs, which are *General, Server, Advanced, Proxy,* and *SSH/SSL*. For more details on each individual option, the integrated help is recommended and the power tip *Configure FTP/SFTP in UltraEdit and UEStudio*, which also contains a helpful video: `www.ultraedit.com/support/tutorials-power-tips/ultraedit/configure-ftp`.

As soon as the account is set up, the FTP Browser allows to search and navigate through the structures of the FTP server (see Figure 9-9).

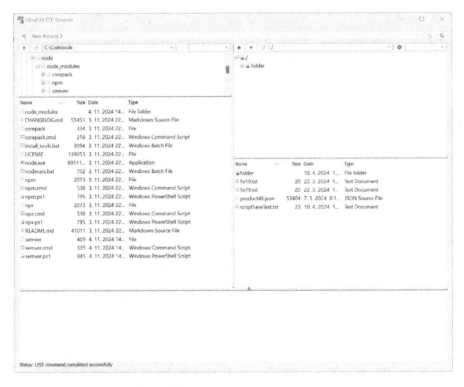

Figure 9-9.   *UltraEdit's FTP Browser*

This FTP Browser consists mainly of four panes:

- Top left pane: Displays the directory tree for the local system

- Top right pane: Displays the directory tree on the remote system (FTP server)

- Panes directly below these (to the left and right): Display the contents of the active/selected folder in each respective directory tree

- Bottom pane: Displays the progress for active transfers

In addition, FTP servers can be accessed from the *File explorer*, which can also be opened with the keyboard shortcut Ctrl+U. The *Remote* category is located in the lower area, and the various FTP accounts with the FTP server structures below them are listed.

In addition to the FTP Browser, there are various core commands for handling remote files on an FTP server:

- Open from FTP: This command opens a file via FTP and displays a custom dialog that allows the selection of the site/account to browse.

- Save to FTP: This command saves an open document/ file via FTP and presents a custom dialog that allows the selection of the site/account to browse.

- Save and upload to server: This command saves the current file and uploads it to the FTP server.

Within the FTP integration, there is an option to link remote directories to local directories. To do this, the user first needs to create an FTP/SFTP account with the Account Manager. Then certain steps must be performed in the following order:

- Open the project: The user needs to open their project from the project menu. If no project was created previously, this can and should be done in the *Project* tab (Ribbon mode) or the *Project* menu (both Contemporary and Traditional menu modes).

- Add a folder: By doing a right-click on the project, the function *Add Folder* needs to be launched.

- In the *New Folder* dialog: The folder which should be linked to the remote directory must exist on the local system. It is suggested to create a new empty directory on the system to avoid any conflicts. To do that, the user can either enter the path to the directory or navigate to the directory. In order to link to the remote directory, the option *Link Folder to FTP/SFTP location* needs to be enabled. Just below the FTP/SFTP account a remote path needs to be specified. After clicking the *OK* button, the folder added to the project appears.

- Download the files: The files are not automatically downloaded/uploaded after configuring the above folder settings. The user can download or upload the files by right-clicking on the folder (in the project view) and selecting *Download/Upload.*

- Finished: After choosing the option to download/upload the files, the *FTP Command Progress* dialog will appear and notify when the operation is complete. The FTP download/upload does run in the background and will therefore allow editing files in UltraEdit.

After the folders are linked, the user can right-click on the folder in the project pane and select from the various upload/download and sync options. These options are the end result for the linking process of remote directories to local directories and reflect a powerful workflow for text editing, even if the files are in a remote location.

Note   For step-by-step instructions, see the power tip "Link remote directories to local directories" at this address: `www.ultraedit.com/support/tutorials-power-tips/ultraedit/sync-local-to-remote`.

PowerShell Terminal

PowerShell is a cross-platform framework for the automation, configuration, and management of IT systems and was introduced by Microsoft in 2006. A command-line interpreter – the so-called Windows PowerShell – can be used to enter a wide range of commands and execute scripts.

UltraEdit offers an integrated solution with the terminal, which can be used in parallel to text editing without having to switch to an external PowerShell command line.

The terminal can be opened via the *Layout* tab ➤ *Terminal* (Ribbon mode), via *Layout* ➤ *Terminal* (Contemporary menu mode), or via *View* ➤ *Views/lists* ➤ *Terminal* (Traditional menu mode). Once the terminal has been created, the terminal window can be moved as wished by holding down the mouse button in the window header. It can be docked into different areas of the UltraEdit frames by dragging it onto the docking symbols displayed and then releasing the mouse button.

Figure 9-10 shows an exemplary PowerShell terminal after the first launch, which is not yet docked and is positioned then in the center of the screen until it will be docked.

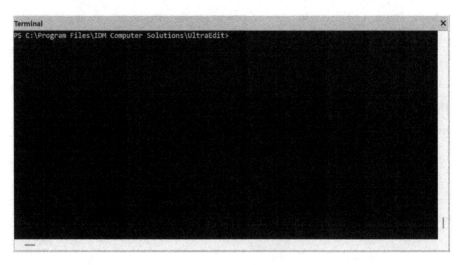

Figure 9-10. *UltraEdit's PowerShell terminal*

We do not want to describe the PowerShell syntax including all commands at this point, as this would go beyond the scope of this book and there is already sufficient literature on the subject. The following books are particularly recommended for this:

- PowerShell for Beginners by Ian Waters, Apress 2021, Softcover ISBN 978-1-4842-7063-9, eBook ISBN 978-1-4842-7064-6

- PowerShell Fast Track by Vikas Sukhija, Apress 2021, Softcover ISBN 978-1-4842-7758-4, eBook ISBN 978-1-4842-7759-1

- Pro Windows PowerShell by Hristo Deshev, Apress 2008, Softcover ISBN 978-1-59059-940-2, eBook ISBN 978-1-4302-0546-3

- Pro PowerShell for Database Developers by Bryan Cafferky, Apress 2015, Softcover ISBN 978-1-4842-0542-6, eBook ISBN 978-1-4842-0541-9

- Pro PowerShell for Microsoft Azure by Sherif Talaat, Apress 2015, Softcover ISBN 978-1-4842-0666-9, eBook ISBN 978-1-4842-0665-2

- Pro PowerShell for Amazon Web Services by Brian Beach, Apress 2014, eBook ISBN 978-1-4302-6452-1

What we want to discuss instead, in contrast to the entire PowerShell command syntax, are ten useful PowerShell commands that can enhance the workflow of any user who works with UltraEdit and uses the integrated PowerShell terminal:

- 1. Get file information:

  Get-Item -Path "file_path" | Select-Object Name, Length, LastWriteTime

  Usage: Displays basic information about the current file (name, size, last modified time)

- 2. Search for a string in files:

  Select-String -Path "directory_path*.txt" -Pattern "search_term" -CaseSensitive

  Usage: Searches for a specific term in all text files within a directory

- 3. Replace text in a file:

  (Get-Content "file_path") -replace "old_text", "new_text" | Set-Content "file_path"

  Usage: Performs a text replacement operation on a file

- 4. Open a file in UltraEdit:

  Start-Process -FilePath "UltraEdit.exe" -ArgumentList "file_path"

  Usage: Opens a file in UltraEdit directly from the terminal

- 5. List recently modified files:

  Get-ChildItem -Path "directory_path" -File | Sort-Object LastWriteTime -Descending | Select-Object -First 10

  Usage: Lists the ten most recently modified files in a directory

- 6. Backup a file before editing:

  Copy-Item -Path "file_path" -Destination "file_path.bak"

  Usage: Creates a backup of the file before making changes

- 7. Count lines in a file:

  (Get-Content "file_path").Count

  Usage: Counts the number of lines in a file

- 8. Monitor a log file in real time:

  Get-Content "log_file_path" -Wait

  Usage: Monitors changes to a log file in real time

- 9. Compare two files:

  Compare-Object (Get-Content "file1_path") (Get-Content "file2_path")

  Usage: Compares the contents of two files and shows the differences

- 10. Convert file encoding:

  Get-Content "file_path" | Set-Content -Encoding UTF8 "output_file_path"

  Usage: Converts a file to UTF-8 encoding, which is often required for compatibility

How can these commands help in the UltraEdit workflow? There are four exemplary answers:

- Automation: Replacing, searching, and monitoring files can save time compared to manual operations.

- File management: Commands like creating backups and counting lines make file management more efficient.

- Integration: The ability to open UltraEdit directly from the terminal improves productivity.

- Debugging: Monitoring log files and comparing file contents are invaluable during debugging or code reviews.

These commands can be easily customized to fit specific workflows and integrated into UltraEdit's scripting or macro capabilities.

Processing of Very Large Files

One of the greatest strengths of UltraEdit is the editing of extremely large files with the so-called Large File mode. This is accomplished with relatively small amounts of memory being used. UltraEdit is a disk-based editor and only loads a small portion of the file into memory at one time. Normally, UltraEdit copies a file that is being edited to a temporary file and, at the end of the editing session, deletes the file after copying back to the appropriate original file. To speed up editing of very large files, the UltraEdit settings allow to specify editing without using temporary files. This removes the time necessary to copy the file to a temporary file. When editing files of many megabytes or even gigabytes, this can be an advantage.

This functionality can be configured in the UltraEdit settings in the category *File handling* ➤ *Large files*, and we have already discussed these settings in detail in Chapter 4 (see also Figure 9-11).

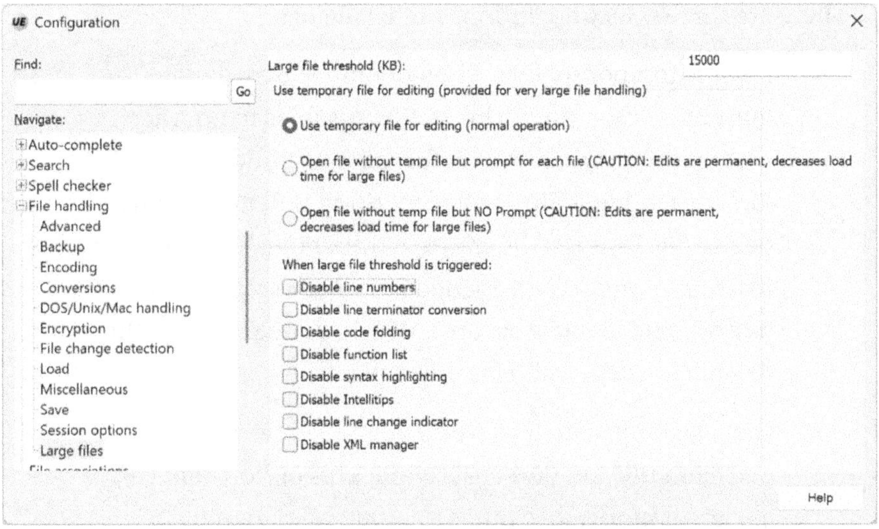

Figure 9-11. *UltraEdit settings for the Large File mode*

If we now load a large file as an example (in our case, a 6 GB CSV file), the *Temporary file handling* dialog appears first, in which the handling of temporary files can be adjusted again (see Figure 9-12).

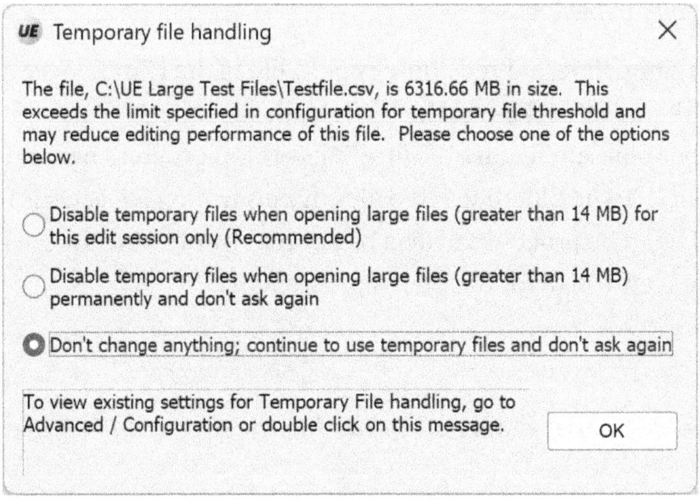

Figure 9-12. *Temporary file handling dialog*

There are three selection options in this dialog:

- Disable temporary files when opening large files for this edit session only: This option disables temporary files for this edit session. In this case, UltraEdit works directly with that file so all the writing is done directly on the file. This is a difference to other mechanisms, where the whole file is loaded into memory and causes performance issues, because Windows needs to use the pagefile if memory is running out.

- Disable temporary files when opening large files permanently and don't ask again: This option behaves like the option above but is not only valid for the current edit session but also permanently for large files opened in the future.

- Don't change anything; continue to use temporary files and don't ask again: This option retains the current values of the UltraEdit settings and does not change any behavior.

At the same time, a direct jump is possible to the UltraEdit settings from this dialog by clicking in the lower dialog area.

Another pleasant feature of UltraEdit is that a progress bar appears at the bottom left when loading large files or performing file actions (such as file searches). The process can also be aborted by pressing the Escape key. Please see Figure 9-13 for this status progress bar.

Figure 9-13. _Status progress bar during the processing of large files_

This is advantageous in that the user is constantly informed about the progress and does not get the feeling that something is frozen. UltraEdit handles large files very transparently and stably, which makes this function a real achievement.

Summary

In this chapter, we have described some of the advanced UltraEdit functions that make daily work easier. These include syntax highlighting, multi-caret editing, the Command palette, FTP integration, the PowerShell terminal, and the processing of very large files.

If the user is familiar with the basic operation of UltraEdit, these advanced functions offer considerable added value for increasing productivity and optimizing every user's workflow.

CHAPTER 10

Further Help

After describing the technical aspects of UltraEdit in the previous chapters, this last chapter deals with the support options provided by UltraEdit as software and UltraEdit as manufacturer.

With regard to the UltraEdit software, we will talk about hints and the integrated online help.

With regard to UltraEdit as a manufacturer with its online presence, we will talk about further help such as online forums, wiki documentation, video tutorials, whitepapers, power tips, and the Frequently Asked Questions (FAQ). All in all, this represents an incredible knowledge base that leaves hardly any wishes unfulfilled and questions unanswered.

If something cannot be found, or potential errors have been found, or simply suggestions for improvement are made, a support form is available at `www.ultraedit.com/support` as well as the email address `support@ultraedit.com`.

Hints

Hints are an effective tool (not only in UltraEdit) to display help texts for various program functions. When UltraEdit is started or when a file is opened, a rectangle in the lower center area of the screen is immediately noticeable, which is primarily referred to as a hint (see Figure 10-1).

© Devid Espenschied 2025
D. Espenschied, *Mastering UltraEdit*, https://doi.org/10.1007/979-8-8688-1160-9_10

Figure 10-1. *Hint at the lower center area of UltraEdit*

These hints contain valuable tips and assistance for all facets of UltraEdit. There are various buttons:

- Got it, don't show again: Marks the current hint as read and closes the hint window

- Next hint: Jumps to the next hint

- Previous hint: Switches back to the previous hint

- Turn these off: Deactivates the hint display for the next UltraEdit program start or when the next file is opened

---

Tip   This hint window is activated by default but can be deactivated manually. That can be done either by clicking the *Turn these off* button or via the menu. When UltraEdit is working in Ribbon mode, the help and support menu is located in the upper right corner, and the help icon opens the help menu. In that menu, the option *Show hints* can be toggled.

When UltraEdit is in Contemporary or Traditional menu mode, this menu item exists in the standard help menu, which is the last entry in the menu bar on the right.

At the same time, hints have another meaning in the IT world, namely, to provide short descriptions of program functions. These description hints are used in Ribbon mode and the Contemporary and Traditional menu modes. In Ribbon mode, they appear as soon as the mouse pointer hovers over the icons on the ribbon tabs (see Figure 10-2).

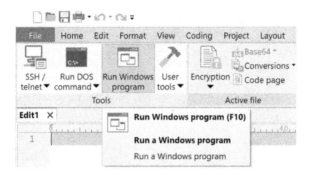

Figure 10-2. *Hint for the Run Windows program function in Ribbon mode*

The hint texts are partly divided into several sections, with a main category in bold at the top, a possibly available keyboard shortcut in brackets behind it, as well as a subcategory in bold and a short description below it.

When UltraEdit is in Contemporary or Traditional menu mode, short hint texts appear in the left-hand area of the status bar at the bottom of the screen when the user navigates to menu items using the mouse pointer or keyboard (see Figure 10-3).

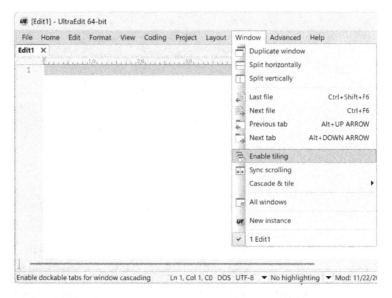

Figure 10-3. *Hint for the Run Windows program function in Contemporary menu mode*

Online Help

UltraEdit's online help can be accessed from within any program function by pressing the F1 key. Ideally, this will provide the exact help page for the respective topic.

Note   The help file is located in the UltraEdit program directory and is named uedit64.chm for the 64-bit version of UltraEdit. The extension "chm" stands for compressed HTML files with text, images, hyperlinks, and other content.

The online help is subdivided into three tabs: *Contents, Index,* and *Search* (see Figure 10-4).

Figure 10-4. *UltraEdit's Online help with three tabs on the left top*

The three tabs in the top left corner allow you to navigate through the basic help texts:

- Contents: Contains the entire online help subdivided into topic groups and subchapters

- Index: Contains an index directory with alphabetically accessible help pages

- Search: Allows a search for text terms

Another feature lets the user install and access additional help files in UltraEdit. On Windows, UltraEdit allows to add up to 20 help files which are then added to the *Help* menu drop-down at the top right of the application.

This happens via the *Add help files* dialog, which allows to add help files (extension "chm" or "hlp") by file name and path or browse for a help file. The user can also enter a URL to a help system or a knowledge database. Presets for MSDN Online and Google exist for this (see Figure 10-5).

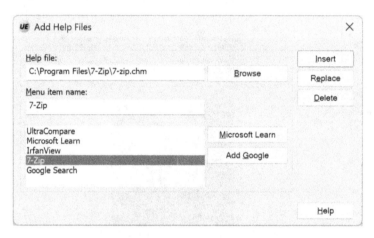

Figure 10-5. *Add Help Files dialog*

As can be seen in Figure 10-5, three help files have been added for the applications 7-Zip, IrfanView, and UltraCompare. To do this, the corresponding "chm" or "hlp" file is selected using the *Browse* button, a name is entered in the edit field *Menu item name* and the *Insert* button is pressed. The following elements are available in the *Add Help Files* dialog:

- Help file: Contains the path and file name of the help file or a URL for any web page (the identifier *$K* can be used to represent the search term/query string inside the URL)

- Browse: Opens a browser dialog in which the user can navigate to the desired file and copy the file name and path into the edit field *Help file*

- Menu item name: Contains the name under which the help file can be accessed via the UltraEdit help menu

- Insert: Inserts a new help file if a name was entered

- Replace: Replaces a currently inserted help file with the new file

- Delete: Deletes the selected help file from the help file list

- Microsoft Learn: Uses the default settings for the Microsoft search engine

- Add Google: Uses the default settings for the Google search engine

Figure 10-6 shows the effect of the help files added in Figure 10-5 on the help menu.

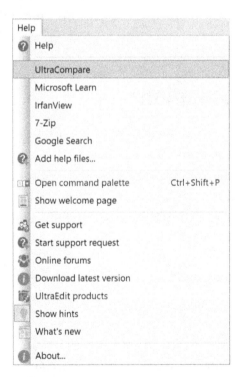

Figure 10-6. *UltraEdit's Help menu with three added help files*

Online Forums

UltraEdit provides an online forum at `https://forums.ultraedit.com`
where users can exchange information and provide each other with
mutual assistance.

The forum is divided into the sections *Important announcements,*
UltraEdit, UEX - UltraEdit for Linux, UltraEdit for Mac, UEStudio,
UltraCompare, UltraFinder, and *UltraFTP,* each with various subsections.

All forum threads can be read as a guest, and as soon as the user wants
to write their own texts, a registration is required. This can be done by
clicking the *Join* button in the top right corner and can be done using an
existing Facebook or Google account or with an email address.

The forum software is based on Tapatalk by Everforo Inc., for which
there is also a smartphone app in the Apple App Store and Google
Play Store.

Wiki Documentation

A very comprehensive and valuable collection of knowledge exists in the
form of a Wikipedia at `https://wiki.ultraedit.com`.

This wiki has been around for many years and provides invaluable
information on all facets of UltraEdit and UEStudio. The wiki is divided
into four categories, which can be accessed in the center left:

- General
- Ribbon commands
- Ribbon, menus, and toolbars
- Settings

Also highlighted are the popular topics, which are located below and
represent common topics.

Other useful tools in this wiki are the search function in the upper right corner, which allows to conveniently search for wiki content. Below that is a translation plug-in, which is powered by Google Translator and allows to translate into any language.

Video Tutorials

There are people who learn better through visual impressions, and videos and tutorials are ideal for this.

UltraEdit offers its own YouTube channel for this purpose, which can be found at `www.youtube.com/ultraedit`. This channel includes product demos, various videos (such as the top ten new features), and a range of tutorials on UltraEdit and UltraStudio, UltraCompare, and UltraFinder.

Separate playlists for events such as Dev Days of Summer, webinars, product demos, and tutorials make it easier to sort through the many videos.

Whitepapers

Whitepapers represent separate tech guides, analysis, statistics, and case studies published by UltraEdit.

At the time of writing, two white papers are available at `www.ultraedit.com/whitepapers` with the following content:

- Everything you need to know about editing big data

- Securing Your Digital Assets: UltraEdit's approach to digital security

In the future, this area will certainly be expanded and more white papers will be added.

To download these as PDF files, the download button opens a form page where the user can enter their contact details and afterward UltraEdit will send an email with the download link.

Power Tips

So-called power tips are bundled knowledge reports that reflect many long-standing user requests. In the past, users have often requested more detailed information about specific features supported in UltraEdit products. By providing an archive called Power Tips, another knowledge base is created with detailed information on useful, time-saving features in the growing range of powerful UltraEdit products.

The Power Tips can be found at `www.ultraedit.com/support/tutorials-power-tips`, and there are different categories for each of UltraEdit, UEStudio, UltraEdit Mac/Linux, UltraCompare, and UltraFinder. At the time of writing, there are almost 200 Power Tips, and we will list the first ten below to give the reader a feel for the variety of topics:

- Keyboard shortcuts: Maximize your speed and efficiency by utilizing UltraEdit's keyboard shortcuts. We list the default keyboard shortcuts in this guide, but you are able to customize them to your liking.

- Smart Templates: UltraEdit includes Smart Templates, a way to automatically complete your code. Type the template text and UltraEdit will automatically suggest the template!

- Vertical & Horizontal Split Window: This is a convenient feature when you're manually comparing files, when you want to copy/paste between multiple files, or when you simply want to divide up your edit space.

- Tabbed Child Windows: Declutter your edit space by using the tabbed child windows feature.

- Auto-Hide Child Windows: When you're deep in your code, the most important thing is editing space. The all-new auto-hide child windows allow you to maximize your editing space by hiding the child windows against the edge of the editor.

- Quick Open: UltraEdit and UEStudio provide multiple methods to quickly open files without using the standard *Open File* dialog. A favorite method among power users is the *Quick Open* in the File menu. The benefit of the quick open dialog is that it loads up extremely fast and allows you to type the name of the file and open it quicker than using the standard open dialog.

- Column Markers: The benefit of a column marker is that it can help you to format your text/code, or in some cases to make it easier to read in complex nested logic.

- Customizing toolbars: Did you know that you can not only change what is on UltraEdit's toolbars, you can also change the icon used, as well as create your own custom toolbars and tools?

- File tabs: Understand how file tabs can be displayed, controlled, and configured through the window docking system in UltraEdit/UEStudio.

- Create user/project tools: Execute DOS or Windows commands in UltraEdit or UEStudio.

FAQ

The FAQ category for Frequently Asked Questions summarizes questions that are regularly and repeatedly asked to UltraEdit, and the `www.ultraedit.com/support/faq` page has been provided for this purpose.

This page contains three question types: *Licensing, Downloads/ Installation,* and *Functionality.* For Licensing, a link is provided to the separate page `www.ultraedit.com/products/ultraedit/licenses-and-faqs`, which also contains a matrix for comparing licenses (subscription vs. perpetual). The license page also explains important terms, for example:

- What is maintenance?

- Renewing and opting out of maintenance

- Subscription vs. maintenance

- What are upgrades? Can I upgrade my old license?

- Refund policy

- UltraEdit All Access subscription

- Concurrent licenses

- Multi-user licenses

- Promos, discounts, and education offers

Summary

In this chapter, we have described the many tools that are available within UltraEdit to assist the user. This ranges from the various hint variants to the integrated online help.

At the same time, we have described the online ecosystem available to support users. This includes online forums, a wiki as a knowledge base, video tutorials, whitepapers, power tips, and FAQs.

As anyone can see from this unlimited source of knowledge, with UltraEdit, the user doesn't only get an extremely stable and powerful editor but also technical support and knowledge sources in many different forms. This combination makes UltraEdit one of the most flexible, powerful, and secure text editors nowadays.

Index

© Devid Espenschied 2025
D. Espenschied, *Mastering UltraEdit*, https://doi.org/10.1007/979-8-8688-1160-9

E

Editing text
  active line
    duplicate line command, 246
    join lines, 246
  clipboards, 242
  copying
    HTML, 240
    HTML document, 240
    RTF, 240
  cut, 241
  deleting data
    bookmarked lines, 245
    functions, 245
    line, 245
  paste
    HTML source, 241
    RTF, 241
  read-only command, 251
  Redo command, 242
  selecting data
    persistent selection, 244
    select all command, 243
    select line command, 243
    select next occurrence
      command, 243
    select range command, 243
    select word command, 243
  spell checker, 248–251
  undo command, 242
  Word count and character
    info, 251–253
  word wrap, 247

F

File change polling
  always on top, 315
  auto-scroll polled files, 315
  full screen, 316, 317
  toggle file change polling,
    314, 315
File explorer
  buttons, 34
  extension groups, 36
  file tree view, 36, 38
  filter settings, 35
  open files, 39, 40
File management
  closing files, 213, 214
  contemporary menu mode, 203
  context menu, 206
  customize dialog, 206, 207
  deleting files, 213
  encryption/decryption
    function, 215–217
  favorite files, 234–236
  format conversions, 221, 222
  group marker, 207
  printing files, 227, 228, 230–233
    classic theme, 234
    line numbers, 233
    margins, 233
    page break code, 234
    2 pages in 1 sheet, 233
    syntax highlighting, 233
    wrap the text, 233
  Quick Open Bar, 208–211

W, X, Y, Z